Project Management JumpStart

Third Edition

Project Management JumpStart

Third Edition

Kim Heldman, PMP

Wiley Publishing, Inc.

Acquisitions Editor: Agatha Kim
Development Editor: Kim Beaudet
Technical Editor: Terri Wagner
Production Editor: Eric Charbonneau
Copy Editor: Kim Wimpsett
Editorial Manager: Pete Gaughan
Production Manager: Tim Tate
Vice President and Executive Group Publisher: Richard Swadley
Vice President and Publisher: Neil Edde
Compositor: Jeff Wilson, Happenstance Type-O-Rama
Proofreader: Jen Larsen, Word One
Indexer: Ted Laux
Project Coordinator, Cover: Katherine Crocker
Cover Designer: Ryan Sneed
Cover Image: © Fiona Jackson-Downes / Cultura / Getty Images

Copyright © 2011 by Wiley Publishing, Inc., Indianapolis, Indiana
Published simultaneously in Canada

ISBN: 978-0-470-93919-2 (pbk)
ISBN: 978-1-118-09445-7 (ebk)
ISBN: 978-1-118-09447-1 (ebk)
ISBN: 978-1-118-09446-4 (ebk)

For general information on our other products and services or to obtain technical support, please contact our Customer Care Department within the U.S. at (877) 762-2974, outside the U.S. at (317) 572-3993 or fax (317) 572-4002.

Wiley also publishes its books in a variety of electronic formats. Some content that appears in print may not be available in electronic books.

Library of Congress Cataloging-in-Publication Data is available from the publisher.

10 9 8 7 6 5

Dear Reader,

Thank you for choosing *Project Management JumpStart, Third Edition*. This book is part of a family of premium-quality Sybex books, all of which are written by outstanding authors who combine practical experience with a gift for teaching.

Sybex was founded in 1976. More than 30 years later, we're still committed to producing consistently exceptional books. With each of our titles, we're working hard to set a new standard for the industry. From the paper we print on, to the authors we work with, our goal is to bring you the best books available.

I hope you see all that reflected in these pages. I'd be very interested to hear your comments and get your feedback on how we're doing. Feel free to let me know what you think about this or any other Sybex book by sending me an email at nedde@wiley.com. If you think you've found a technical error in this book, please visit http://sybex.custhelp.com. Customer feedback is critical to our efforts at Sybex.

Best regards,

Neil Edde
Vice President and Publisher
Sybex, an Imprint of Wiley

To BB, my best friend and forever love

Acknowledgments

Writing a book, like any project, requires a dedicated team of folks working together to produce the end product. Once again I've had the privilege to work with the talented staff at Sybex to write the third edition of this book. They're the best project team around.

First, I'd like to especially thank Neil Edde, vice president and publisher, for giving me the opportunity to write this book. Thank you to Agatha Kim, acquisitions editor. Her support and encouragement were a great help to me. Kim Beaudet, our developmental editor, was terrific. She kept me on track and managed this process like a true project manager. Eric Charbonneau, production editor, kept a keen eye on my grammar and sometimes not-so-funny puns. His insights were very helpful.

Another special thanks to Terri Wagner, who reviewed every word of this book for accuracy and adherence to sound project management principles. Terri is an expert in the field of project management, and her suggestions based on her consulting and training experience helped make the book stronger and clearer. Thanks again, Terri, for another great job.

As always, there's a host of behind-the-scenes folks who put a great deal of effort into making this book the best that it can be. Thanks to these folks as well: Pete Gaughan, editorial manager; Connor O'Brien, editorial assistant; and Kim Wimpsett, copy editor.

Last but not least, thank you to my husband and best friend, BB. You are truly an inspiration to me, and without your support, encouragement, and prayers, I wouldn't be where I am today.

About the Author

Kim Heldman, PMP, is an IT Director for the Governor's Office of Information Technology, State of Colorado. She oversees delivery of information technology services to four departments including Natural Resources, Public Health and Environment, Agriculture, and Local Affairs. She has more than 20 years of project management experience in the information technology field. She's managed small, medium, and large projects over the course of her career and shares her breadth of experience and knowledge in her books through examples, stories, and tips.

Kim Heldman is the author of other project management books, including the best-selling *PMP: Project Management Professional Study Guide, 6th Edition*, and co-author of *CompTIA Project+*. You can learn more about Kim at her website: http:/KimHeldman.com.

Contents

Introduction

This book was written with those of you in mind who are exploring the project management field or perhaps have been assigned to your first project.

Project management encompasses almost all aspects of our lives, not just our working lives. If you think about it, many things you do — from organizing a dinner party to planning a child's birthday celebration to bringing a new product to market — are projects. The principles you'll learn in this book will help you with all the project work you'll find yourself involved with.

Project management crosses all industries. My own personal searches on some of the popular job-hunting websites have shown that organizations are understanding the importance of employing skilled project managers. In these tight economic times, organizations are less likely to take on risky projects, and they want assurances that if they do take on a new project, it will be successful. Reading this book will give you a solid footing in project management practices. If you apply the principles you'll learn here, you'll give your future projects a much better chance at success.

If you find that this topic interests you and project management seems like a career worth pursuing, I strongly recommend you consider becoming certified through the Project Management Institute (PMI). They are the de facto standard in project management methodologies. You'll find in your own job searches that many organizations now require a PMP certification. PMP stands for Project Management Professional and is the designation that PMI bestows on those who qualify and pass the exam.

Reading this book will give you a jump start on understanding the principles of project management. From here, you can build on this knowledge by taking project management classes, reading other books on project management, and networking with others in your organization or community involved in project management work. This book is based on the project management guidelines recommended by PMI, and many of the terms, concepts, and processes you'll read about in this book are based on PMI's publication, *Guide to the Project Management Body of Knowledge (PMBOK), 4th Edition*.

For a more detailed exploration of project management in general and the PMP certification specifically, pick up a copy of another book I've written called *PMP: Project Management Professional Study Guide, 6th Edition*, also published by Sybex.

NOTE

Whether you choose to pursue certification or not, a basic understanding of project management practices is invaluable. During the course of your career, you'll be involved in several projects. Even if you are not the one managing the project, understanding how project management works, what a project life cycle is, and how to plan and execute a project will enhance your ability to communicate with others on the project team and know what process should be followed to assure a successful outcome.

Who Should Read This Book

This book was written for those of you fairly new to project management and lays the foundation for an understanding of the basic principles of good project management methodologies. Even if you've had some experience in the project management field, you'll find the example projects, templates, and checklists included in this book immediately applicable to your next project.

The fact that you purchased this book means you're interested in learning new things and furthering your career. Having a solid understanding of project management practices will help you increase your marketability. Your knowledge and practice of the principles outlined in this book will help assure employers that you understand how to bring a project to a successful closure, thereby saving them time and money. If you choose to take this endeavor one step further and become certified, you will increase your chances for advancement and improve your odds for landing the higher-paying project management positions. Potential employers will interpret your pursuit of project management knowledge and certification as assertive and forward-thinking, and they know that this will ultimately translate to success for their organization.

What This Book Covers

This book walks you through the project life cycle from beginning to end, just like projects are performed in practice. We've included many useful examples, tips, and hints that will help you solve common project management dilemmas. The chapters are designed to follow the project life cycle. Here's a high-level overview of what this book entails:

Chapters 1–2   These chapters lay the foundation of project management and delve into definitions, project life cycles, and the skills that all good project managers need for success.

Chapters 3–4   This section deals with the Initiation and Planning processes of the project life cycle. Here you'll learn why project charters are important and how to set project goals and document the requirements.

Chapters 5–7   These chapters walk you through breaking down the work of the project into manageable components, acquiring resources, and identifying and planning for risks.

Chapters 8–9   A large part of the planning work is done. Now you'll pull it all together into a final project plan, including a project schedule, final estimates, and the project budget.

Chapters 10–11   Now the work of the project begins. Here we'll cover the Executing and Monitoring and Controlling processes, including such tasks as team building, reporting project status, monitoring project performance, and taking corrective action.

Chapter 12   Finally, the book wraps up with the project closeout process.

Making the Most of This Book

At the beginning of each chapter, you'll find a list of topics that the chapter will cover. You'll find new terms defined in the margins of the pages to help you quickly get up to speed on project management–specific terminology. In addition, several special elements highlight important information.

Notes provide extra information and references to related information.

NOTE

Tips are insights that help you perform tasks more easily and effectively.

TIP

Warnings let you know about things that you should do — or shouldn't do — as you perform project management tasks.

WARNING

You'll find several review questions at the end of each chapter to test your knowledge of the material covered. You can find the answers to the review questions in Appendix A. You'll also find a list of terms to know at the end of each chapter that will help you review the key terms introduced in each chapter. These terms are defined in the glossary toward the end of the book.

We've also provided all the templates you'll encounter throughout the book in Appendix B. Appendix C contains all the checklists. These are ready for you to use or modify according to your needs.

Chapter 1

Building the Foundation

In This Chapter
- ◆ The definition of project management
- ◆ Different organizational structures
- ◆ The project management process groups
- ◆ Project criteria
- ◆ Constraints and their impacts
- ◆ Project management certification

Welcome to the world of project management. Chances are you've already had some experience with project management, whether you've called it that or not. Maybe you've helped organize your company's annual conference or been involved with a new product launch. At some point in your personal or professional life, you've probably used some sort of process to get from the beginning of the project to the end results.

You'll discover through the course of this book that you may already use some of the processes we'll talk about, but you may never have realized they were formalized procedures. I'll add some new twists and tricks to those processes that you'll want to try. You'll also learn some new techniques and procedures that will enhance your project management experiences and help you run your next project smoothly and effortlessly. (OK, that might be stretching it a bit, but your project will run more efficiently.)

In this chapter, we'll start building the foundation of good project management processes.

The Project Management Journey

project management
The process of applying knowledge, skills, tools, and techniques to describe, organize, and monitor the work of the project in order to accomplish the goals of the project.

Start your engines — we're ready to lay the foundation for building and managing your project. In this chapter, we'll start with a definition of a project, and then we'll take a high-level look at some of the processes and plans you'll build throughout the rest of the book and how you'll benefit from using solid project management techniques when managing your next project. We'll also cover organizational foundations before moving on to the project processes themselves. Here we go.

Is It a Project?

How do you know whether your new work assignment is a project or whether it's going to benefit from *project management* techniques? If you're like most of us, once you get to work and settle in for the day, you check your email and voice mail and touch base with some of the other folks on your team. The boss may drop by and ask for a status report on a problem you've been working on, gently nudging you to get back to it. All of these tasks are everyday work. They don't really have a beginning or end; they're ongoing. Projects are not everyday work. In order for work to be considered a project, it must meet a certain set of criteria.

Projects set out to produce a unique product or service that hasn't been produced before. They have a limited timeframe and are temporary in nature. This means that projects have a definite beginning and ending. You can determine that a project is complete by comparing its end result or product to the objectives and deliverables stated in the project plan.

Everyday work is ongoing. Production processes are an example of ongoing operations. Maybe you love popping a handful of chocolate drops into your mouth mid-afternoon for a quick treat. Producing those chocolate drops is an example of ongoing operations. The production line knows how many candies to produce, what colors to coat them with, how many go in a package, and so on. Every day, hundreds of thousands of those little drops make their way into bags, onto the store shelves, and eventually into our mouths — yum. But the production of these candies is not a project.

Now let's say that the management team has decided it's time to introduce a new line of candy. You've been tasked with producing the new candy flavor and shape. You assemble a research team to come up with a new candy formula. The marketing team gathers some data, which shows that the new candy has real potential with the consumers. The candy is produced according to plan, monitored for adherence to the original formula and design, and shipped to the stores. Is this a project or ongoing operations?

The answer is, this is a project even though candy making is something the company does every day. The production of chocolate drops is considered an ongoing operation. The new candy, however, is a unique product because the company has never produced this flavor and shape of candy. Remember that projects are originated to bring about a product or service that hasn't existed before. The new candy project was kicked off, carried out, monitored, and then ended when all the requirements were met. Candy production didn't stop there, though. At the end of this project, the production of the candy was turned over to ongoing operations and absorbed into the everyday work of the company. The project ended in this case by being assimilated into the ongoing operations of the company. Table 1.1 recaps the characteristics of projects versus ongoing operations.

Table 1.1 Projects versus ongoing operations

Projects	Ongoing operations
Definite beginning and end.	No definitive beginning and end.
Temporary in nature.	Ongoing.
Produces a unique product, service, or result.	Produces the same product, service, or result over and over.
Resources are dedicated to the project.	Resources are dedicated to operations.
Ending is determined by specific criteria.	Processes are not completed.

Where Are We Going?

When you start out on a journey, it helps to have the destination in mind. We've embarked on a project management discovery journey, so I'd like to start by describing where we'll be when we've finished.

The end of the project is the time to reflect on the processes used to complete the activities, to determine whether the *customer* is satisfied with the product the project set out to produce, and to document the lessons learned throughout the course of the project (among other things). You will be able to use this book to guide you from start to finish through your next small or medium-sized project so that you can easily assess those factors not only at the end of the project but as you progress through the project as well. (I consider large projects to be along the lines of building rocket ships, constructing major highways, or writing the latest, greatest software program that will automatically do your grocery shopping and monitor your golf swing all at the same time.) If you're just starting out in project management, you probably aren't heading up a large-scale project. But rest assured that all those small and medium-sized projects will teach you a great deal about project management and will start you well on the way to bigger and better opportunities as your experience grows.

customer
The end user or recipient of the product, service, or result of the project. Customers may be internal or external to the organization.

NOTE When you're just starting out, don't discount the experience you'll gain by working on small projects. Large projects are really a lot of smaller projects all lumped into one. The stepping stones to large project work are created by a history of success with small and medium-sized projects.

Included in this and each subsequent chapter you'll find discussions of the process at hand, examples so that you can apply what you're learning, and templates that you can use or modify to complete your project documentation. Now let's take a high-level look at a completed project.

A Bird's-Eye View

Our first example of a project is this book you're holding. You haven't yet read the entire book (unless, of course, this is your second time through). No doubt you're asking yourself, "Will this book give me the information I'm looking for?" or perhaps, "Will I be able to run my next project more efficiently as a result of reading this book?" Of course, I think the answer to both of these questions is, "Yes," but you don't know that yet. After you've finished the book, you'll know the answers to these questions and be able to reflect and discover that you did learn some new things and your project management tool bag is much better equipped for your next project. In other words, you've satisfied your curiosity and increased your knowledge of project management.

Projects work the same way. As the project manager, your primary concern throughout the project and particularly at the end of the project is, "Did I meet the customer's requirements to their satisfaction?" If you've followed the appropriate project management processes correctly, you're well on your way to having a successful answer to that question. At the end of the project, you'll document the things you've learned for use in future projects, which will help you improve the process the next time around.

Projects come about as a result of a need, and that need relates to the customer's expectations concerning the end result. But how do we get there? How do we know the customer is going to be satisfied? Table 1.2 is a bird's-eye view checklist that outlines the plans we'll create and the processes we'll practice during the course of a project. Don't worry that you may not understand everything on this list — I'll describe each of these areas in detail as we go. We'll revisit this list in a similar format one more time later in this book in Appendix C, "Sample Project Management Checklists."

NOTE You can also download this checklist of project processes from www.sybex.com/go/projectmanagementjumpstart3.

Table 1.2   Checklist of project processes

Complete	Process or document name	Notes
❏	Project charter	Created by project manager with input from the project sponsor and key stakeholders. Describes project purpose and outcomes.
❏	Cost-benefit analysis	Created by project manager with stakeholder input. Determines whether the project is financially beneficial to the organization. Sometimes this is done prior to the project to determine whether the project should even be undertaken.
❏	Assumptions and constraints	Created by project manager with stakeholder input. Describes assumptions and project constraints.
❏	Project scope statement	Created by project manager. Signed by project sponsor and stakeholders. Project manager works with project team and stakeholders to define and document project deliverables in the scope statement.
❏	Critical success factors	Defines what must be done to determine whether the project will be deemed successful. Can be included with the scope statement.
❏	Communications plan	Created by project manager. Describes the information needs of stakeholders and the project team and how the information is distributed.
❏	Work breakdown structure (WBS)	Created by project manager. Formatted as a deliverable-oriented hierarchy that defines the work of the project.

Table 1.2   Checklist of project processes *(continued)*

Complete	Process or document name	Notes
❏	Roles and responsibility matrix	Created by project manager. Ties roles and responsibilities of project team members with WBS elements.
❏	Resource plan	Created by project manager. Describes physical resources and human resources needed to complete the project.
❏	Procurement plan	Created by project manager or procurement team. Describes resources or services to be purchased from an outside provider.
❏	Risk management plan	Created by project manager or risk analysis team. Identifies, describes, and plans for project risks.
❏	Quality plan	Created by project manager or quality team. Describes how quality will be assured and measured.
❏	Project schedule	Created by project manager. Displays task dependencies, task durations, and milestones. Used to determine the critical path.
❏	Project budget	Created by project manager or financial team. Determines targeted costs of project.
❏	Change management plan	Created by project manager. Describes how changes will be identified and managed.
❏	Implementation checklist	Created by project manager. Describes issues to be discussed at turnover to internal departments or the customer.
❏	Lessons learned	Created by project manager with input from sponsor, stakeholders, and team members. Provides information to improve performance on future projects.

Charters and schedules and budgets, oh my! If you're thinking this looks like a great deal of work, you're correct. But anything worth doing is worth the time and effort to perform correctly and thoroughly. And remember that the size of the project will dictate how much effort should go into each of the items on the checklist. You might be happy to know that some of these processes can be combined or scaled back for small projects, depending on the project and the impact on your career growth if the project isn't successful.

This list may appear daunting right now, but by the end of this book you'll have a better understanding of the importance of each of these elements and why you need to incorporate them into your next project.

Know the Structure of Your Organization

It's important for project managers to understand the kind of organization they work in. Each structure has its own pluses and pitfalls that influence your effectiveness as a project manager. Organizations and their cultures are as unique as the projects they carry out. Functional organizations are the most traditional company structure. However, there can be deep layers of bureaucracy in this type of culture, and project managers may find themselves having little to no authority to make work assignments or complete the tasks needed to finish the project. Projectized organizations are structured with a project-oriented focus, but they also have their own unique advantages and disadvantages. Matrix organizations are yet another type of structure that mixes some of the features of the functional organization with the projectized organization. Let's take a further look at each of these organizational structures.

Functional Organizations

Functional organizations group similar work operations together into departments. For example, there's an accounting department, staffed with folks who know how to count the money and keep track of expenditures and such; maybe a human resources department; an information technology department; and so on; in this type of organization. The departments themselves are organized around similar work processes, and the employees who work in these departments have similar skill sets, albeit ranging from beginners in the field to seasoned experts.

Chances are you work for a person, known as the boss, who has some level of authority over your work assignments. Chances are your boss works for a boss who works for the big boss. This is an example of a functional organization. All the employees report up through their own departments to bosses who report to the big cheese at the top. Most organizations are structured this way; it's the most common form of organizational structure.

functional organizations
A traditional organizational structure that is hierarchical in nature. Employees report to one manager who reports to a higher-level manager.

Project managers who work in functional organizations usually have other responsibilities besides the project at hand. When the manager of human resources receives approval to undertake a project implementing an automated leave request system, not only will she have to manage the project, but she'll also continue to manage the duties of her regular position. This makes the project management tasks easier since she's the one who assigns the work to her staff, but her job responsibilities become more complicated since she's juggling functional duties and project management duties. Here is a typical organizational chart for a functional organization:

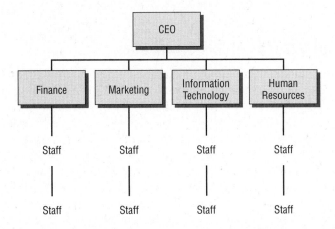

If you find yourself working as a contract project manager in this type of organization, be aware that corporate culture may dictate strict adherence to the chain of command. This means you must speak with the functional managers directly and should not go over their heads for answers unless they instruct you to do so. And rather than taking the initiative and rallying the employees in the department around the project, you'll likely need to get permission from their boss before you speak to them.

Advantages of a functional organization include the following:

Clear Chain of Command   Project team members have one supervisor, and they clearly understand the lines of authority.

Cohesive Team   Team members know one another because they work in the same department. Because their skills and talents are known, task assignment is easier.

Separation of Functions   This setup allows team members to fine-tune specific skills and eventually become experts.

Disadvantages of a functional organization are as follows:

Project Managers Are Typically Functional Managers Also   This arrangement tends to pull a manager in several directions and can cause projects to suffer from lack of attention. If the project manager is not a functional manager, the project team may not respect their authority, which can lead to poor project performance.

Layers of Bureaucracy   This structure slows down the project progress because of the time it takes to get approval or make decisions.

Competition for Resources   When multiple priorities and projects are undertaken, the department can become stretched thin under the load, which can adversely affect all the work of the department. (To be honest, this problem can occur under any organizational structure.)

Project Managers Have Limited Authority   Project managers in a functional organization usually have to rely heavily on negotiating skills in order to obtain resources from functional managers. They also typically have little or no authority to hold team members accountable.

Projectized Organizations

Projectized organizations are structured just the opposite of functional organizations. If you're a project manager in this type of organization, you probably report directly to a vice president of project managers or perhaps to the CEO.

In this type of environment, the project manager has full authority over the project, and supporting functions such as accounting and human resources report to the project manager instead of to a functional manager in that area of expertise. Organizational structures like this focus on projects as their top priority. As a result, project managers have the authority to form project teams, assign resources, and focus on the work of the project. All the team members assigned to the project report directly to the project manager, and their sole responsibility involves project-specific activities. At the conclusion of the project, team members are assigned to new projects or to other assignments.

Project teams are typically *collocated* in a projectized environment. This facilitates communication and decision-making processes because everyone works together and reports to the same project manager. The following graphic is a typical org chart for a projectized organization.

projectized organizations
Projectized organizations focus on the project itself, not on the work of the functional department. Project managers have the most authority in this type of structure, and other functions, such as accounting or human resources, may report to the project manager.

collocated
Project team members are physically located together at the same site.

Projectized structures can exist within an otherwise functional organization. Perhaps the company is undertaking a mission-critical project and needs a dedicated team of folks to work on nothing but that project. A project manager is appointed who reports directly to an executive manager, the team is chosen and assigned, and off you go with a projectized team structure within the functional organization.

NOTE

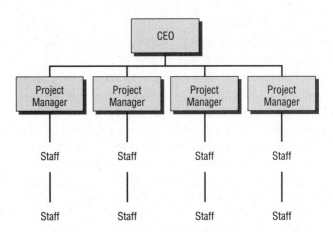

Advantages of a projectized organization include the following:

Project Managers Have Ultimate Authority   Team members have one boss (you and only you) and clearly understand the lines of authority. Teams are typically collocated, which makes communication very clear.

Project Managers Are the Primary Decision Makers   This makes communication, problem resolution, and priority setting clear-cut. The buck stops here.

The Focus of the Organization Is Project Work   Resources are focused on the projects and the work of the project. Loyalties are formed to the project and to you as the project manager.

Disadvantages of a projectized organization are as follows:

Reassignment of Team Members   When the work of the project is complete, team members need to find new assignments. There may not be another project available to the team members right away.

Idle Time   Team members with highly specialized skills may be required only at certain times or for specific activities on the project. What they do with their time otherwise is a tough issue to resolve in this type of organization.

Competition   Project managers compete against each other for the best resources available within the organization when forming their teams and acquiring materials. This could have a negative effect on the external customer who is unfortunate enough to have the project manager who drew all the short straws for their project.

Matrix Organizations

Matrix organizations are a result of combining the best of the functional and projectized organizations while downplaying the disadvantages inherent in both. Many organizations use this type of structure for project work. Like the projectized organization, projects are the focus of the work in a matrix structure.

The biggest disadvantage of this type of structure is that project team members report to more than one manager. I don't know about you, but having one boss is difficult enough, let alone two or three. (Sorry, boss!)

matrix organizations
An organizational structure where employees report to multiple managers, including one functional manager and at least one project manager.

NOTE

The idea here is that project team members are assigned to the project and thus report to the project manager for all project activities. They may still have duties to fulfill at their old functional job and thus report to their functional manager regarding those duties.

Let me give you an example. Suppose your project is to install a new piece of equipment in the remittance processing area. (They're the folks who take your money and credit your account for making the payment.) This project cuts across the lines of several departments: remittance processing, information technology, customer service, and accounting. In order to accomplish this project, team members from each of these functional areas are assigned to the project. Let's say you're the project manager and must make sure all the team members focus on this project to meet the implementation deadline. However, Sara in accounting really doesn't want to work on this project and has a particular loyalty to her functional manager. She spends most of her time on her functional duties, claiming priority issues or emergencies, and never seems to get her project activities completed on time. I think you're getting the picture.

Organizations operating under a matrix structure that place a strong emphasis on project work can eliminate the problem discussed in the preceding paragraph. When the emphasis is on project work, team members are relieved of their old functional duties during the course of the project. Functional managers are responsible for collecting time reports and monitoring the low-level administrative work of their team members. However, project assignments come from the project manager. At review time, the project manager will deliver an evaluation of project team members to their respective functional managers. This becomes input into the employee's annual review. Functional managers are responsible for holding formal reviews and rating their employees.

Project managers working in this environment should be certain to work closely with the functional managers when preparing project plans, setting schedules, and determining the staff members needed for specific activities. If you don't work closely with the functional manager or are lacking in negotiating skills, you may mysteriously find that the resources you need are never available when you need them.

When the functional department managers have good working relationships with the project managers and the company culture is focused more on the work of the project than on departmental work, this structure can work well. A project-focused matrix organization is known as a strong matrix organization. Project managers usually have more authority in a strong matrix structure than the functional department managers, and that makes it easier to settle disputes, assign resources, and focus on the work of the project. Here is a typical org chart for a matrix organization:

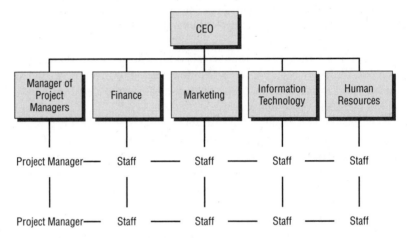

Advantages of a strong matrix organization include the following:

The Focus of the Organization Is Project Work   Resources are focused on the work of the project.

Specialty Skills Can Flourish   Employees with specialized skills are able to use these skills across the organization in various projects and remain up-to-date in their specialty. This benefits both the employee and the organization.

Opportunities for Growth   Employees just starting out their careers are exposed to various departments within the organization, which isn't as easy to do in a functional organization. They become well rounded in their perspectives and have a better understanding of how the organization operates.

Disadvantages of a strong matrix organization are as follows:

More Than One Boss   Team members report to more than one manager, which can lead to conflicts or delayed project activities later if they feel a strong loyalty to one manager.

Confusing Duties   Team members may be easily confused about their work priorities if the project managers and functional managers are not working together well.

Conflicts Between Managers Struggles over resources and priorities can affect the relationships between project managers and functional managers, thereby jeopardizing the project. If the managers have a particular dislike for one another, things can get very interesting.

As a project manager, it's important for you to understand the kind of organization, or project reporting structure, you're working under. Knowing the structure will help you understand your level of authority and why it's harder to get things done in certain organizations. Just being aware of the advantages and disadvantages of each type of organization will help you to navigate through some of the bumps in the road that you'll inevitably encounter.

Benefiting from Project Management Practices

We'll begin our journey into the world of project management by discussing what project management is and how to take advantage of established practices and tools of the trade. Perhaps you've been recruited to work on your organization's upcoming annual conference. You're working as an assistant to the project manager in charge of making arrangements for the vendors to attend, assigning their exhibit spaces on the conference room floor, and assisting them in making arrangements with the hotel for their hospitality functions on different evenings during the conference. Things progress relatively well until the evening before the conference begins and you discover that several of the vendors' booths are not wired for electricity. To make matters worse, the hotel informs you that it has another conference going on at the same time in another area of the hotel and all its personnel are busy working on those issues and they'll get to you when they get to you.

Applying good project management processes and techniques to your project could have prevented this mishap. That's not to say you'll never experience problems during your projects, but using good project management techniques will make you much better equipped to deal with problems as they arise. And, if you've really done a good job with project planning in particular, you won't be taken by surprise because you will have already accounted for the unexpected.

Project management means applying skills, knowledge, and established project management tools and techniques to your project and the processes used to carry out the project to produce the best results possible. You're going to learn all about those tools and techniques throughout the remainder of this book. Applying these skills once you've learned them is up to you. One thing I can assure you is if you're currently practicing project management by the seat of your pants, you'll notice a big difference in the way your projects play out, and in their success, if you'll apply some of the strategies outlined here (particularly the planning processes). If you haven't yet delved into project management, following the processes and techniques you're about to learn will make you look like an old pro.

You might be thinking that this whole project management process sounds like a lot of extra time added to the project. Why not just jump in and get started with the real work? In reality, that thinking is incorrect. Remember that time is money, as the old saying goes. Properly planning, executing, and monitoring your project along the way will save you lots of time in the long run. You'll have the tools at hand to measure your success as you go (and to know what you're looking for in the first place). Proper planning and follow-up will prevent mistakes or unplanned events that could creep up on you unexpectedly. At the very least, the impact of those unplanned events (also known as risks) is lessened if they do occur. And if you've saved the company time, what else have you saved?

NOTE   **Utilizing good project management techniques puts you in the driver's seat. Instead of your project running wildly out of control and bumping into every obstacle in its path, you'll steer it to a successful completion by applying the tools and techniques of an established project management process.**

Again, good project management techniques put you in the driver's seat. They allow you to control and apply the resources of the project and assure that you and your team are headed for the right destination. As the project manager, you'll realize several advantages when working through your next project by employing good project management techniques. Here's a brief list of the advantages of establishing sound processes in your organization:

- Improves overall project performance
- Reduces the time to complete projects
- Reduces project risk
- Increases quality
- Improves communication and provides an open environment for communication
- Provides standard methodologies for everyone in the organization to follow
- Ensures consistency in reporting
- Improves accuracy of project reports

Today, there are several established project management processes to pick from. A host of vendors and companies exist solely to sell you their solution and/or consulting time, to establish project management procedures in your organization. If your company doesn't have an in-house project management expert, this might be one way to get a framework for project management established. Most of these products and processes are easily adaptable to your organization's needs. There are also consultants aplenty who will gladly come in and organize project management processes for your company.

You don't have to purchase someone else's solution, however. With a little time, some elbow grease, and the blessing of your management team, you can develop your own procedures following standards already set out by such organizations as the *Project Management Institute (PMI)*. PMI is the international de facto standard for project management, and I'll rely heavily on PMI guidelines, process, and terminology throughout the rest of this book. There are other project management methodologies besides PMI that will work just as well. Later in this chapter, I'll list several websites you can visit to look at their ideas and approaches to project management.

Keep in mind that the exact process you use isn't what's important. What is important is that you follow an established procedure and that you properly plan and monitor the work of your project and follow through with good communicating skills and documenting techniques.

Project Management Institute (PMI)
Project Management Institute is a worldwide organization dedicated to promoting the use of standardized project management techniques across industries.

Tools of the Trade

Just as there are established project management standards and practices in existence today, there are several tools and resources available to assist you in various stages of the project. Project management tools are no different from the tools you'd buy if you were building a shed out in your backyard. You should know how the tool is used to derive the most benefit from it, and you shouldn't expect one tool to do everything. You wouldn't use a hammer to screw hinges to the door frame; in the same way, you shouldn't expect a project-scheduling tool to perform risk analysis for you. Above all, no tool takes the place of a good project plan. You can pick up that hammer and start nailing away at boards all day long, but if you don't have a good plan to work from, you may end up with a doghouse instead of a shed.

No tool, no matter how whiz-bang it is, will take the place of good project management practices.

NOTE

With that caveat behind us, let's take a look at a few of the tools available to help make your next project a success.

Project Management Software

Go ahead, check it out for yourself. Bring up your favorite Internet search engine and type in the words *project management software*. You'll be greeted with a host of products from scheduling to time tracking to risk assessment and more. The products abound. Are they all necessary? Are they all good? Well, that depends.

Way back in ancient times, there weren't any computers and thus no computer software programs. People did everything on — can you guess — paper! The point here is that the tool is only as good as the effort you put into it. Automating processes certainly helps your scheduling, planning, and tracking functions (to name a few), but you still need an understanding of how the results you see on the screen are produced. Elementary schools all over the country today teach children how to perform math calculations by hand and require them to memorize the multiplication tables. Why do they do that when they could issue calculators to every child on the first day of school? It's because the kids need to understand why 4 pops up on the calculator screen when they plug in 2×2. (And that always brings up the question, what happens when the aliens invade and mess with Earth's electromagnetic field and all the computers become art deco paperweights? Who will do all those calculations?) If you understand the formulas, processes, and theories used to produce the results, you'll have a much better grasp of the impact changes and risk may have on the project.

NOTE   **One of the best-known project management software tools is Microsoft Office Project. In later chapters, we'll be looking at different aspects of this software and how it can make project scheduling easier for you. This product is widely used in many different industries today and has practically made *Gantt chart* a household term. The strongest features of this product are its scheduling ability and its resource assignment and usage functions. We'll dive into these functions later in the book.**

Other software packages are available that perform some of the same functions as Microsoft Office Project, and I encourage you to check them out. Remember that the outputs from these software packages are not the project plan itself — they are part of the overall project plan. One more thing you should remember is that if you plug bad information into the tool, you're going to get bad information out.

Templates for Project Forms

Did you ever play with stencils when you were a kid? You'd take your trusty No. 2 pencil in one hand, hold the stencil down tight against your paper, and trace away, drawing almost perfect shapes. Templates are like stencils. They provide a consistent format to follow for everything from scope statements to progress reporting and are reusable from project to project. You'll be seeing several examples of templates throughout this book. If these whet your appetite and you'd like to see more, you can search for templates, information, and articles on project management on several websites. Here are a few to check out:

www.gantthead.com
www.techrepublic.com
www.tenstep.com
www.pmi.org

www.allpm.com

www.projectconnections.com

Pull up your favorite search engine to see if you can find more.

Project Notebooks

This is one of my favorite tools. Project notebooks are a handy way to maintain all of your project documentation and archive projects in the project library. You can quickly pull them off the shelf when the boss pops in unexpectedly asking about the project.

Project notebooks should be organized the way your project logically unfolds. Order a few of those trusty three-ring binders, available in any office-supply store, and some divider tabs. Start the notebook with a minimum of eight tabs, adding more as you build the project. The first section contains all the documents pertaining to the origination of the project, the next section contains the project planning documents, and so on. You'll get more familiar with each of these documents and the project notebook sections as we proceed through the coming chapters.

Printing and filing documents in a three-ring binder may seem antiquated to you, but I know many project managers who still use this method today, along with their electronic storage counterparts. Microsoft's SharePoint product is perfect for storing, sharing, and controlling project documents. Set up separate folders that correspond to your project processes and save your documents to the SharePoint site as the documents are created and modified. The goal is to maintain all the project information in one place that's easily accessible to the people who need it.

For long-term archiving, I recommend saving all project information on your organization's server. You'll need to check with your IT group to find out the procedures for storing information you want to keep long term.

Understanding Project Processes

All projects progress through five project management process groups: Initiating, Planning, Executing, Monitoring and Controlling, and Closing. We'll take a closer look at each of these momentarily. First, let's see how they all work together in the big picture.

The production and printing of this book is an example of a project. This book started with an idea that was submitted for approval and then given the "go" after examination and selection based on various selection criteria (Initiating). Then a plan was produced that also received a review and approval (Planning). Each chapter was written (Executing) and reviewed by technical experts for accuracy. When errors were found or passages discovered that could be clarified, notification was sent to the author for correction (Monitoring and Controlling).

Corrections were made and resubmitted for review and approval (repeat of the Executing and Monitoring and Controlling processes). Finally, the book was completed, reviewed, approved, printed, and distributed to local booksellers (Closing).

Every project, whether it's building a bridge, publishing a book, constructing a building, or creating a new software program, progresses through a *project life cycle*. The phases of the life cycle will differ depending on the industry. For example, the construction industry has phases within a project life cycle with titles such as *initiating, designing, building,* and so on. At the end of each phase, the project manager and others determine whether the project should continue to the next phase. This phase-to-phase progression is called a handoff. Each phase serves as a checkpoint of sorts to determine whether the project is on target before the handoff to the next phase occurs. If things are not progressing as planned, decisions need to be made to determine whether some of the phases should be repeated or the project should be scrapped altogether.

The project management process groups work much the same way. Each process has its own characteristics and produces outputs that serve as inputs into the next group of processes or, in the case of the Closing process, serve as the final approval for the project. Let's take a quick look at the purpose of each process and what it produces.

Initiating Process

Project initiation begins at the beginning. The *Initiating process* determines which projects should be undertaken. It examines whether the project is worth doing and if it is beneficial to the company when all is said and done. Most important, the Initiating process acknowledges that the project should begin and commits the organization's resources to working on the project. Some of the things that are accomplished during this process are:

- Defining the major goals of the project
- Determining project selection criteria
- Assigning the project manager
- Writing the project charter
- Obtaining sign-off of the project charter

Planning Process

Project planning is the heart of the project management processes. The *Planning process* tells everyone involved where you're going and how you're going to get there. I'm a strong advocate for a good project plan. It isn't unheard of to spend a good deal of project time in the Planning process; however, for the record, the majority of project time and costs is usually spent in the Executing process. The documents produced during the Planning process will be used throughout the remaining project processes to carry out the

project life cycle
All the phases of a project when taken together from the beginning of the project through the end.

handoff
The transition between each phase of the project life cycle.

Initiating process
Initiating is the first process group and is where the project is requested, approved, and begun.

Planning process
Project plans are created and documented, the project deliverables and requirements are defined, the project budget is established, and the project schedule is created.

activities of the project and monitor their progress. Some of the things that are accomplished during this process are:

- Determining project deliverables
- Writing and publishing a scope statement
- Establishing a project budget
- Defining project activities and estimates
- Developing a schedule
- Determining the special skills and resources needed to accomplish project tasks
- Identifying project risks and creating plans to address them

Executing Process

Executing is the process where the work of the project is produced. Here, you'll put all the plans you devised during the planning processes into action. Your team members are assigned and raring to go, and the project manager keeps them on task and focused on the work of the project. The *Executing process* is where most of the project resources are utilized and most of the budget is spent. Be aware that this process is where you'll likely run into scheduling conflicts. Some of the things that are accomplished during this process are:

Executing process
In this process group, team members perform the work of the project. Teams are assembled, tasks are assigned, and the work is carried out.

- Developing and forming the project team
- Directing and leading the project team
- Obtaining other project resources
- Conducting status review meetings
- Communicating project information
- Managing project progress
- Implementing quality assurance procedures

Monitoring and Controlling Process

The *Monitoring and Controlling process* of the project is where performance measures are taken to determine whether the project deliverables and objectives are being met. If not, corrective actions are taken to get the project back on track and aligned with the project plan. This means you might have to revisit the project Planning and Executing processes in order to put the corrective actions into place. Change management also takes place during this process and involves reviewing, managing, and implementing changes to the project. Some of the things that are accomplished during this process are:

Monitoring and Controlling process
This process group concerns monitoring project performance to make certain that the outcomes meet the requirements of the project. Change requests are monitored and reviewed during this process.

- Measuring performance against the plan
- Taking corrective action when measures are outside the limits

♦ Evaluating the effectiveness of the corrective actions

♦ Ensuring that project progress continues according to the plan

♦ Reviewing and implementing change requests

Many project managers, including myself, sometimes collapse the Executing process and the Monitoring and Controlling process into one process. Some projects, especially small projects, lend themselves well to this approach. My projects are information technology–based and usually involve some type of new programming and/or the installation of hardware and such. Combining Executing with Monitoring and Controlling makes a lot of sense on this type of project because you need to test and control outcomes as you go. Other projects or industries may not lend themselves well to this structure. Be aware that these processes are not set in stone, nor are the templates you'll come across throughout the book. Use good judgment to decide what's appropriate for your project. If you're in doubt, it's better to err on the side of too much planning and monitoring throughout the project than too little.

Closing Process

Closing process
The last process group, where final approval is obtained for the project, the books are closed, and the project documentation is archived for future reference.

The *Closing process* is the process that is most often skipped. It seems that once the product of the project has been produced and the customer is satisfied, the books are closed and everyone moves on to the next project. However, Closing is an important process. It's during this process that you'll want to celebrate the success of the project, document what you've learned, and obtain a final sign-off on the project deliverables. Some of the things that are accomplished during this process are:

♦ Obtaining acceptance of project deliverables

♦ Documenting the lessons learned over the course of this project

♦ Archiving project records

♦ Formalizing the closure of the project

♦ Releasing project resources

TIP

You may have a substance for poison control hiding in the back of your medicine cabinet called syrup of ipecac. You can easily remember the project management process groups with this mnemonic: IPECC (Initiating, Planning, Executing, Controlling, Closing), which sounds like the syrupy lifesaver. (Note, you'll have to remember to add "Monitoring and" back to the Controlling term to make this work.) Effectively using these processes on your next project could be a project lifesaver.

As stated earlier, project phases recur throughout the project. As an example, let's say our book project has progressed to the Monitoring and

Controlling process. While reviewing one of the chapters, an editor discovers that an important topic was missed. In order to determine where the topic should be inserted, she revisits the Planning processes. After she figures out where to insert the new information, the Executing process is also repeated (the new material is written) and then the Monitoring and Controlling process is performed again to review the new additions for accuracy. At the end of the project, the Closing process is performed, and sign-off is achieved. All projects follow this kind of process. The most often repeated processes are the Planning, Executing, and Monitoring and Controlling processes.

When you're performing a multiphase project, the Closing process feeds back into the Initiating process. At the conclusion of each phase of the project, there's an additional opportunity to make a go/no-go decision. Closing is the time to examine the project objectives and the progress to date and determine whether the next phase should be initiated.

The next image shows how these process groups interact. Initiating has outputs that become inputs into the Planning process, Planning outputs are inputs to Executing, and so on. You'll notice that the Monitoring and Controlling process has outputs that are inputs back into the Planning and Executing processes. This shows their recurring nature.

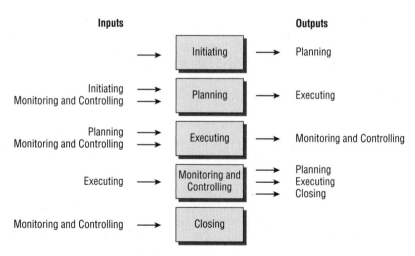

Project Management Process Group

Some project management methodologies combine the Executing and Monitoring and Controlling processes. There's nothing wrong with that as long as you're careful not to skip anything along the way. We'll discuss each of these processes later in the book as separate processes so you can see the unique characteristics of each. Then you can decide for yourself if you'd like to combine these processes into one.

Twenty-first Century Project Management

Is project management different today than it was hundreds of years ago? My guess is there probably isn't a lot of difference in the way the projects are managed today than when the Pharaohs built the pyramids or when the medieval castles were designed and constructed. We have many more tools available to us today, such as computers and software planning tools, than our ancient counterparts did, but I believe the core processes we use now are the same as they were then.

Ancient project management went something like this: Someone with lots of time and money on their hands thought up the project — they didn't need approval for the project because the project requestor was usually the ruler of the kingdom and you don't argue with someone like that. An expert was hired (or "recruited") to manage and monitor the execution of the project and then beheaded when it was completed. OK, fortunately we don't behead project managers today, or you and I wouldn't be very interested in this topic. But I can't help but believe that the core processes themselves were the same. The idea was hatched, a plan formed, the work carried out, and the project closed out.

What's Old Is New Again

Even though we may perform some of the same basic processes as our ancient counterparts did, we probably call them by different names. PMI has worked hard to establish project management standards, guidelines, and terminology that can be used across industries. Putting official names to processes and project details helps everyone involved on the project to understand the topic at hand. When you tell me you're having a problem scheduling resources for tasks, I know what process you're talking about and where it falls in the project management process.

stakeholder
Anyone who has a vested interest in the project.

The formula for project success is simple, and it hasn't varied since project work began. Successful projects meet or exceed the expectations of the stakeholders. *Stakeholders* can be anyone from the king or queen who commanded that the project be completed to the customer who is paying you to complete the project for them. As the project manager, you are a stakeholder, as are other department managers, the project team members, vendors, the customer, and so on. Stakeholders have different parts to play in the project. We'll talk more about stakeholders and their roles in Chapter 3, "Initiating the Project."

Constraints

Let's go back to our candy project. The boss comes in and starts giving you some high-level ideas about this project and what the end product should look like. You diligently take notes, and the wheels in your head start spinning as he's talking. Then he says something that astonishes you: "You have an unlimited budget and all the time you need to get this project completed and into production. And quality really isn't a big concern, nor are we that worried about what the end customer thinks of the new candies. Just get the project done and the candies rolling off the line."

Did you have to reread that to believe it? I know what you're thinking, and you're right — this is the stuff of B-grade sci-fi movies! Each of the things the boss mentioned in this unbelievable statement is called a *constraint*. No project manager in modern times has ever worked on a project under conditions like these. All projects have constraints.

Not too long ago, the big three constraints, also known as the *triple constraints*, were *the* project management doctrine preached from the lips of all experienced project managers. The big three constraints are scope, schedule, and cost. However, because the definition of a constraint is anything that restricts or dictates the actions of the project team, you can see that there are probably many more constraints than just these three. These three, plus customer satisfaction, probably have the biggest impact on project outcomes, and that's why they get so much attention.

Keep in mind that the *Guide to the Project Management Body of Knowledge* also uses the term *competing demands* for constraints. It lists the primary constraints of a project as scope, schedule, cost, and quality. It also identifies many other factors such as resources and risk as potential constraints. We'll examine some of the common constraints in a little more detail.

constraint
Anything that limits or dictates the actions of the project team.

triple constraints
The three constraints common to all projects: schedule, scope and, cost. Each of these constraints, or any combination of them, has the ability to impact quality.

Scope

All projects set out to produce a unique product or result. Scope defines what the product or result should be like. Scope considers the goals and objectives of the project and describes what the project is trying to accomplish. These goals are then broken down into smaller components until the work can be easily defined. Scope can often grow or change during the course of a project, which is why it is so important to document scope. (We'll talk more about that in Chapter 4, "Defining the Project Goals.")

Scope often involves trade-offs with the other constraints, and changes in scope will impact time, budget, or both. Changes in budget or time can also impact scope. For example, I'm building a new house on a limited budget. I would like to have granite countertops in the bathrooms, but I don't have enough in the budget. I'll have to modify the scope and choose a different material for the countertops so that I don't go over budget.

Schedule

Most projects operate under some type of deadline. If your project entails building a new shopping center that must open in time for the holiday shopping season, your project is time-constrained. Schedules are built on units of time, so you will often find the word *time* used in placed of the word *schedule* when referring to the triple constraints. This time deadline determines the way project activities are scheduled and completed.

The stakeholders, or perhaps the project requestor, have stated that the new center must open by October 1. You work hard on the project schedule and come up with a plan that allows for all the activities to complete by the deadline. Be aware that time constraints, which usually involve scheduling activities, can cause some interesting problems for the project manager. If your schedule calls for paving crews at a specific point in the plan but no paving crews are available at the scheduled time, you'll have a dilemma on your hands. We'll talk about how to solve dilemmas like this when we look at project scheduling in depth later in this book.

Budget

Budgets are a staple on all projects. No matter how small or large the projects, there will always be a budget. You may have $3,500 at your disposal or $35 million, but either way you are constrained by the total amount available for accomplishing the project goals. Utilizing solid project management techniques will help assure you accomplish all the objectives of the project within the allotted budget.

Quality

Quality is sometimes quoted as one of the triple constraints by some project management gurus. Quality can be a constraint but is most often impacted by one of the triple constraints. Quality assures that the end product conforms to the requirements and the product description that's defined during the Planning process.

Taking quality measurements and performing quality control assure that quality requirements will be met. They also assure that the project measures up to the original requirements.

Customer Satisfaction

Customers are the reason companies are in business. Even though we've all had those experiences where we could swear otherwise, customers, and their satisfaction with the company's products or services, are the key to achieving success. This is true for project management as well. Scope, time, and budget may all track exactly as planned, but if the customers aren't satisfied, they aren't going to come back.

You might be thinking that if the requirements of the project have been met according to the product description, and if the product or service was delivered on time and under budget, how could the customer not be satisfied?

I'll answer that question two ways: first, communication problems, and second, relationship building. These two topics go hand in hand. If a project manager alienates the customer because of poor communication skills or poor people skills, the customer will not be satisfied with the project. They might love the product but dislike the way the project process was carried out. When you dig deep enough, you'll see that the roots of customer dissatisfaction (when they are otherwise happy with the product itself) can be attributed to communication problems and differences in interpersonal skills. We'll devote entire sections of this book to these topics later, but for now keep in mind that good communication skills can avert a host of problems on your project. Commit yourself to brushing up and improving these skills soon.

Juggling Acts

Managing under the triple constraints may seem like a real juggling act for project managers. One minute all the balls are in the air, and the next minute one of them drops to the floor and bounces into the corner. Typically, though, constraints are give-and-take. If budget is the primary constraint, then time and/or scope may have to give a little. If time is the biggest constraint, then it might take more money than originally thought to complete the project according to the deadline. You can keep all the balls in the air and manage project outcomes by understanding the constraints and their impacts. Constraints limit every project, but they shouldn't prevent you from accomplishing the work of the project.

An important step you can take early on in the project process is to determine which of the constraints is the primary constraint. Knowing that time is the primary constraint, for example, will help you address issues concerning budgets and scope as they come up.

It's sometimes difficult to determine which constraint is the primary driver. Here's an example: Your boss has assigned you to a new project to get the company network upgraded. He tells you that you have until November 1 to get the network converted to the latest technology, and the budget for the project cannot exceed one nickel over $150,000. How do you know which of these is the primary constraint? At first glance, you don't. Both time and budget are constraints on this project. To determine which one is the most important, ask the boss this question, "Boss, if you could have only one of these two alternatives — project completion by November 1 or we won't exceed the budget — which would you choose?" If the boss answers that you must stick to the budget, you know that money is the primary constraint for this project. Does that mean you shouldn't try to meet the deadline? No, but it does mean that if there are problems down the road, you might be able to convince the boss to bend a little on the deadline, whereas you know the budget is not going to change.

Constraints can include things other than the triple constraints. The management team may issue directives that restrict the project team. Technology may dictate what type of equipment must be used for your particular project. Government regulations may dictate the actions of the project team. What's important is that you're aware of the project constraints so that you can plan, estimate, and control your project activities appropriately. Constraints are one of the items documented and filed in your project notebook.

And don't forget to continue to communicate the condition or status of the constraints with your sponsor. We'll cover this again in the Planning phase of the project.

Where Do You Go from Here?

Once you've gained some experience in the project management field, you may want to consider becoming a formal project manager by way of a postgraduate certificate program or a professional certification. Many industries are realizing the importance of project management and project management certification, and many organizations are now requiring certification as part of their hiring criteria.

Many colleges now offer project management certificate programs. Just like any academic program, it consists of a series of courses, some of which may require a dictated amount of outside project time, and multiple exams. These programs (or even a few courses) are excellent additions to any professional's resume. Those who are serious about becoming a formal project manager will likely be targeting certification. It could be, though, that the effort of obtaining certification might not appeal to you. In this case, a few courses may suit your needs. Either way, many college extension programs are recognized PMI providers, so your option of certification is readily available.

PMI's Project Management Professional (PMP®) certification is the most recognized certification in the field. I highly recommend obtaining the PMP certification if you're serious about the project management field. Becoming PMP certified assures potential employers and customers that you have a firm understanding of project management practices and disciplines and that you have experience putting it all into practice. Having the PMP designation will open up doors for career advancement, and it gives your customers, and your company, confidence that you've mastered and established the standard project management processes and disciplines.

There are other certifications besides the PMP that you might want to think about as well. CompTIA Project+ is a project management certification that you might want to consider either independently or to augment the PMP certificate.

Becoming PMP Certified

The Project Management Institute was founded in 1969 with the goal of developing standards for project management practices across industries. It has been successful at its goal, because PMI has set the standard for project management techniques worldwide. The organization has outlined processes and techniques in its own publication, *A Guide to the Project Management*

Body of Knowledge 4th Edition, also called the *PMBOK® Guide.* Numerous other books exist that explore PMI techniques in depth that you might want to peruse after sparking your interest with this book. As previously mentioned, this book follows the techniques and processes defined by PMI because its methods are the industry standard.

PMI requires you to fill out an application to take the PMP exam. You can submit your application online at www.pmi.org. In addition to the application, you need to meet a few other requirements. You'll need to document 35 hours of formal project management education. This can include a combination of seminars, workshops, college classes, or training sessions. You'll need to list course titles, dates, and the number of hours you spent in training on your application.

PMI also requires that you have a certain number of hours of project management experience. At the time of the publication of this book, PMI requires 4,500 hours of project management experience if you hold a bachelor's degree. You'll need to provide proof of your degree as part of your application process. If you do not have a bachelor's degree, you'll need to verify 7,500 hours of project management experience. Visit the PMI website to get the all the forms needed to verify your project management experience.

The exam itself is held in testing centers in major cities across the country. You can find a center near you by contacting PMI or looking it up on its Internet site. At the testing center, you are required to show two forms of photo identification and to place your personal belongings in a locker. You are not allowed to take anything with you into the testing area. The testing center will furnish you with a calculator, pencil, and scrap paper. The exam is scored when you've finished, so you'll know whether you passed before leaving the center. You have up to four hours to complete the exam, which consists of 200 randomly generated questions on the five process groups (Initiating, Planning, Executing, Monitoring and Controlling, and Closing) and an area called Professional Responsibility. Only 175 of the 200 questions are scored. A passing score requires you to answer 106 of the 175 questions correctly. Twenty-five of the 200 questions are "pretest" questions that will appear randomly throughout the exam. These 25 questions are used by PMI to calculate statistical information and to determine whether they can or should be used on future exams. All unanswered questions are scored as incorrect answers, so it benefits you to answer them all even if you have to guess at an answer.

If you're seriously considering taking the PMP exam, I recommend you pick up a copy of another Sybex book titled *PMP: Project Management Professional Exam Study Guide, 5th Edition* (written by yours truly) to help you prepare for the exam. It has hundreds of sample questions, many real-life examples that help you apply what you've learned, and a project case study at the end of every chapter that applies the project management processes talked about in the book.

PMI has several requirements for certification. You should check its website for the most up-to-date information regarding the requirements.

Even if you aren't going to sit for the exam, consider becoming a PMI member and getting involved with a local chapter. (You do not have to be PMP certified to become a member of PMI.) Today, PMI has more than 265,000 members from 170 different countries. Local chapters exist in most major cities in America. You can visit the PMI website (www.pmi.org) to find a chapter that meets near you. I encourage you to get involved with your local chapter. You'll have the opportunity to share experiences with other project managers and learn new skills and techniques. PMI works hard to maintain standards and promote ethics, and it offers a host of publications, training, seminars, and more to train new project managers and keep experienced project managers current in the latest processes.

Certifying with CompTIA's Project+

CompTIA is an organization dedicated to certifying individuals in the general principles and knowledge of the information technology industry. It does not test on any particular brand of hardware or software (with the exception of the Linux tests) but instead tests on general knowledge regarding these topics. (As an example, you may have heard of CompTIA's A+ certification test regarding general knowledge of PC hardware.)

The Project+ exam tests on general knowledge and principles of project management based on PMI's project management methodology. The Project+ test is ideal for people who are new to project management. You might consider taking this exam first to get yourself acquainted with certification testing because it's not as intense as the PMP exam.

CompTIA does not have any specific requirements to take the exam other than a strong knowledge of PMI's project management techniques and terminology. You can visit its website at www.comptia.com to get further information.

If you're considering taking the Project+ exam, you might want to get a copy of the Sybex book titled *CompTIA Project+ Study Guide, 2nd Edition*, by yours truly and William Heldman to help you study.

Formal Education Programs

There are numerous educational programs on the topic of project management. Many institutions offer everything from certificates in project management to master's degrees. Whatever your interest level, you can find educational programs to meet it. Try your local colleges and universities to see what they offer. If going back to the classroom doesn't sound like something you want to do, then search the Internet for an institution that offers online classes on project management. You'll be amazed at the number of classes available to you in this format.

Terms to Know

Closing process	matrix organizations
collocated	Monitoring and Controlling process
constraints	Planning process
customer	project life cycle
Executing process	project management
functional organizations	Project Management Institute (PMI)
handoff	projectized organizations
Initiating process	stakeholder
	triple constraints

Review Questions

1. What is project management?

2. What are some of the benefits of a projectized organization?

3. What are the five project management process groups?

4. Name three of the things that you'll accomplish during the Planning process.

5. Name three of the things that you'll accomplish during the Executing process.

6. Which project management process is the one most often skipped?

7. Name at least three criteria for determining whether your work assignment is a project.

8. What is the definition of a constraint?

9. Name the triple constraints and other common competing demands.

10. What does it mean when a person has a PMP?

Chapter 2

Developing Project Management Skills

In This Chapter
- General management skills
- Organizing techniques
- Communication skills and styles
- Exchanging information
- Active listening

Project managers are multitalented folks. You need to master several skills for success in the field of project management. Many of the skills that we cover in this chapter are the same kind of skills you'd need in most any profession. (Skills specific to project management will be covered in subsequent chapters.)

By far, the most important skill you'll need in order to succeed as a project manager is communication. This chapter discusses the importance of communicating effectively, and it will remain the underlying theme for all of the topics we'll cover in this book. Organizational skills are probably the second most important skills you'll need for a successful career in project management. These include things such as employing time management techniques, setting priorities, and managing information.

At the end of this chapter, you'll have a solid foundation of management skills to help you on your next project.

A Little Bit of Everything

Applying project management techniques to your projects involves combining a unique set of skills and talents. Reading this book will help you develop some of those skills — or at least expose you to them so you can research and maybe even practice the ones you're not familiar with. After reading this book, you should have a feel for what life as a project manager is like, and you will be able to do some self-assessment to determine whether you're ready to take the plunge.

If you enjoy working with people at all levels of the organization, performing a variety of activities, managing and controlling outcomes, and solving problems, you'll love the world of project management. It's a diverse career, because no two projects are ever the same. You might apply the same techniques, but the product is different, the stakeholders are different, and maybe even the company or the country you're working in is different.

Organizations often make the mistake of promoting their top technicians to project managers. The thinking is that if the employee excels at programming, engineering, or research, then they must automatically be good at project management. That is not necessarily true. You may very well be an accomplished programmer with the natural skills to move into project management, but I've witnessed many situations where just the opposite happens. Expert technicians are put into the project management role and flounder. This doesn't have to happen to you, however. After some diligent study on project management techniques and a little practice, your projects will pass with flying colors.

Project management allows you to learn about and potentially gain experience in many different industries. As a project manager, you don't necessarily have to be an expert in the industry you're working in because your expertise is in managing projects. However, most hiring managers look for candidates with some experience or knowledge in the industry. You don't need to be an expert on everything about that industry, but some exposure will give you a leg up when competing against other candidates. If you find yourself working in a new field, remember that you'll rely on the technical experts in that industry to provide you with the information needed that's specific to the project at hand. They'll give you the details regarding the activities you need to plug into the project plan and provide you with activity estimates.

Some of the most important skills you'll need as a project manager are strong oral and written communication skills, good organization skills, general management skills such as budgeting and team building, negotiation and problem-resolution skills, and people skills. Project management is not so much about having one set of skills or knowing one way to do a thing; it's really more about knowing a little bit about a lot of things. Project managers have been characterized as "a mile wide and an inch deep." That sums up the breadth of skills you'll need in order to successfully manage your next project.

Project managers are a mile wide and an inch deep — their skills cover a broad range of general management disciplines.

Communication Is the Key

By far, the most important skills a project manager possesses are communication skills. These encompass good verbal skills as well as good writing skills. As the project manager, you'll be the one generating almost all of the communication that will take place on the project. You'll talk to stakeholders, team members, customers, vendors, senior management, and so on. You'll also create status reports, generate project documents by the truckload, generate reports, write email, and more. The better you are at communicating, the smoother your project will go. Does this mean you won't experience problems along the way or get into tussles with stakeholders or team members? Absolutely not. But it does mean that everyone will know exactly what's expected of them, and everyone will understand what the project status is at any time and what's still to come.

Communicating the right information to the right people at the right time helps assure project success. You can never over-communicate when you follow this rule.

We'll talk about good and bad communication techniques — and many other communication skills — in more detail in the second half of this chapter.

Organizing Techniques

"Where did I put my keys?" Have you ever asked yourself that question as you're rushing out the door on the way to work or an important meeting? I used to until I put up a hook next to the garage door to hang my keys on the minute I walk in. Although this may be a minor example, it illustrates how organizational skills will help you when managing projects. If I'm wasting time hunting down my keys every morning, something else isn't getting done (like getting a jump on rush-hour traffic). This applies to project work as well. If I'm always spinning my wheels looking for project documentation that's buried in piles and spread out all over the office or if I find I spend half the day addressing unimportant issues and email, I'm wasting valuable time that could be spent elsewhere.

So, how do you get a handle on all that project information and differentiate between important messages and problems during the course of the day? Some basic organizational techniques will get you off to a good start. Remember back in Chapter 1, "Building the Foundation," when we talked about the different ways to assemble project information using project notebooks or the company's intranet? That's one organizational technique you can use right away for all your project documentation. Putting all that paperwork together in one location will keep you organized almost automatically (provided, of course, that you actually put the information in the book or in the proper folders on the server). We'll work on the project notebook, including what gets filed and how it gets filed, throughout the remaining chapters of this book. That will take care of organizing your project documents, but what about time management and all those emails and voicemails and the constant interruptions, just to name a few?

Organization is a topic that spans many areas, including time management, priority setting, and information. Let's look at some of the techniques in each of these areas.

Time Management

How many times do you get to the end of your day and wonder, "Where does the time go?" You glance over at the clock and it's 5:15, but you feel you haven't accomplished a thing. If this describes you, it's possible that your day is managing you instead of the other way around.

Each of us has only 24 hours to accomplish our tasks for that day. However, it seems some folks can get twice the amount of work done in that amount of time as others. They don't have more time available to them than we do, so how do they do it? They accomplish this with good time management techniques. Time management is a process you use to control the priorities over your time. This might sound pretty basic, and it is. It starts with keeping your calendar up-to-date and maintaining a task list of things to do each day. These two things alone can go a long way toward keeping your day from getting out of control. I find that writing down a list of tasks for the day helps me prioritize where my time should be spent and helps me know which activities to focus on.

Several time organizer tools are available on the market. At a minimum, most include a calendar, task list, notes, and a contact list. You can find these organizers in paper and electronic formats. I'm a fan of the electronic version because not only can I keep my appointments, to-do lists, and contacts all in one place, I can also keep a copy of the latest project status report, important project information, and a high-level project plan with me at all times. If someone happens to catch me in a meeting on another topic but has a question about the project, I have the latest information at my fingertips.

Remember our rule from Chapter 1, though: The tool is useful only if you know how to use it.

TIP   Use one organizer tool for all your appointment, task, and contact lists. Combine your business and personal information in one organizer, not two, so that you don't end up with scheduling conflicts.

The rule for this chapter is to use only one tool! I knew a project manager who used three separate organizer tools. It drove her crazy because she never knew where she was supposed to be. One organizer was for project-specific appointments, tasks, and notes. Another organizer was for her regular management duties. (Pop quiz: What kind of organization is this describing?) And she kept yet another one for her personal affairs! You can only imagine what happened when it was her turn to pick up the kids from soccer practice (recorded in organizer number three) as she was rushing to a project meeting scheduled for the same time (recorded in organizer number one). Keep all of your appointments and tasks in one organizer. If you're using an electronic tool such as Microsoft Outlook, you can flag your personal items as such, and they'll be hidden from public view if you so choose.

Dozens of classes and books are available for further information on the subject of time management. I really encourage you to take a time management class if you never have, even if you think you're good at it. You're bound to pick up some useful tips and hints that will make you a better time manager.

Setting Priorities

Prioritizing your time according to the importance and urgency of the item you're dealing with will help you focus on the right issues.

Most priorities fall into four zones. I call these zones the firefighting zone, the planning zone, the time-waster zone, and the looking-for-a-new-job zone. Let's look at a description of each of these:

Firefighting Zone   A fire needs to be dealt with now, or else the problems will only get worse. You need to drop everything you're doing to go fix the problems springing up around you. You'll likely find issues such as emergencies, unplanned risks, and business or service interruptions occurring in this zone. You want to spend as little of your time as possible in this zone because it's a time killer. You can accomplish that by spending more time in the planning zone.

Planning Zone   Every day brings a new list of things to do along with all the tasks you didn't get to yesterday. Taking a few minutes each morning to review the tasks you need to complete and determining their priorities will help you set the tone for the day. Ask yourself, "What must be accomplished today?" to help establish priorities. If possible, delegate tasks that don't need your personal attention to other team members. Planning puts you in control. Think of this zone more like earthquake retrofitting than firefighting; it's important that you create a sound structure, but thankfully the structure is not currently under immediate threat. Put a high importance on planning activities, and they will keep you out of the firefighting zone. It's important to continue to review the items and prioritization on this list, too. Things that one day seemed high-priority sometimes move lower on the list as time goes on.

Time-Waster Zone   The alarm is going off, but there is no actual crisis. This zone might include things like unnecessary meetings, unimportant email and voicemail, junk mail, drop-in visitors discussing their recent trip to Hawaii, and so on. Apply a little discipline and hit the Delete key — you really don't have to read every email that comes your way, do you? Let your co-worker know you're simply dying to hear all about their trip to Hawaii and ask whether you can take time during lunch, a break, or after work to devote your full attention to his pictures and stories. Try to stay out of this zone because it's a time killer, and you're really not accomplishing much.

Looking-for-a-new-job zone   No alarms are going off, no crisis is at hand, and there's no motivation to spend time planning. Heck, there's no motivation to do anything! You can probably imagine what this zone includes: things like cube hopping, Internet surfing, showing pictures of your Hawaii trip to anyone passing by, extraneous documentation, frivolous email, and so on. If you find yourself in this zone often, it's time to ask yourself some hard questions: Are you enjoying this job? Are you performing meaningful and fulfilling work, or are you simply killing time? When you find yourself in this zone often, it's probably time to consider looking for some new challenges.

Using these categories to classify your issues as they arise can help you decide what should be dealt with immediately and what can wait. The process works something like this: Those items that are of high importance and high urgency should be dealt with first; you have to fight the fires. However, if you find yourself in firefighting mode often, you're probably not spending enough time planning — or you have a runaway project on your hands that's screaming out for drastic measures. For example, it might be time to reexamine scope, reexamine the purpose of the project, or kill the project. Try to stay out of this zone by concentrating on the planning zone. Write in time for planning activities on your calendar and a to-do list every day. Spending the first part of your day in the planning zone will likely save you a lot of time in the long run.

TIP   **Avoid spending all of your project time in the firefighting zone by using proper planning techniques.**

Your two biggest time wasters are those things found in the time-waster and looking-for-a-new-job zones. Limit the amount of time that you allow yourself to get caught up with these things, and you'll have more time to plan and fight fires when necessary.

You can use these zones to help make decisions about which project activities to undertake as well as which tasks to complete, email to answer, phone calls to return, meetings to attend, and so on. If the activity is unimportant or frivolous, don't waste your time with it.

Managing Information

I confess, I'm an information junkie. I love learning new things and digging out all the facts. But it's important to know what information really is important in order to sort out the good from the not-so-good. If you don't manage what's coming your way, it can drown you in a sea of useless details.

Today, we're bombarded with a plethora of information, and it comes in mainly two forms: email and voicemail. I'll give you some tips on how to deal with all this information next.

Email

Information comes from a variety of sources, and projects have a way of accumulating information rapidly. Email alone could fill a room or two with three-ring binders. Should you print all those emails and file them in the project notebook? Well, that depends. Personal preference has a part to play in the decision as does the priority and importance of the email. If it's an email that has the potential to cause major problems for the project team, pertains to late shipments, or shows that a functional manager is being a little less than cooperative, then I recommend keeping a printed copy for reference.

Handle every piece of information one time and do something with it immediately — delete it, respond to it, or file it.

NOTE

One of the best tips I've ever come across for information management is this idea of handling every piece of information one time, be it email, voicemail, interoffice mail, or regular mail. When I first learned about this tip, it applied only to regular mail and interoffice memos because email and voicemail didn't yet exist. Yikes, does that show my age? But I've found that it's a good tip for all the information that's likely to come across your desk — regular mail, email, voicemail, and so on. Once you've read the email, act on it. If you need to save it, move it to a project folder. If you need to print it, then print it, file it, and move it to the project folder. If it's not productive information or it's something you don't need, then delete it. The same goes for information you receive on paper. Handle it one time. Read it and then do something with it.

Email is a great tool and has some handy features that you can put to use on your next project. Most email systems allow you to create personal folders. I recommend setting up a folder for your project and maybe even a set of subfolders within the project folder for email from various sources — maybe folders for vendor communication, team member communication, customer communication, and so on. Use the email system's functionality to help you deal with the volume of email you receive. For example, you might want to create rules that move important email to a specific folder. Flag junk mail immediately so that the filter sends this mail and future mail it catches the Trash folder. Setting up rules like these will save you lots of time. You won't be tempted to open the mail just because it's in your inbox, and you won't waste time having to manually delete it either.

Rules are a handy tool because they let you easily move your messages to folders you designate, change the color of incoming messages (I've set all the messages coming from my boss to red so I don't overlook them), or delete those items you don't want to look at. Unfortunately, though, rules can't tell you how or when you should respond. That's something you'll have to determine based on the email, the person who sent it, and the content.

You might want to set aside certain times during the day for reading and responding to email. You may decide that every two hours is often enough to check email and in between those times you'll work on other productive things. But I'll warn you, this is hard to do. If you're like me, the minute you have a "new mail" notification, you'll jump right to the inbox. This can be a time-waster, though, because it breaks your concentration on whatever else you're working on (such as the project plan or schedule). You stop what you're doing, go read the email, get lost down a rabbit trail, respond, and then maybe stew about it and forget what you were doing before you stopped to read the email. Try setting a schedule to review email every two hours, or some other time increment, that works for you.

Voicemail

Voicemail is another potential time killer. There isn't an easy way to filter the voicemail you receive, but you can still practice some of the same principles we've already discussed. Listen to the voicemail one time and then act on it. Either return the call, delegate it, or delete it.

When leaving voicemail messages, speak clearly and slowly and get in the habit of repeating your phone number twice. It's annoying for a listener to have to keep backing up the message or repeating the message to catch the phone number.

Here's another trick I learned from a friend of mine several years ago that's really handy. Many times when I'm at home doing things other than work (yes, you should have a life outside your current project), something will pop into my head about the project I'm working on that I don't want to forget. Maybe it's a call I need to make or someone on the project team I need to catch up with. Call yourself at work and leave yourself a voicemail detailing the thing that you want to do tomorrow. (Just don't start asking yourself how you are doing, and you'll be all right.) Shhh, don't tell, but I use a modified version of this in reverse too. If I'm at work and think of something at home that I don't want to forget to do, I send myself a text message to my personal cell phone and then I have a handy to-do note waiting for me when I get home.

Use voicemail or text messaging as a handy reminder tool. Leave yourself voicemail or text when you think of something that you need to take care of and don't want to forget.   *TIP*

Odds and Ends

We've already introduced the idea of the project notebook. This is a great project management organizational tool. Checklists are another useful tool. The checklist table shown in Chapter 1 details most of the things you'll put together for the project notebook and can be used to make sure that you don't forget something along the way.

Remember that the project notebook can be in electronic form if you choose. I'll use references to the project notebook throughout the remainder of this book, and the techniques I'll talk about can be applied to paper or electronic formats.   *NOTE*

This may sound routine, but having a routine is another good way to keep everyone involved in the project on track. Set up your project progress meetings for the same time — the first and third Tuesdays at 10 a.m., for example. Schedule team meetings at consistent times as well. Once everyone attends a time or two, they know what's expected and what type of information you're going to be looking for in the meetings, and they'll come prepared.

I like Albert Einstein's theory on information management. He used to say something like, "Why remember it when I can look it up?" I believe it's been said that he didn't know his own phone number because he could look it up in the phone book. That might be going a little far, but why take a chance on remembering things that you can easily write down or record? Get in the habit of carrying your organizer or PDA with you everywhere so that you can jot down ideas or things to do as they occur to you. If you don't have your organizer with you, leave yourself voicemail.

General Management Skills

Project managers wear a lot of hats. This implies that you need to have a basic understanding of general management skills, and that covers a lot of topics. You'll be preparing budgets, coaching teams, negotiating for resources, communicating with vendors and customers, and providing customer service. As such, you need to have some general knowledge of each of these areas.

Budgeting skills are necessary when estimating the resources and materials you'll need for the project. Most stakeholders want to know how much it's going to cost to implement the project, and the project manager is usually the one responsible for coming up with the initial estimate. This doesn't mean that you need to be a certified public accountant, but you'll want to have some understanding of how accounting and finance work. Most organizations have accounting departments that are responsible for anything that has to do with money and budgets. You'll work very closely with those folks to come up with initial estimates, set a project budget, and monitor expenditures. If you understand their lingo, it will make your job easier.

As a project manager, you'll sometimes wear the leadership hat and sometimes the manager hat. Leadership skills are different from management skills. *Leaders* tend to focus more on the big picture, or the strategic direction of the company. They have the ability to inspire others and rally them around a common goal or vision. Once that vision is planted, leaders get things accomplished through others who are committed to the vision, are loyal to the leader, and have a good deal of respect for the leader. Good leaders tend to have a directive approach; in other words, they tell you what the end result is expected to look like and they make certain everyone understands the goal, always keeping them focused and driven toward accomplishing the goal. They impart the vision and let the team members work together to make it happen. You'll find that most good leaders have very strong interpersonal skills.

Managers, on the other hand, are usually task-oriented and concerned with accomplishing the job at hand to the satisfaction of the customer or stakeholders. They focus on things such as planning, budgets, and human resource management and are concerned about following established policies and procedures.

leaders
Create and inspire vision while encouraging and motivating others to fulfill the vision.

NOTE

Leaders are inspiring and lay out the overall direction of a project. Managers complete tasks, create plans, and monitor performance. Project managers need to exercise both of these skills to survive in the project management world.

managers
Those who carry out the details of the leader's vision by completing the tasks and activities associated with the vision and by managing the day-to-day operations to the satisfaction of the stakeholders.

You'll need both of these skills — leadership and management — in your tool bag at different times throughout the project. In the beginning, you'll rally the team around the project goals and convince them of the merits of the project. Sometimes teams will experience a lull midway through the project or after setbacks that impede the progress of the project. You'll need to whip out those leadership skills again and refocus the team on the initial vision.

At other times, you'll use your management skills to develop plans, monitor activities for adherence to the plan, and so forth. The management of the project itself takes on the form of project planning, scheduling activities, assigning work, monitoring tasks, reporting progress to stakeholders, and so on. You'll use these skills throughout the project.

Customer service skills are important because all of your stakeholders, those people who have something at stake in your project, are really your customers. Simple things such as using proper phone etiquette, being courteous, and not speaking poorly of the folks you work with are common sense. Nonetheless, it's important to remember that customers are the reason you have this great project management job in the first place. Whether those customers are internal or external to the company shouldn't matter. The end goal is still the same — satisfying their expectations and delivering the project on time and on budget.

People Management Skills

People management is a vast topic. The majority of your workday will be spent interacting with people, so it's important to understand how people tick, what motivates them, and how to keep them focused and on task. Some of the things you learned in grade school apply here, such as saying "please" and "thank you," using people's names, and not interrupting while others are talking. Other skills, such as motivation, delegation, managing upward, following through, and equating authority to responsibility, are just as important for you to master.

People management skills are something you'll have to master if this doesn't come naturally to you. And when people are involved, there will be conflict. Negotiation techniques belong in your bag of tricks as do problem resolution skills. Each of these will help you deal with conflict and resolve those issues that can become real sticking points on the project. We'll cover these topics in depth in Chapter 6, "Planning and Acquiring Resources."

Some of your guidance in dealing with others on the project, particularly vendors, stakeholders, and customers, comes from professional responsibility principles, which we'll cover in more detail in Chapter 10, "Executing the Project." For now, remember that people like being recognized for their contributions to the team, and they like feeling as though their work is important to the project.

Communicating Your Style

Have you ever experienced a situation in your personal or work life where you found yourself saying, "If I just knew what was happening with this situation, I'd know what action to take"? Suppose you're up for a big promotion. You've been dying to hear the final outcome of the interview process, but nothing is forthcoming. You don't know whether to book that upcoming business trip because you may be in your new position by the time you need to go on the trip. What you are looking for is information, some kind of communication from the hiring manager to help you determine which course of action to take.

Or imagine that you're a stakeholder on a project. You haven't heard from the project manager in weeks, so you assume everything is progressing well. One rainy afternoon (isn't it always raining in the movies when something bad is about to happen?) the project manager shows up at your door, head in hand. "Uh-oh," you think, "Something is up." The project is in big trouble, and this is the first anyone beside the project manager has heard of it. Imagine how frustrated you are. All along you've believed the project is on track, and now the project manager is telling you the problems are so insurmountable that the project is in jeopardy. I don't recommend running your next project in this manner, because you may not have many new assignments coming your way after a project blunder like this one.

Clear and honest communication could have prevented this situation from happening. It may be true that the problem is one that is insurmountable and is a potential project killer. But informing the stakeholders of project status should occur throughout the project so that no one is taken by surprise. If the project manager had been communicating with the stakeholders all along in the preceding scenario, the stakeholders or senior managers could have helped the project manager by working on a solution or workaround to the problem. But if they don't know anything about the project status, it's difficult for them to come to the rescue at the 11th hour. It doesn't bode well for the project manager's future employment endeavors either. Keep the stakeholders informed and be honest about the project status; don't sugarcoat it.

There is almost no way you can communicate too much as long as the information is clear and focused. You can communicate incorrectly, poorly, or not at all, but almost never too much. Sharing the right information with the right people at the right time is never out of place. There are lots of examples of poor communication. One of my pet peeves — I'll bet it's yours, too — is broadcast email to everyone in the company on every single topic related to the project. Ugh, don't do that!

Some estimates show that as much as 90 percent of a project manager's time is spent communicating. Based on my own personal experience in project management, I'd say this is true. You'll be conducting team meetings, writing reports, generating documents, holding progress meetings, informing stakeholders about issues and problems, helping resolve problems, and negotiating for resources, just to name a few. This next section looks at several aspects of communication, including one of the most critical aspects — listening. We'll top it off with 10 tips for effective communication.

Exchanging Information

sender
The person or group formulating the content of the message.

receiver
The person or group the message is intended for.

Communication, in a nutshell, is the exchange of information. You (the *sender*) have something (the message) to tell me, and I (the *receiver*) have something I need to hear. As the sender and receiver, we each have a part to play in the exchange. In addition, the form the communication takes, as well as the way information gets from the sender to the receiver, also has an impact on the exchange.

Communication Methods

The message is at the center of the communication exchange, and the content can take various forms. The two primary forms of communication are verbal and written. We might exchange information verbally with the spoken word in meetings, on the telephone, or in face-to-face situations, or we can use written forms such as email, memos, or reports. Depending on the circumstances, both verbal and written communication might be formal or informal exchanges.

Verbal Communication

Project managers should generally take an informal approach when speaking with stakeholders individually. The same is true when communicating one-on-one with project team members. Keeping these types of communication informal makes you appear approachable and friendly. This openness can come in handy later in the project when there are problems that team members might be afraid to report. If they've had a history of face-to-face communications with you that are open and easy-going, they're much more likely to share problems later. If they feel that every communication with you is so rigid and formal that they're wondering when the ax is going to fall, you're not likely to find out critical project information until it's too late.

When it comes to project team meetings and project status meetings, you should use a more formal approach by setting an agenda ahead of time and keeping everyone on topic. This helps keep order during the meeting, and the formal structure of the communication conveys a sense of importance and seriousness.

Project managers should conduct project team meetings and do status reporting using a formal, consistent communication style.

NOTE

Written Communication

Written communication is usually more formal than verbal communication, with the exception of some email. Email can take on the tone and form of casual conversation. I recommend you limit this type of email because it can quickly pass over into the noise category. Keep email brief and informative, not chatty. And never, ever write something in an email message that you wouldn't want everyone in the entire company to know!

Written communication is a useful tool when you need to convey complex, detailed information. If extensive instructions are necessary or detailed explanations are needed for certain project activities, use the written form of communication. A contract is a form of written communication, as are letters, memos, invoices, and books.

The advantage of using written communication is that complex information can be conveyed in a detailed manner so that it's easier for the receiver to understand. Written messages force attention to the thought behind the message, whereas verbal communication does not. The reader can also go back over the material as many times as needed for clarification. All of your project documentation, project plans, and status reports should be written, so brush up on those business-writing skills if need be.

Using language is one way to get a message from the sender to the receiver. Language is an example of how messages are *encoded*, or put into a format the receiver will understand. Receivers then decode the message in order to comprehend what the sender is saying. However, language is only one method of transmitting information. Pictures, graphs, charts, and videos are examples of how senders might transmit information to receivers in visual form, or senders might use a combination of visual tools and language. Part of good communication is knowing which tool, or transmitting method, to use in a given situation. As a general rule, informal communication can take the form of verbal messages, while complex information such as project plans should take the written form. When in doubt, put it in writing.

Senders

The sender's responsibility is to make certain the information is clear and precise. They should also make sure the information is presented in such a way that the receiver will understand it. Equally important is making certain you're sending the right information to the right people.

Suppose you're working with a vendor on your current project. Some minor issue has come up regarding a shipment of telecommunications equipment. The late shipment will have no impact on the final project schedule because this activity is not critical for completion of the project. Now the question is, should this information be broadcast to the entire project team and all the stakeholders? The answer is, of course, no. However, the project team members who have a part in this activity need to know about the delayed shipment. And if you need the assistance of the telecom manager (a functional manager) for this activity, then you should inform him that the shipment is going to be delayed and what your expectations are regarding the new arrangements. But does the VP of marketing need to know about this just because she's a stakeholder of this project? Probably not. This is what I mean by sending the right information to the right people. Anything else is just noise.

Back in the pre–cable TV days, stations used to go off the air for several hours during the night. When the station signed off for the evening, your TV screen turned into a snowstorm of magnificent proportions. Along with the snow, a steady scratchy noise blasted out of the TV speaker. If you were unlucky enough to fall asleep with the TV on and then the station signed off for the night, the blast of static would come on so loud it would wake you from the dead. Static is noise. And information that's sent to someone who doesn't need it is nothing more than noise in their already busy day. If no usable information is being transmitted to a particular receiver, it's just noise, but it's so distracting that it grabs their attention. If you continue sending very much noise, the receiver eventually learns to ignore it and might end up missing something important or ignoring it altogether, like the boy who cried, "Wolf!"

Be a noise reducer. Aim the information you're distributing to the right audience.

NOTE

Examine the information and the impact it has on the situation you're relaying to the various parties involved, and make smart decisions about who should get what information. If you're in doubt or find yourself wondering whether stakeholder X really needs to know, err on the side of sending them the information. If you get a nastygram back about cluttering their inbox with unnecessary information, you'll know next time that they aren't interested in receiving this kind of information. Or better yet, if you're able, just ask them if they'd like to see the information before sending it to them.

Receiving uninformative communication is not the only form of noise. Other examples of noise include the following:

- Distractions during verbal communication
- Interruptions
- Disruptions in meetings
- Personal issues that interfere with a person's ability to absorb the message
- Stress
- Organizational issues

I'm sure you could add more to this list. Remember that when you're sending written messages, you should reduce the noise by sending the information to the right people. When your message is verbal, be sure to eliminate or control the distractions so everyone can remain focused on the actual message. The rule for all communication is to keep the message clear and concise. If the receivers have to dig for the gems that you've buried in a lot of extraneous information, they may pass and miss the main point of the communication.

Receivers

Senders use language or some other form of transmission to frame the message and send it to the receivers, who then decode it. It's the job of the receivers to make sure they understand what's been communicated. While the sender should make sure the message is clear and well written, the receivers are responsible for understanding the content of the message and making sure they have all the information they need to act on the communication. If there is a misunderstanding or something doesn't seem clear, receivers should ask the sender to clarify what is meant or enhance the communication to make it easier to understand.

Receivers filter the information they receive in many ways. In other words, their own personal perceptions, the emotional state they're in when they hear the message, or cultural differences between sender and receiver have an effect on the way they interpret the message. Senders should keep this in mind when preparing their communications so that they can make the information as clear as possible. Here are a few of the ways receivers filter information:

◆ Knowledge of the subject

◆ Personal perceptions

◆ Cultural influences

◆ Personal values

◆ Language ability

◆ Emotions and attitudes

◆ Stress

◆ Geographic location

Receivers should attempt to interpret the information sent to them at face value whenever possible. This is especially true when working with team members or stakeholders who might be from other cultures or countries. What is a natural, customary manner of speech or writing style for them may seem brash, abrupt, or even rude to you. Keep these differences in mind before reading between the lines.

If the message is cluttered with noise and extraneous information, ask the sender to clarify it. Chances are, if you don't understand, others do not either. And remember, as the project manager, your communication is a model to others and should be free of noise, clear, and to the point.

A Little of Both

The project manager is both a sender and receiver of information. Table 2.1 highlights the things you should remember when sending and receiving communication.

Table 2.1   Sending and receiving communication

Senders	Receivers
Be clear and precise.	Read for understanding.
Reduce noise levels.	Avoid jumping to conclusions.
Target the information for the right audience.	Ask clarifying questions.
Avoid unnecessary detail and technical jargon.	Control your filters and emotions.

Senders and receivers are equally important in the communication exchange. Senders are responsible for sending clear, precise communication. If you find that your message was misunderstood, go back and examine the message content. Was it written clearly? Did it convey what you meant? Were there too many technical terms for the audience for which you intended this message? If the message was delivered verbally, maybe the delivery of the message — your body language or facial expression — said something that the words didn't, and others drew conclusions you didn't intend. Be on the lookout for these problems, and stop them before they have a chance to adversely affect your message.

The receivers have the responsibility of making sure they understand what was communicated and for making certain they have all the information they need. Project managers spend the majority of their time communicating, so keep in mind both of these roles when preparing or receiving your next message.

A lot of information is exchanged between the project manager and the project team. I recommend giving everyone on the project team a copy of the chart in Table 2.1. Take it along to the first team meeting to explain what's expected of them when they're in these roles.

Active Listening

Active listening means more than just hearing what was said or reading what was written. Active listening involves your powers of observation as well. Let's say you run into one of your team members, Henry Lu, in the lunchroom. You exchange the normal greetings, and then you remember that Henry is waiting for a business analyst to answer some questions before he can proceed with his scheduled activity. You ask Henry about it and he replies, "Oh, they're working on it." He casts his eyes aside when he says this, and his body language tells you something different. You probe a little further with some clarifying questions: When did you speak with them last? Did they give you a date? Henry spills the beans. The analyst came unglued when Henry asked her for the information. Henry is gun-shy about prodding the analyst any further since the attack was pretty uncomfortable.

If you hadn't practiced active listening in this situation, you might not know the real story. When Henry's deadline came and went, you'd be concerned with Henry's performance and not necessarily thinking there was another cause. Because you found out early, you're able to intervene — using your superb powers of communication — and resolve the problem. Queue up those powers of observation and be on the lookout for nonverbal clues lurking under the surface.

Active listening will tell you more than what the words alone convey.

TIP

Listening involves interpreting the information you're hearing and paying attention to the conversation. We often think we're listening when we really are not. We're planning our next sentence, thinking about dinner later that night, forming the speech we're going to give to the boss that justifies our reasons for a much-deserved raise, or thinking a host of other thoughts at that moment. Noise, such as phones ringing, interruptions, or the boss walking by, can prevent us from listening as well. And don't forget our own personal perceptions or biases. Even our opinions of the person talking or sending the information can prevent us from listening or understanding the message the way it was intended.

Listening Techniques

Listening is a critical skill for all project managers. You'll receive input from everyone involved on the project, from team members to stakeholders to the final customer. You could have potential project disasters on your hands if there is a discrepancy between the message being sent and what you thought you heard. Listening well is as important as clearly conveying your own messages to others. The following is a list of things you can do to improve your listening skills and help you avoid potential pitfalls on your next project:

Show Genuine Interest   Let the speaker know you're interested by nodding in agreement, asking questions when appropriate, and letting them know ahead of time that you're looking forward to hearing what they have to say.

Let Others Have a Turn   One person dominating the meeting or conversation is usually not effective unless you're in a large lecture hall. This scenario does not go over well at stakeholder meetings or team meetings. Limit the amount of time you spend speaking and give others a chance to participate.

Eliminate the Noise   Keep distractions to a minimum. Close the door when you're having a team meeting. Refrain from rushing to answer the phone when someone is in your office. Give them your undivided attention. Make sure the information you're sharing is appropriate for the audience.

Refrain from Interrupting Others   Interrupting others sends the message that what they have to say is not important and isn't worth the time to listen to. You can't expect others to listen to you when your actions tell them they're not important enough to hear out.

Ask Clarifying Questions   This is a great technique to make certain you've interpreted the information correctly. Ask questions that get the sender to elaborate their main points and to verify that what you're thinking matches up to their intent.

Paraphrase What You Heard   This one goes hand-in-hand with asking clarifying questions. Periodically rephrase what you heard and tell the sender in your own words what you think they're saying.

Maintain Eye Contact   Look at the speaker when they're speaking. This helps put them at ease and lets them know you're interested in what they have to say.

How Many Connections Are There?

There's a party game where all the participants stand in a big circle and the starter leans over and whispers something to the person next to them. That person then whispers what they heard to the next person and so on all around the circle. When the message gets to the last person, they state the message out loud for the group to hear. Laughter erupts from the group because the message the last person heard is usually very different from the message the starter of the game whispered to the first person.

This party game illustrates the importance of communicating clearly and using active listening techniques. In all fairness, you can't ask clarifying questions during the game, but I think you see the point. The party game also illustrates the impact that the number of people in the communication chain has on the message and its interpretation. The more people passing the message back and forth, the more places for misunderstanding and misinterpretation to occur. This image shows the lines of communication among five participants.

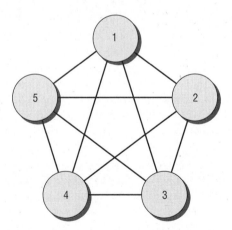

The circles, or nodes, are the participants, and the lines between the nodes illustrate the *lines of communication* between the participants. This project has five participants. That means there are 10 lines of communication between the five team members. It also means that there are potentially 10 places to

lines of communication
The number of channels between the people involved in the communication exchange.

introduce errors in the message. The bigger your group, the more lines of communication, and hence the more room for error.

You could draw a figure similar to mine to figure out how many lines of communication there are in your group, but that could get messy if you have more than six or seven people on your project. There is a simpler way. Here's a formula to determine the number of lines of communication:

$$(n \times (n - 1)) \div 2$$

If you plug in the number of participants in your project for the variable n, you'll see that there are 10 lines of communication:

$$(5 \times (5 - 1)) \div 2 = 10$$

As I mentioned previously, the more folks you have on the team, the higher the number of lines of communication between them. Six participants give you 15 lines of communication, 8 participants give you 28 lines, and 10 participants give you a whopping 45 lines of communication. The more people you're communicating with, and who are communicating with one another, the clearer the communication should be. I also recommend using formal written methods of communication when you have messages or information to send to this many people. If you deliver the message verbally and they all get to talking among themselves about what you really meant, you'll likely end up with numerous variations and interpretations of your original message.

Ten Tips for Communicating Effectively

This section wraps up our formal discussion on the topic of communication. Keep in mind that good communication is the underlying theme of good project management techniques. If you've mastered excellent communication skills, then you can succeed in almost any project in any industry.

I've known project managers who have worked in industries where they've had little technical or hands-on experience and have brought multimillion-dollar projects to a successful close. Their ability to communicate effectively, interact with team members, and manage the project is what counted.

You don't have to be a programming expert, for example, to successfully lead an information technology project to completion. Although it's helpful for you to have some knowledge and exposure in the industry, as a project manager, you're not expected to be the head technician; you're expected to manage and lead the project to a successful conclusion. You'll have expert technical folks on your team who can assist with estimating and defining specific technical tasks. Make sure you interact regularly with all your team members and especially the technical experts. Require your team members to provide you with updates and always ask to see their accomplishments. If you're a good communicator and interact well with your team members, you'll likely lead the project to a successful conclusion.

Because your biggest job as the project manager is communicating and it takes up 90 percent of your time, your single most important skill is excellent communication. Let's take a look at 10 ways to communicate effectively:

1. Deliver the right information to the right people at the right time. Unnecessary information is distracting, and if it's not needed by the receiver, it's simply junk mail, or noise, that's cluttering up their day. Target your communication to the right audience.

2. Use proper email etiquette. Keep your messages brief and to the point, and send the email only to the folks who really need to know its content. See tip 1.

3. Paraphrase what you think you heard the speaker say for clarification. This tells the speaker that you're really listening and that you're interested in understanding the information correctly.

4. Ask pointed questions. This tells the speaker that you heard what was said but you need more information to fully understand the meaning. It's also useful for clarifying what was said.

5. Use proper voicemail etiquette. Leave short, descriptive messages. Speak clearly, and leave your phone number twice so the listener doesn't have to back up the message to get it all.

6. Eliminate noise. Noise is distracting and can interfere with the communication at hand. Focus on the person you're meeting with and give them your undivided attention.

7. Practice active listening. Active listening includes such things as making eye contact, nodding to show you're paying attention and interested, asking questions, and being observant of nonverbal messages.

8. Make your messages clear and to the point. Eliminate technical jargon and industry-speak in your messages whenever possible. Use the following public speaking technique to help keep the message clear and drive home your main points: Start by telling your audience what you're going to tell them, then tell them, and then tell them what you just told them.

9. Combine communication methods. Use visual aids when you're speaking and include graphs and charts in your written materials. Bringing together two or three communication methods is very effective in getting people to remember what you communicated.

10. Be patient when communicating complex ideas or technical information. Sometimes you have to get into the technical aspects of a situation. When this occurs, be patient with your listeners, and go the extra mile to explain what you mean. You know exactly what you mean, but your listener may have little or no experience with the technical issues, and that'll require extra patience on your part.

There are a couple of more important points for you to consider before wrapping up the chapter. The first thing to keep in mind is that important messages need to be repeated. It's good to keep pointing out the important messages or important points in your messages. The average person needs to hear the message three to seven times before it sinks in. Keep this in mind when you're communicating, and consider how many times the message should be repeated so that everyone gets it.

I know we've covered a lot of information about communications here. You don't have to keep all this in your head, however. Much of what we've talked about in this section should be documented in the communications plan. We'll talk more about this plan in Chapter 4, "Defining the Project Goals."

Terms to Know

leaders	receiver
lines of communication	sender
managers	

Review Questions

1. What is the most important skill that a project manager can possess?

2. Why is time management important?

3. What are some examples of firefighting priorities?

4. What are some examples of looking-for-a-new-job zone activities, and why should you avoid them?

5. What is an excellent rule to remember for information management?

6. Name the elements involved in information exchange.

7. What are some of the things senders are responsible for when communicating with team members or stakeholders?

8. What are some of the things receivers are responsible for in receiving information?

9. Name three effective listening techniques.

10. Name three effective communication techniques.

Chapter 3

Initiating the Project

In This Chapter
- Selecting projects and assigning priorities
- Sponsoring a project
- Determining stakeholder roles and responsibilities
- Creating the project charter
- Holding the project kickoff meeting

You've determined that your new work assignment is a project according to the criteria detailed in Chapter 1, "Building the Foundation." You've dusted off your communication and organizational skills and bought yourself a cool new organizer tool. You're set to go. Now what?

Your next stop is the Initiating process. This is the first set of processes you perform for the project. This is where you determine whether the project is worth doing, select which projects should be worked on and in what order, and publish the project charter.

This chapter covers all the aspects of the Initiating process.

Selecting Projects for Success

The Initiating process is the first set of processes in the life of a project. We've already addressed the initial question, "Is it a project?" So, this process serves as the official project kickoff.

The *Initiating process* acknowledges that the project should begin or that the next process of a project already in progress should begin. For example, prior to the handoff from planning to executing, the Initiating process is revisited to determine whether the handoff should occur.

There aren't any formal rules for Initiating other than publishing the project charter and documenting a high-level definition of the project objectives in a preliminary project scope statement, which we'll cover later in this chapter. Generally what occurs during this process is that a project is proposed because of a need or demand. A selection committee — or perhaps the senior director or manager — reviews the project request and its accompanying details and then decides whether to undertake the project. Following a go decision, the project charter is created and approved, resources are committed, and a project manager is assigned.

The following graphic illustrates how the Initiating process works. Needs or demands create requests for projects, and that in turn kicks off the Initiating process of the project. The output of this process is the project charter. The project charter becomes an input into the Planning process, which is the next stop in the project management process cycle.

> **Initiating process**
> The process where project requests are generated and approved or denied. Once the project is approved, the project charter is produced during this process, the project manager is appointed, and the organization recognizes that the project should begin.

NOTE   **Projects that are considered small to medium in size or complexity for your organization may be approved by an individual on the management team. Once you receive their approval, you can start work on the project charter. Large projects, especially those that are risky or have significant costs associated with them, may require a more extensive approval process including creating a business justification, a feasibility study, and/or a cost-benefit analysis. We'll cover all these topics later in this chapter.**

How Projects Come About

The VP of sales strolls into your boss's office one day and asks for a little assistance. The VP is interested in purchasing a system that will help her staff profile potential customers. The sales department has satellite offices over a six-state region, and each of these offices needs access to the system. Because this is an IT system and you work in the IT department, the VP thinks it's a good idea to let your department run with the project.

Your boss was mightily impressed with the last project you successfully completed and decides you'd be the perfect candidate for this project. It will stretch your skills and give you even more experience in the project management arena. You jump at the opportunity.

You know that this is a project: There are definite beginning and end dates, it's unique, and it's temporary in nature. Even though Ms. VP is planning to purchase this system from a vendor, the implementation of the system is a project that will require the participation of members from both the sales department and the IT department. This new system will interface with existing systems that the IT department manages currently.

This project came about as the result of a business need. Ms. VP would like to increase sales for the organization, and she thinks this new tool will help her sales team accomplish that goal. Organizations are always looking for new ways of generating business. It seems that some of the most common business concerns today include operating more efficiently, saving time or money, and serving customers with higher levels of excellence than their competitors. These are some of the reasons behind new project requests. Let's look at all the categories of needs and demands that generate projects.

Project Generators – Needs and Demands

Several needs or demands drive almost all projects. Needs or demands are also known as strategic considerations because the resulting projects they bring about are usually aligned with the strategic goals of the organization. Understanding why a project came about will sometimes help you clarify the goals and scope of the project (which we'll cover in Chapter 4, "Defining the Project Goals"). For example, if you understand that a project is being driven by a legal requirement, you'll know that the project is required to be completed according to specific conditions and that there are certain aspects of this project that cannot be compromised. The new law may require certain specifications, and those specifications become the requirements for the project. The following is a brief description of the categories of needs and demands that bring about projects:

> **Business Need or Strategic Opportunity**   The customer-profiling project that this section opened with came about because of a business need. This organization would like to increase sales by examining its customer base and allowing sales team members to use the information to improve the number of "Yes" responses they get. Business needs (such as improving efficiency, reducing costs, and utilizing resources efficiently) and strategic opportunities are very common reasons for new project requests.

> **Market Demand**   The needs of the marketplace can drive new project requests because of changes in the economy, changes in the supply and demand cycles, and so on. As an example, the auto industry may initiate a new project to design and create cars that run on a combination of electricity and gasoline because of a decrease in the supply of oil.

Customer Request   Customer requests can generate any number of new projects. Keep in mind that customer requests can come from internal customers or from customers who are external to the company. If you're looking at it from the perspective of the vendor, the customer-profiling project given in the opening of this section is an example of a customer-driven project. Your organization — the customer — has purchased a profiling system from the vendor. Your organization has some specific requirements that must be met regarding this system prior to installation. From the vendor's viewpoint, you are the customer, and the purchase and customization of this product to suit your own organization's purposes (a customer request) are what are driving this project.

Legal Requirement   Projects driven by legal requirements come about for as many reasons as there are laws on the books. Perhaps Congress passes a new law requiring warning labels to be placed on certain electrical appliances cautioning users of potential hazards. Producing the labels and attaching them to the appliances, when none were required previously, is an example of a project driven by a legal requirement.

Technological Advance   We live in an age of technological advances that seemingly take place almost overnight. Things never dreamed of just a generation ago, such as talking on a wireless phone from almost any location, are taken for granted today. Technological advances in the software available for the handheld devices may generate a project to create and introduce a new line of services for business customers that takes advantage of the new software capabilities and generates more profits for the organization.

Social Need   Projects driven by social needs may include things such as designing and presenting public awareness campaigns about the prevention of infectious disease or creating educational programs for underprivileged children. Social needs can be driven by concerned customers or concerned citizens. Perhaps the organization's customers put pressure on the company to develop new methods of testing that reduce environmental hazards or protect water supplies in the countries where the company operates.

Ecological Impacts   Ecological impacts such as "greening" initiatives, utilizing alternative energy sources, requirements regarding the use or disposal of certain materials, and the like, may drive project requests.

NOTE   **Determining the need or demand, or strategic consideration, that's driving the project will help you define the project goals.**

Whatever the reason for your project — whether it's a business need or customer request — make certain that you understand the priority of the project and how it fits with company's strategic plans. Sad to say, most organizations do not have an established process for selecting and prioritizing projects. "Someone" decides the project is important and must be done until the next "someone" (or sometimes even the same "someone") comes along and tells you to drop everything because this new project is the highest priority. A while later, the first "someone" comes back and asks what the status of their project is. You stand and stare, because you really don't know what else to do, and finally you muster up the courage to say you're working on another project with higher priority. If your organization doesn't have a formal selection and prioritization process for projects, I can promise you'll find yourself in this situation. Take some time to establish a process and formalize how the project will be prioritized so you don't find yourself working on one project when you really should be working on another.

Project Requests

Let's go back to the beginning of the customer-profiling project that was requested by the VP of sales. Projects in this organization go through a two-step process before they become projects. First, the project is submitted to a review committee on a project request form, or a *project concept document*, similar to the one shown here:

project concept document
Outlines the objectives and high-level goals of the project. Used in the selection process to determine whether the project should be approved or denied.

Project Concept Document

I. General Information

Project name:_____   Project number:_____
Requestor name: _____   Date of request:_____
Requestor's contact information:_____

Section One — To be completed by the requestor

II. Business Justification   *State the reason this project is needed and what problem or issue the project will resolve. Describe the impacts to the organization if the project is not approved.*

III. Project Description   *Provide a high-level overview of the project objectives. Include a brief list of desired project outcomes.*

IV. Project Costs   *Provide high-level estimates if known.*

V. Timeframe   *Is there a critical completion date?   Y/N   Date required:_____*
Desired completion date if not critical:_____

――――― **NOTE** ――――― **You can also download the template for the project concept document from** www.sybex.com/go/projectmanagementjumpstart3.

On the first page of the project concept document, you can record general information about the project, including the project objectives and overview, so that review committee members can decide whether to actually commence working on the project and where it should fall in priority with the other project work of the organization. The review and prioritization is the second step of the process and occurs prior to actually beginning the work of the project.

The project concept document is the first template that we'll talk about in the project's Initiating process. You may want to make changes to this template to suit your organization's needs. Keep in mind that the information provided here should be high-level only. The intent of this document is to capture enough detail to initiate a project and determine whether its benefits are worth pursuing. Detailed descriptions and objectives will be required later in the project charter and scope statement. This document should not exceed two pages, so don't let the requestor get too carried away with the amount of information on this form, because you don't know yet whether the selection committee is going to approve the project. The concept document should contain enough information to make a go/no-go decision but should not detail every requirement of the project. You'll be creating other documents during the Planning process that will give the details of the project, including deliverables, requirements, and so forth. The project concept document form should contain these basic elements:

◆ Project requestor, department or company name, and contact information.

◆ Date of the request.

◆ Project name. You may want to include room for a project number for tracking purposes within your department.

◆ Business justification. This should include the need or demand that brought about the project and answer the question, "What business problem or issue will this project solve?" This section can include a subsection describing the impact to the organization if the project is not undertaken. Business justification should also contain appropriate financial information such as return on investment, cost-benefit analysis, or internal rate of return to justify the project and help the selection committee make a determination on the project. We'll cover these concepts in the next section.

◆ Project description. This is a brief overview of the project objectives and what outcomes the requestor is hoping this project will produce. This should include a list of high-level objectives that the project must meet in order to be considered successful.

◆ Project costs. This information may or may not be available at this point. If the requestor has a limited budget amount, they should note that here. If the requestor knows that a contractor is required for this project or that services need to be purchased outside the organization, they should list those initial cost estimates here if known.

◆ Required or requested completion date.

The second or last page of the concept document has two sections. One is for the project manager — or perhaps a functional manager if a project manager has not yet been assigned — to fill out. This section should include high-level planning estimates. This will give the review committee an idea of how long the project is going to take to complete. It should also include a list of the other business areas in the organization that will be impacted if the project proceeds.

The second section of this page is for the review committee. This section has an area that indicates that the review committee has reviewed the request, the date reviewed, and whether the project has been accepted or denied. Providing an area for signatures is a good idea as well. Here's an example of what this portion of the form may look like:

Project Concept Document—page 2

Section Two — To be completed by the business unit manager or project manager

VI. Planning Estimates   *Provide a high-level estimate of project completion.*

VII. Business Areas Impacted   *List all business units impacted by this project.*

Section Three — To be completed by the review committee

VIII. Selection Committee Review

Date of review:
Comments:
Project reviewed/denied:
Project priority:

IX. Signatures of Review Committee

This is the first document you will file in your project notebook or repository. It's an official project document that can be shared with anyone who asks. Some of the elements you've included here are used again in the project charter. I know this seems a bit redundant, but you really can't write the project charter without having the project approved first. And you can't get the project approved without sufficient detail. Your management team has this funny habit of wanting to know what the project is about, how much it might cost, and how long it might take before they give the team the go-ahead to work on it. The project concept document is a great way to capture all that information and request an official review of the project. Once the selection committee gives you the official nod, you'll prepare the project charter.

Selecting and Prioritizing Projects

Project selection is the next step in the process. Many organizations do not have a formal selection process. Rather, the CIO, or some other senior executive, merely says, "Do it," and you have a project on your hands. That's not really the best way to select or prioritize projects. If your organization does not have a formal method for project selection, consider adopting the techniques outlined in this section. You'll likely have more success with the projects that you do undertake, and your organization will benefit by weeding out the unprofitable or potentially unsuccessful projects before they even start.

The first task is to establish a selection committee. Review committees or steering committees are formed to review the project concept documents and decide, based on a myriad of criteria, which projects should go forward. Selection criteria can be as simple as someone in the top ranks of the company saying that the project will be done to complex scoring models with multiple criteria to determine which projects are chosen. We'll look at a few of these methods shortly.

Most projects are subject to some type of financial review as well. Organizations are in business to make a profit, unless of course they're a non-profit organization or a government agency. If they're in business to make money, they're going to be concerned about choosing projects with the greatest potential for revenue. Nonprofits and government agencies aren't concerned with making profits, but they are concerned about getting the greatest utilization out of their operating funds as possible. That means they want to select projects that provide the most benefit for the least cost. Not altogether different from their profit-making partners, their motivation to use resources to their fullest extent possible while receiving the greatest return possible is the same.

Let's look at the first category of selection criteria that organizations might use to choose their projects.

Calculating Return

Profit and nonprofit companies alike have limited resources and limited amounts of time. As such, they're interested in knowing that if they invest the time and resources to produce the product of the project, it will be a good investment. Financial calculations can tell you whether the project is likely to produce a good return on your investment. In other words, are you going to get more out of it over the life of the project (or the product the project is going to produce) than you put into it? Financial calculations are also used as selection criteria when comparing and deciding among several projects.

The most common financial methods used as selection criteria include *pay-back period*, cash-flow techniques, cost-benefit analysis, and internal rate of return. The following is a brief explanation of each of these techniques. It's beyond the scope of this book to go into the detailed formulas behind each of these calculations. If you're interested in sitting for the PMP exam or the CompTIA Project+ exam, you'll need to know these formulas, so I recommend picking up a copy of *PMP: Project Management Professional Exam Study Guide, 5th Edition* (Sybex) or some other text that explains these formulas.

> **Payback Period** The payback period is simply the amount of time it takes for the project to pay itself back. The payback period compares the total project costs to the revenue generated as a result of the project and calculates how long it will take for revenues to pay back, or equal, the initial investment. When comparing one project to another of similar size and scope, typically the project with the shortest payback period is chosen.

payback period
The amount of time it takes to recoup the original investment.

> **Discounted Cash Flow** This goes back to the old saying that time is money. The *discounted cash flow* technique takes into account the time value of money to determine whether the potential revenue stream for the project is worth more than what it costs to produce the product or service of the project. The idea is straightforward. Money in your hand today is worth more than money you might receive tomorrow. Because you have access to the money today, you could invest it and make a profit, put it in the bank and draw interest, start a small business, and so on. Therefore, money you may receive tomorrow needs to be related to what it's worth today.

discounted cash flow
A financial calculation used to determine the project's worth or profitability in today's value. Used as a selection criteria technique when choosing among competing projects.

> Discounted cash flow takes into consideration all of the potential future revenue streams related to today's dollar. As an example, $1,000 two years from now, given a 7 percent interest rate per year, is worth $1,145 (rounded up) today. This technique is used to compare projects of similar size and scope; typically, you'd select the project with the highest return on investment. If you were choosing between this project with a value of $1,145 and one with a value of $1,023, you'd choose the $1,145 project since it has the higher return value — given that all the other criteria

were equal. Your projects will likely have much greater values than these, but I'm keeping the numbers simple in order to more easily convey the concepts.

Cost-Benefit Analysis   Cost-benefit analysis compares the costs to produce the product or service of the project to the financial benefits gained from doing so. You should consider all costs when analyzing the cost benefits, including the costs to produce the product, costs to market the product, and ongoing support costs. This is a simple decision tool. If the costs are lower than the expected return, the project will receive a go recommendation.

internal rate of return (IRR)
The discount rate when the present value of the cash inflows, or the value of the investment in today's dollar, equals the original investment. Used as a selection criteria technique when choosing among competing projects.

Internal Rate of Return   *Internal rate of return (IRR)* is a very complex calculation that is best determined using a financial calculator. IRR calculates the rate you'd have to apply to the present value of the expected cash inflows (in other words, what the cash inflows are worth in today's dollars) to make the cash inflows equal to the original investment. Generally speaking, the higher the IRR, the more profitable the project. IRR assumes cash inflows are reinvested at the IRR value.

It works like this. Say your initial investment is $10,000. Further, let's say the value of the future cash inflows in today's dollars equals $12,000. IRR calculates the discount rate you'd have to apply to the $12,000 to make it equal to the initial investment of $10,000. (As I said previously, this is most easily determined using a financial calculator.) Internal rate of return, like the other techniques, compares projects of similar size and scope. Projects with the highest IRR are the projects that should be chosen. For example, Project A produces an IRR of 5 percent, while Project B has an IRR of 6 percent. In this case, if the project size and scope are similar, Project B should be chosen.

Return on Investment   *Return on investment (ROI)* measures the amount of savings or profit the project will generate. It can be expressed as a simple percentage calculation that works like this: If your initial investment is $20,000 and the profit generated equals $30,000, the project has generated a 50 percent ROI.

Financial calculations are an easy way to tell the selection committee whether the project is going to be profitable, and they provide a basis to choose among projects. Some organizations set specific standards for the financial goals of a project. For example, the organization may automatically reject projects with an IRR of less than 5 percent. Or perhaps all projects must have payback periods of less than 18 months. If you're proposing a project that has an IRR of 3 percent, you know that it will not receive approval as soon as you do the calculation.

Selection Methods

Financial calculations are one method used to select projects, and they usually carry the most weight. Other methods of selecting projects include scoring techniques based on a series of questions or models that score company goals or project goals against criteria determined by the selection or review committee. Combining scoring methods with financial calculations gives you a very clear picture of which projects to choose. However, neither of these methods is an indicator of project success. You can have great financial numbers and high selection scores but still experience project failure. Good project planning will help you avert potential obstacles as will good follow-through and taking proper corrective actions at the right time. But we're getting ahead of ourselves.

TIP

High scores during the project selection process do not ensure project success. Project success comes about by following standardized, methodical project management processes.

Scoring models can take on many forms, including questionnaires, checklists, and complex models where weights are combined with scores. Table 3.1 shows an example of a simple weighted questionnaire.

Table 3.1   Selection questionnaire

Rating criteria	Score
Business problem appropriately addressed or resolved	5
Customer satisfaction easily achieved	4
Profit potential	4
Marketability	5
Easily produced or supported	3
Total score	**21**

In this example, the review committee members examine the various criteria against the project concept document and assign scores on a scale of 1–5, where 5 is the best score. The scores are totaled and then used to make a final determination regarding the project. The organization may have predetermined rules for project selection such as one that says all projects with scores lower than 18 are automatically rejected.

Another example is shown in Table 3.2, which is a simplified weighted selection-scoring model. This table shows the same criteria as Table 3.1, but the criteria have been assigned weights according to the goals of the company or as defined by the selection committee.

Table 3.2 Weighted selection-scoring model

Weight	Rating criteria	Points	Score
25%	Business problem appropriately addressed or resolved	90	22.50
25%	Customer satisfaction easily achieved	90	22.50
20%	Profit potential	85	17
15%	Marketability	95	14.25
15%	Easily produced or supported	75	11.25
	Total score		**87.50**

The first column in this chart shows the weight the selection committee has assigned to each of the selection factors. The first entry determines whether the project will adequately address the problem or issue stated in the business justification section of the project concept document. Points in this case are assigned a value of 0–100. The first factor was given 90 points. The weight for this factor is 25 percent, making the final score 22.50 (90 points × 0.25). Each factor is assigned points, and the total score is calculated by adding together all the scores. Finally, all the forms are collected, and all selection committee scores are added together for a final overall score for the project.

Selection can take several forms. Perhaps the selection committee feels that one of the factors is so important — say the customer satisfaction factor — that scores lower than 20 are an automatic rejection. Along the same lines, another method might look at total score. All projects with scores that fall below a certain number are automatically rejected. If the committee is choosing between projects of similar size and scope, projects with the highest score will be chosen.

Selection methods can also be used to prioritize projects. Financial calculations and scores can be used to rank projects in the order of most profitable, highest return, or greatest potential for market penetration, for instance.

Every organization has powerful members who seem to get what they want when they want it. There's a dynamic at work here that no one can explain, but if this particular person says, "I want Project A," Project A gets done (unless it is wildly out of the realm of possibility). Although your selection committee may use several methods or combinations of methods to select projects, don't underestimate the political pull of some managers to get projects approved without following a formal process — maybe even without the approval of the selection committee.

Other Selection Criteria

Scores and financial impacts might be a big part of the picture, but other factors should be considered when selecting projects as well. In fact, some of the things we'll talk about here could easily be added to a weighted scoring model and rated for selection purposes.

Strategic Plans

One of the issues that should be addressed regarding all projects concerns choosing projects that are in line with the organization's strategic plans and goals. In some cases, this might seem obvious. For example, say you work for a pharmaceutical company and someone proposes a project to research and develop a new allergy medication for hay fever sufferers. Since researching and marketing new drugs is the company's bread and butter, it's a no-brainer that this project will at least make it to the selection committee for review. Other reasons may exist that could kill the project in the selection stage, but it is fundamentally in keeping with the company's strategic plans.

Now let's suppose that you work for a small pharmaceutical company whose focus is researching and developing medications for particular blood diseases. If the hay fever project were proposed to this selection committee...well, the person who proposed it would probably get a little visit from their manager to remind them of what the company focus really is. Chances are this project proposal would never make it to the selection committee, because it wouldn't be in keeping with the organization's strategic plans.

Project requestors should be conscious of the overall strategic mission of the company prior to submitting a project proposal. Selection committees might use adherence to strategic plans as one of the criteria in their project selection models as well.

Risks and Impacts

Another area that concerns most organizations is risks and impacts. Risk comes in many forms, but what concerns the selection committee at this stage is risk to the company — be it financial risk, bad publicity, potential product flops, and the like, or project risk, such as the potential failure to complete the project or incompatibility with their customers' business practices. A project that puts the company at risk financially will more than likely not be selected. But keep in mind that organizations have risk-tolerance levels just like you and I do. What may seem risky to one company may not be considered high risk at all to another. Be aware of the risk and impacts to the company and the risk-tolerance levels of the organization when submitting projects for selection. We'll cover risk much more in depth in Chapter 7, "Assessing Risk."

Constraints

Constraints either limit or dictate the actions of the project team. Organizations may have preestablished guidelines (constraints) for project work estimates, budgets, and resource commitments. For example, perhaps the organization will not take on any project work internally with completion estimates longer than one year. The same type of restrictions may apply to budgets in that no projects in excess of certain dollar amounts will be approved, or there might be preestablished limits on the number of internal resources allowed for project work. Be aware of constraints that might kill the project before it's even started.

Other constraints may include things such as priority conflicts with other projects already in progress; actions or outcomes that would violate laws, regulations, or company policies; and lack of skills in the technologies needed to create the product of the project.

NOTE

Not all projects should be worked. Timing issues, constraints, political events, and a variety of other reasons may prevent a go decision from the selection committee.

Lack of support from upper management or the project sponsor is another huge red flag. Although this may not kill the project up front, it's something you should watch for right from the beginning. Lack of support or commitment tells you right away that you're going to run into problems later in the project. If you aren't getting much support for the project at this early stage, opt out if at all possible. We'll cover project sponsorship in the next section.

Feasibility Study

feasibility study
A preliminary study that examines the profitability of the project, the soundness or feasibility of the product of the project, the marketability of the product or service, alternative solutions, and the business demands that generated the request.

Some projects are much more complicated than the organization feels comfortable undertaking. However, the project has such merit that the selection committee doesn't want to just toss it out — in other words, the project sounds good on the surface, but more information is needed before a go/no-go decision is made. In these types of situations, a feasibility study might be requested. The *feasibility study* is sometimes conducted prior to the selection committee review process in anticipation of their concerns, or it can come about as a result of a selection committee recommendation.

The purpose of the study is to find out more of the project details, including digging deeper into the business need or demand that brought about the project and to propose alternative solutions. A feasibility study is generally needed when projects are complex in nature, are larger than the normal projects that the organization ordinarily undertakes, require large sums of money to complete, or seek to do something that the organization has never attempted before. Feasibility studies look at things such as the viability of the product of the project, the technical issues surrounding the project or product of the project, and the reliability and feasibility of the technology or product proposed.

Feasibility studies should not be conducted by the same people who will make up the final project team. The reason is that project team members may already have formed opinions or have built-in biases toward the study outcome and will sway the results to line up with their biases. I know you would never do this, but you should watch for strong biases among the feasibility team members. If you see personal opinions starting to influence the study outcomes, voice those concerns so that the project gets a fair shake and the results and findings are accurately reported to the selection committee.

Eliminate bias in the feasibility study by choosing different people to conduct the study than those who are going to work on the project.

TIP

Some organizations hire outside consultants to conduct their feasibility studies. This is a great way to eliminate personal opinions from influencing the results of the study. Keep in mind, however, that if you hire a consultant to perform the feasibility study, you should not use that same consultant, or their company, to work on the project. Consultants will approach your project having their product or services in mind as the end result of the study (there are those personal biases again) if they know they're going to work on the final project.

The completion and approval of the feasibility study marks the beginning of the Planning process. Before we jump into Planning, though, we have a few more areas to cover in the Initiating process.

Meeting the Stakeholders

Stakeholders are people or organizations who have a vested interest in your project. Stakeholders have something to either gain or lose as a result of the project. You as the project manager are one of the stakeholders in the project. The majority of this book is about your role on the project, but, simply put, you're the one responsible for getting the project completed to the satisfaction of the customer on time, on budget, and within the quality constraints. Some of the other primary stakeholders you'll find on most projects are the project sponsor, functional managers, the customer, the project team, and suppliers or contractors who are critical to the completion of the project.

Stakeholders come from all areas of the organization and can include folks outside the organization as well. If your project involves producing products or services that are potentially hazardous, for example, or your industry has specific regulations that it must follow, you'll need to include industry or government representatives on your stakeholder list also. Let's look at the role of the project sponsor first, and then we'll explore the responsibilities of some of the other stakeholders you'll have on your project.

Working with the Project Sponsor

project sponsor
An executive within the organization who has the authority to make decisions, assign resources, and assign budget to the project.

We know that projects come about as a result of a need or demand. But someone has to propose the project and describe the results the project is intended to produce. Someone has to win the support of management and convince them to support this project and dedicate time and resources to it until the project is completed. That person is the *project sponsor*.

The project sponsor rallies support from the upper ranks and generates a lot of fanfare. The project sponsor finds supporters who'll pledge their involvement and resources and who understand the importance of the project. Finally, support is gained, the project is approved, and the hands-on work is passed off to you — the project manager. The project sponsor doesn't go away at this point but instead becomes a partner with you during the project. The sponsor will serve as an escalation point for decisions and has the authority to assign resources and budget to your project. They will also help keep the stakeholders committed to the project.

The project sponsor usually has the most involvement in the Initiating and Planning processes of the project. This person introduces the project, publishes the project charter, and serves as an advisor to the project manager throughout the project. The Executing and Monitoring and Controlling processes don't require as much involvement on the part of the sponsor except when problems arise. By this point in the project, if everything is going according to plan, meeting with the sponsor and keeping them updated on progress may be the extent of the sponsor's involvement until the celebration phase of the Closing process.

The project sponsor is your best friend, and you'll be doing yourself a favor by treating them as such. This is the person who will go to bat for the team when things aren't going well. This executive will steer you through the inevitable roadblocks that will arise during the course of the project and assist you in getting more resources or put pressure on suppliers to perform if needed.

TIP **The project sponsor is your partner throughout the project and shares responsibility with you for a successful outcome.**

The project sponsor will oversee all the project documents you produce and may assist you with the development of the scope and planning documents in particular. A project sponsor typically has the authority to make decisions and to settle disputes. If a problem cannot be resolved any other way, the project sponsor is the one who makes the final call.

In exchange for the support and trail-blazing on the part of the project sponsor, your responsibility as the project manager is to keep the sponsor informed. Don't wait even a minute to inform the sponsor of potential problems or issues. The project sponsor should be the first to hear about project trouble or conflicts and should never hear about these things secondhand. Because the sponsor is generally an executive who has the authority to settle disputes and make decisions, don't hesitate to bring problems and issues to his attention to get matters resolved quickly. The sponsor has a vested interest in the success of the project and will work with you — not against you — to help resolve the problems.

Documenting Stakeholder Roles and Responsibilities

Each stakeholder has a different role in the project, and you should clearly understand and document those roles. This will reduce confusion and serve as a reference for the project team when questions come up later in the project about who does what. This information should be filed in your project notebook so it becomes part of the project documentation. When the information is written down, it ensures that everyone on the project understands what their role is. And there's no danger of forgetting the information because you've written it down. Remember Einstein's rule — you don't have to memorize things that you write down or can look up. If you haven't gotten used to the idea of documenting yet, you will by the time you get to the end of this book. Documenting is going to become your second-best friend after the project sponsor.

Try to keep the list of stakeholders to a reasonable number. For example, one representative from the supplier's company might be all you need to list. But you should include all the functional managers who will contribute deliverables or provide the services of their department to the project.

Some of these stakeholders will serve on a project oversight or steering committee that's charged with overseeing the management of the project. Not all stakeholders will serve on this committee. You should meet with the project sponsor, who chairs the oversight committee, to decide which stakeholders should be included in the steering committee. The purpose of this committee is to make decisions outside the realm of the project manager's day-to-day issues and to ensure that the organization's resources are being applied correctly to meet the project goals and objectives. Remember that if controversy or conflicts arise among the steering committee members, the project sponsor has the final say in all decisions and has the authority to override the decisions of the steering committee if needed.

Make a list of stakeholders (include their names on your chart) and their responsibilities, similar to the example shown in Table 3.3, and include this in your project notebook.

Table 3.3   Stakeholder roles and responsibilities

Stakeholder	Responsibility
Project manager	Manages project, creates project plans, creates various management plans related to the project, measures project performance, takes corrective action, controls project outcomes, manages project team, and reports status.
Project sponsor	Executive who initiates and oversees the project. Serves as an advisor to the project manager; can resolve issues and make decisions. Issues the project charter. Serves on project oversight or steering committee. Has the authority to assign resources and budget.
Functional managers	Responsible for completing project activities and producing deliverables. May serve on project oversight or steering committee to help oversee management of the project.
Customer	Provides project requirements. Approves project deliverables and verifies that they meet requirements. Serves on project oversight or steering committee.
Project team	Responsible for completing the activities of the project.
Suppliers	Provide goods or services to assist project team in completing project.

Your stakeholder list should be more specific than the one shown in this example. I've outlined the generic responsibilities of each of these groups of stakeholders, but you should list their actual responsibility in the project. For example, maybe one of the functional managers on your project will be responsible for installing a new piece of hardware. List that under the Responsibility section of your chart. Keep in mind that you aren't going to know everything that's required of the stakeholders at this point, but what you do know should be noted. You'll have an opportunity later to update this chart and to provide additional documentation on responsibilities in the Planning process.

Keep your stakeholder list within reach throughout the project. Stakeholders may change as the project progresses, or some may have involvement only at certain times during the project. Update your list of stakeholders and their roles and responsibilities periodically so everyone is on track with what's expected of them. It's a good idea to review the stakeholder list occasionally as well. If there are stakeholders on the project whose participation isn't needed until the end of the project, reviewing this list will prompt you to open up the communication channels with that sponsor at the right time, preparing them for their project role.

Competing Needs of Stakeholders

Because stakeholders come from various areas of the organization, they have competing needs and interests. This means that one stakeholder's concerns are focused on the aspects of the project that impact their department — information technology as an example — and that another stakeholder has completely different concerns. As the project manager, you'll have to balance these needs and concerns and use those communication skills we talked about in Chapter 2, "Developing Project Management Skills," to keep everyone informed and working together cooperatively.

Stakeholders are not always in favor of your project. Get to know the stakeholders, and open the lines of communication with them as early as possible. Stakeholders are influential people, and negative comments regarding your project can take hold quickly, generating a lack of cooperation or a lack of commitment from stakeholders and functional managers you're relying on to help the project succeed.

WARNING

Stakeholders have a lot of other responsibilities on their plate besides this project that occupy their time and attention. And unfortunately, sometimes not all stakeholders are supporters of the project. They may not agree with the project, they may not like the project sponsor, they may think their own projects have much more merit than this project, they may not like the impact that the project will have on their department, or they may have other higher priorities and don't want to be bothered with project duties. There are dozens of reasons why a stakeholder may not be behind the project.

Your job is to get to know the stakeholders and establish an open, trusting environment as soon as possible. If you make the extra effort to get to know the stakeholders and understand their issues and concerns, they're much less likely to cause problems later. If they feel you are really trying to incorporate and address their concerns and you treat them with respect, they'll likely reciprocate. Get to know your stakeholders and the business processes they oversee, because this will help you make decisions later on regarding the scheduling of activities and resource requirements in the Planning process.

Creating the Project Charter

We've covered a lot of information before getting to the project charter. The project has been proposed, outlined at a very high level, passed through a selection committee, and finally approved. You know who the sponsor is, and by now you are likely to know the primary stakeholders and have an idea of their role in the project. As you get further into the project's Planning process, more stakeholders may come to light whom you'll want to add to your stakeholder list. Now it's time to produce the project charter.

project charter
The official, written acknowledgment and recognition that a project exists. It gives the project manager the authority to proceed with the project and commits resources to the project.

The *project charter* is an official, written document that acknowledges and recognizes that a project exists. It's usually published by the project sponsor but can also be published by another upper-level manager. It's important that the charter is published by a senior-level manager because it gives more weight and authority to the document, and to you as the project manager, and it demonstrates management's commitment and support for the project.

The charter contains several pieces of information about the project that are more in-depth than the project concept document but not as detailed as those found in the scope statement. As you can see, we've started at the 50,000-foot view with the project concept document, and now we're closing in a little tighter with the project charter by refining some of those elements even further. By the time we get to the project scope statement, we'll know all the precise requirements of the project and what elements will be used to determine whether the project is successful at completion.

Before we get into the particulars of what goes into the charter, let's take a look at some of the purposes for the project charter.

Purposes for the Charter

The primary purpose of the project charter is twofold: It acknowledges that the project should begin, and it assigns and empowers the project manager. Let's look a little closer at all the project charter purposes.

Acknowledges That the Project Should Begin   The charter announces to all the stakeholders that the project has received approval and been endorsed by upper management. It serves as official notification to the functional business units that their cooperation is needed and expected.

Commits Resources to the Project   The project charter commits the organization's resources to the work of the project. This includes time, materials, money, and human resources.

Ensures That Everyone Is on the Same Page   This may seem obvious, but you'd be surprised by how many projects get started without a project charter and very few requirements. Perhaps half of the stakeholders think that the purpose of the project is to upgrade the network, and the other half think that the purpose of the project is to move the servers in the computer room to a new location. That might be a stretch, but you see the point. When the purpose, objectives, and an overview of the project are written down and agreed upon, everyone understands the purpose from the beginning, and confusion is eliminated.

Appoints the Project Manager   In many cases, the project manager is known prior to the creation and publication of the project charter. However, the project charter serves as the official notification and appointment of the project manager. The project sponsor formally assigns authority and responsibility for the project to you, the project manager. This means stakeholders are put on notice that you'll soon be requesting resources from their areas. Also, stakeholders and team members alike know that you're calling the shots on project issues. Does this mean you're automatically a born leader and everyone is going to do what you say? No, just because you have the authority doesn't mean that people will respect (or respond to) that authority. We'll look at how to overcome these issues when we cover leadership skills in Chapter 10, "Executing the Project."

Provides an Overview of the Project and Its Goals   The project charter is the first detailed stab at describing the project purpose, overview, goals, and high-level deliverables. While the concept document covered some of these things in a high-level fashion, the project charter goes into more detail.

All this points us back to good communication skills. A well-documented project charter keeps the team on track and helps maintain the focus on the purpose of the project. It helps keep the requirements definition, created in the Planning process, in line with the goals of the project.

You may be asked to write the project charter document, but it should be published under the name of the project sponsor or other executive manager.

NOTE

Even though I stated earlier that the project charter is published by the project sponsor, don't be surprised if you're asked to actually write the charter contents. If you are asked to write the charter, be certain that you put the project sponsor's name on the document. Remember that the purpose for this document is to acknowledge the project, commit resources, and assign you as project manager. This needs to come from an executive who has the authority to direct people's work. You don't have that authority until the project sponsor appoints you.

In the case of the charter, you'll be exercising those written communication skills. In an upcoming section, you'll find a project charter template. Although the template will provide you with the elements that should be included in the charter, you'll need to make certain the content within each area is clear and concise and easily understood by the recipients. (Refer to Chapter 2 if you need a review on effective communication techniques.) We'll discuss what goes into the project charter next.

Essential Elements of a Project Charter

To write a good project charter, you or the sponsor will need a couple of other documents at your disposal: the project statement of work, which includes the product scope description, and the organization's strategic plan. Let's look at each of these.

statement of work (SOW)

Contains a description of the products, services, or results produced by the project; a description of the work of the project; and concise specifications of the product, services, or results required. Often used with contracts to describe the work of the project.

Statement of Work   The project *statement of work (SOW)* describes the product, services, or results the project intends to create. The project request or sponsor typically prepares a statement of work when the project is internal to the organization. When the project is external to the organization, the SOW is usually provided by the customer as part of the request for bid process.

You essentially created a statement of work when you wrote the project concept document. The statement of work describes the work of the project and the overall objectives and includes the business need for the project. The SOW also includes the product scope description and a reference to the organization's strategic plan.

product scope description

Lists the characteristics of the product, including specifications, measurements, or other details that identify the product.

Product Scope Description   The *product scope description*, as you might suspect, describes the product of the project. The details and characteristics of the product, service, or result of the project are contained in this document. This is not necessarily an official project document, but you certainly should put a copy in your project notebook or repository. The product scope description is usually completed at roughly the same time as the project concept document but before the project charter. It will begin to give you clues to some of the objectives of the project.

A product scope description should be clear and concise. If your project consists of manufacturing cases for personal handheld computers, for example, the product description would contain specific information as to size, color, materials, and other exact specifications that describe the product.

strategic plan

Describes the organization's long-term goals and plans.

Strategic Plan   The *strategic plan* contains important information about the overall direction of the company. The project manager should consider this information in light of the project goals. For example, if the organization's strategic plan includes opening offices in three European cities within the next year and your project includes upgrading the company's network, you'll want to consider the impact that the three new offices have on your plan.

The project charter has elements that are similar to the project concept document, but the charter should contain more details. All project documents should have a General Information section that contains the project name, number, date, and perhaps fields for the date the document was modified, a version number, and for the author. The remaining sections of the charter should include the following:

Project Overview   The overview includes the purpose of the project (which was documented in the project concept document) and also explains the reason for undertaking the project. It should also describe the product or service of the project and reference the product scope description. Attach a copy of the product scope description to the project charter or let others know where they can get a copy if they'd like one. (Hint: You can get most of this information from the project concept document that you prepared for the selection committee.) The project overview should also include a high-level time estimate for the project. The project schedule will be developed later in the Planning process. The estimate in this section will give your stakeholders a rough idea of the length of this project.

Project Objectives   Project objectives should include the factors that help determine whether the project is a success. For example, you've been charged with implementing a new imaging system in the processing area of your company. Your objectives for this project might read something like this: "Implement a new imaging system that integrates with our existing information technology systems and programs. Implement the new system without interrupting current processing work flows." These objectives should be measurable whenever possible and will be used as criteria to determine whether the project should be approved once all the work of the project is completed. We'll get into specific requirements and deliverables when we produce the scope statement.

High-Level Requirements   Project requirements at this stage are high level. Think of them as a further description of the project deliverables, because they describe the specific characteristics of the deliverables. We'll talk more about requirements in Chapter 4, "Defining the Project Goals." The Requirements section should also state the needs and expectations of the customer, the project sponsor, and the stakeholders, and how those expectations will be satisfied.

Business Justification   It's a good idea to reiterate the business justification for the project in the project charter, including your financial justification — ROI, for example. The concept document isn't officially signed off by key stakeholders, whereas the project charter is (we'll cover the importance of this shortly), so copy the information in the Business Justification section of the concept document to the charter. Remember that this section describes the problem or issue the project will solve. This includes describing the benefits to the organization of taking on the project and the impacts to the organization if it doesn't. (Hint: Copy and paste from the SOW in the project concept document.)

Resource and Cost Estimates   If you have initial cost estimates, include them in this section. This section might include the cost of the feasibility study if one was conducted and the costs of the proposed alternatives. Depending on the amount of information known at this juncture, you may consider including a summary budget in this section that documents costs by major milestones, phases, or deliverables. If you don't have enough detail to create a summary budget, don't worry. We'll establish a project budget and a resource management plan later in the Planning process that will go into detail regarding costs and resources.

Roles and Responsibilities   Include a roles and responsibility chart like the one in Table 3.3, with the names of the participants under each title. Remember that you'll have only one project manager and one project sponsor, but there might be multiple entries for functional managers, vendors, customers, and so on. This is the section that names you as the project manager and officially gives you the authority to begin the project and secure the resources needed for the project.

Sign-off   This section is very important. Include room for signatures from the project sponsor, key stakeholders, senior management, customers, and anyone else appropriate for this project.

Attachments   Attach any other documentation that will help clarify the project, including the product scope description and the feasibility study, if one was performed. Information about project processes, templates, and where project documents are stored can be noted here.

If you have an idea of the milestone deliverables associated with the project, you could include a section for them along with a preliminary schedule of their due dates. It's been my experience that milestone schedules at this stage of the project are not accurate and can backfire on you if your stakeholders are real sticklers for detail. They'll tell you, "You published such-and-such date in the project charter, and I expect you to stick to it." However, be advised that you may have stakeholders ask for a preliminary schedule, so be prepared with a high-level list of the major deliverables, or milestones, associated with the project and a rough estimate of their completion dates. Make certain that you note these dates as tentative or draft or some such wording so that your stakeholders aren't shocked when you get into the project's Planning process and change them.

NOTE   It's possible that the project concept document doesn't sufficiently describe the project. It could be the project manager didn't participate in the project selection process or they didn't create the project concept document. (These documents are sometimes created by another manager or stakeholder.) If so, the project manager should go the extra mile to make sure that these sections are completed to a sufficient level of detail for initiation; if they don't, they'll be sorry later.

Some Specifics on the Project Sign-off

The project charter is not complete until it's signed off. Essential signatures include the project sponsor, the project manager, key stakeholders, senior managers, and the customer. Other signatures can be added as well. Confer with the project sponsor regarding who should sign the document if you're unsure.

Sign-off is important because it assures you that everyone who signs has read the charter and understands the purpose of the project and its primary objectives. Their signatures indicate that they agree with the project and endorse it. It also should mean that you can expect their cooperation on the project and participation in key areas when the time comes.

It's a good idea to hold a meeting to make sure that the stakeholders acknowledge the charter and that they understand the importance of their signatures. It can take an enormous amount of time to get the document routed for signatures if stakeholders have questions or misconceptions about the charter (or project). Holding a meeting gives you, and the stakeholders, an opportunity to ask questions, address issues, and clarify any misunderstandings.

TIP

The project charter is not official until it's signed by the project sponsor and key stakeholders. This ensures that they've acknowledged the project, and it will help ensure their cooperation with project activities.

After obtaining all the signatures, your next step is to deliver a copy of the charter to everyone who signed it. At this time, I would also give copies to the remaining stakeholders (the ones who didn't sign the charter) for review. After delivery of the copies, the fun begins with the project kickoff meeting. First though, let's take a look at a project charter template that you can use for your next project. Modify this to suit your organization's needs and personal style. Oh, don't forget, a copy of the project charter goes into the project notebook as well. If you're also keeping documentation on the intranet for others to see, you should put a copy of the charter there as well.

Sample Project Charter

Let's pull all this together into a template format and see what a project charter might look like. As I mentioned, feel free to modify this to suit your needs. You might want to add your company logo at the top and use some color or shading. The example shown here is pretty bare bones and is just to give you an idea of what information you're gathering and reporting. Get those creative juices flowing, and pretty this up a bit for your use.

NOTE

You can also download the project charter template from www.sybex.com/go/ projectmanagementjumpstart3.

Project Charter

I. General Information

Project name:_____   Project number:_____
Sponsor name:_____   Date:_____

II. Project Overview	*Describe the product or service of the project, the reason the project was undertaken, and the purpose of the project.*

III. Project Objectives	*Describe the overall objectives of the project and what factors will determine the success of the project.*

IV. Requirements	*Describe the expectations and requirements of the customer, sponsor, and stakeholders.*

V. Business Justification	*State the reason this project is needed and what problem or issue the project will resolve. Describe the impacts to the organization if the project is not approved.*

VI. Resource Costs and Estimates	*Provide cost estimates if known, including monies already expended such as a feasibility study or consulting time.*

VII. Roles and Responsibilities	*List the stakeholders and their responsibilities.*

VIII. Signatures	*Include signature lines for the project sponsor, project manager, key stakeholders, customers, and vendors.*

IX. Attachments	*List the attachments to the charter here.*

Holding the Project Kickoff Meeting

The project has officially begun. The charter has been published and distributed, the project manager has been appointed, and you're ready for the next step — the project kickoff meeting.

The purpose of the kickoff meeting is to accomplish verbally what you accomplished in writing, that is, communicate the objective and purpose of the project, gain support and the commitment of resources for the project, and explain the roles and responsibilities of the key stakeholders.

Creating the Agenda

When you announce the meeting time and place, publish an agenda with the announcement. This will be the rule for all project meetings from here on out. It's always good practice to publish an agenda. Everyone knows what to expect from the meeting, and if you're expecting meeting attendees to come prepared with some type of information, note that in the agenda.

Make certain when the meeting is called to order that everyone has a copy of the project charter so they can follow along when you go over each section.

NOTE

A typical project kickoff meeting agenda might look something like this:

Project Kickoff Meeting Agenda

I. General Information

Project name:_____   Project number:_____
Project Manager name:_____   Date:_____

II. Agenda Items

1. Introductions
2. Project charter
3. Project purpose
4. Project objectives
5. Roles and responsibilities
6. Questions

You can also download the sample project kickoff meeting agenda from www.sybex.com/go/projectmanagementjumpstart3.

NOTE

The first thing to do is introduce the key players. Even if these folks have all worked together for quite some time, it doesn't hurt to allow everyone a minute or two to state their name and describe their role in the organization.

Next comes the project overview. Describe in your own words what the project is all about. Include the project purpose and the project objectives in your overview for the group. Then proceed to cover each section of the charter step-by-step and ask for questions when you get to the end of each section. Also, ask for input and concerns as you cover each section in the charter.

Take some time when you get to the roles and responsibilities section. You want to make sure that everyone leaves this meeting understanding what's required of them during the course of the project. Now is the time to clear up any misunderstandings and get folks pointed in the right direction.

The closing agenda item for this meeting is a question-and-answer session. Allow everyone the opportunity to voice their questions and concerns. If questions arise during the meeting that you don't know the answers to, write down each question and let the person know that you'll get back to them. Then follow up with a response as quickly as possible.

Questions you may encounter during this first meeting will include things like the following:

♦ "Can we really do this project?"

♦ "Can we meet the deadline?"

♦ "Do we have the resources for this?"

♦ "Whose bright idea was this anyway?" (This one is my favorite.)

Answer what you can and of course stay consistent with what has been documented in the project charter.

A well-documented project charter gets the project off to a great start. It will also make your job of developing the scope statement much easier. We'll look at scope statements in detail in Chapter 4.

Terms to Know

discounted cash flow	project charter
feasibility study	project concept document
Initiating process	project sponsor
internal rate of return (IRR)	statement of work (SOW)
payback period	strategic plan
product scope description	

Review Questions

1. Name the primary output of the Initiating process.

2. Name at least three needs or demands (also known as strategic considerations) that bring about projects.

3. What is the purpose of the project concept document?

4. What are the most common financial methods used to weigh project selection criteria?

5. Describe the role of the project sponsor.

6. Where should the stakeholder roles and responsibilities chart be documented and filed?

7. State the purpose of the project charter.

8. Who should publish the project charter?

9. Who should sign the project charter, and why?

10. What happens at a project kickoff meeting?

Chapter 4

Defining the Project Goals

We're off and running! The Initiating process is complete, and we're ready to start the processes in the Planning process group.

The process contained in the Planning process group are some of the most important processes in the project. I think most project managers will contend that a well-documented plan that's managed expertly will drive the project to a successful completion almost all by itself. Almost. Don't forget that you're the one who is responsible for developing the plan — with help from the project team — and later monitoring the project for adherence to the plan. But most of the work in project management is in the Planning process group, so we'll spend many of the remaining chapters of the book discussing planning documents.

This chapter kicks off planning with a definition of goals and project deliverables. From there, we break down these elements into requirements and wrap it all up with the creation of a project scope statement.

Agreeing on the Deliverables

Scope definition is the first thing you'll want to tackle in the Planning process. Defining the scope starts with the goals or objectives of the project and continues to refine them, breaking them down into smaller components until at last the deliverables and requirements are defined at a level where they can be accurately estimated, assigned, and controlled. The end product of scope definition is the publication of the project scope statement, which spells out each of the things I just mentioned, plus a few others we'll cover in the coming sections.

Goals, objectives, deliverables, requirements...what's the difference? These terms sometimes get used interchangeably, but there are some differences. We'll spend the next few sections examining what makes up each of these components and what their differences are.

Goals and Objectives

The title gives this one away. Goals and objectives are very closely related and probably can be used interchangeably without a lot of confusion. Goals and objectives define the "what" it is you're trying to produce or accomplish. They are the reason the project was undertaken.

I like to think of objectives as having a little broader definition than goals. Goals, on the other hand, are more precise and are stated in tangible terms. But let's not get too hung up on goals versus objectives, because objectives are subject to the same criteria as goals if you're using the terms interchangeably.

Let's suppose you've been appointed the project manager for the Logan Street Move project. Your company has purchased a new building and made some extensive renovations, and you're ready to move the existing staff, currently in two different locations in your city, to the new building. The objective for this project might read something like this, "Move the existing staff to the Logan Street location with no disruption in service to our customers."

Although that's a good objective statement, it really doesn't qualify as a goal. Goals describe what you're trying to do or accomplish or produce by way of this project. When the goals are completed or accomplished, the project is complete. Goals must spell out exactly what's needed to accomplish the project. That means they must be specific enough to use as the criteria to determine whether the project was a success.

From here on out, I'm going to use the term *goal*, but know that you could use *objective* just as easily, as long as you follow the guidelines outlined in this section for defining them.

Project goals are the heart and soul of your project. Without a clear, written understanding of what the goals are, folks might take off in all different directions, and, before you know it, you have a project disaster on your hands. At best, you'll find a lot of disgruntled team members and stakeholders mumbling their version of the project goals under their breath (or to your boss) and not understanding why you didn't understand that their version of the goals was the correct version. You don't want to go there.

Goals describe *what your project is going to accomplish or produce.*

The Logan Street Move project needs some further definition. Suppose I'm a team member on this project, and I'm working from the objective statement given in the opening of this section. I understand that the move is taking place on two separate days, and I've planned my activities with this understanding in mind. But you, the project manager, know that the move from our two existing locations must occur on the same day. The first problem with this scenario is a lack of communication between the project team and the project manager, but that's another chapter. The second problem is that the goal is not stated clearly enough; it probably wasn't written down nor was it communicated to everyone involved on the project. So let's fix it.

SMART Goals

SMART project managers document the goals of the project and communicate them to all the team members and key stakeholders. You may have seen this acronym before, but it's one that we should review again. Goals should be SMART: specific, measurable, attainable, realistic, and time bound. Each of these is explained in a little more detail here:

S = Specific   Goals should be specific and stated in clear, concise terms. This means that if you were to leave the company somewhere in the middle of the project (this is generally not a recommended career move), another project manager would be able to read and understand what the goal is without confusion.

M = Measurable   Goals are measurable. The results of the goal are verifiable through some means. This could include everything from complicated formulas and measurements to a simple determination that yes, the result occurred, or no, it did not.

A = Attainable   The goal should be attainable for the project team in terms of technology, skills, ability, financial means, and so on. It's reasonable for a goal to be a bit of a stretch for the project team, but if it's beyond their capability, your chances of successfully completing the project and meeting the goal are at risk. You should have a solid understanding of the capabilities of your team members and when outside resources or expertise may be needed in order to assure project success. Goals should also be agreed to. You'll want to gain consensus and agreement from the key stakeholders on the goals of the project. This ensures that everyone understands what the final outcome is and will work toward that end.

R = Realistic   Goals must be realistic. If both of the existing offices need to move on the same day to the new facility and there is only one moving van available, the goal is not realistic. (You would discover this problem during the Planning process, and as a result, you would have to come back and revise your goals and thus the scope statement.)

T = Time Bound   Goals must have a timeframe that they're completed within, that is, an established end date. Just as projects have a definite end date, so do goals.

Now let's take another stab at writing a goal statement for this project using the criteria we just learned. "Move the existing staff from the Third Street location and from the Washington Street location on March 4 to the new Logan Street location with no disruption in services to our customers."

This statement meets all the requirements of a goal. It's specific because it states who, when, and where, and it's written clearly and concisely. It's measurable because either the move will occur or it will not. The service-disruption part of the goal statement is measurable also. It's attainable and agreed to by all the key stakeholders. The goal is realistic, and it's time-bound by the March 4 date.

I like having one, over-arching goal for the project such as the one stated in the previous paragraph. In one sentence, this statement conveys exactly what the purpose of the project is and what we hope to accomplish. It's concise and clear. This is a great motivator to print on attractive paper and hang in prime locations where team members, stakeholders, and management will see it often.

_____ **NOTE** _____

A single goal statement keeps the team focused on the end result of the project. It's the reason that they're assigned project activities — and all project activity should ultimately concern meeting the project goal.

Now that everyone understands the goal of the project, it's time to move on and establish the deliverables.

Deliverables

deliverables
A measurable outcome, measurable result, or specific item that must be produced to consider the project or project phase completed. Deliverables are tangible and can be measured and easily proved.

Deliverables include measurable results, measurable outcomes, or specific products, services, or results that must be produced in order to consider the project complete. Deliverables, like goals, should be specific and measurable.

You can apply the same SMART criteria to deliverables as you do to goals. The clearer and more specific you make the deliverables, the easier it will be to plan and estimate project activities and communicate assignments. Deliverables are like mini-goals in that they describe what it is you're producing or going to accomplish. When all the deliverables are completed, the goal of the project is accomplished.

Now back to the Logan Street Move. Knowing that our goal is to move the staff on a specific day, we can start to document some of the more obvious deliverables needed to make the move happen. Here are a few:

◆ Contract with a local moving company by January 15.

◆ Provide boxes and labeling instructions to all employees by February 7.

◆ Hold weekly town hall meetings to answer questions about the move, starting February 1.

◆ Meet with the management team by January 7 to explain how seating arrangements should be identified.

◆ Obtain floor plans from the management team by February 1 showing employee placements.

◆ Contract with IT specialists by January 15 to coordinate and move network servers, switches, printers, and PCs.

◆ Move telecom equipment, network servers, switches, printers, and PCs the evening of March 3 starting at 5:01 a.m.

◆ Connect and test all telecom and network equipment by 6 a.m. on March 4.

Each of these deliverables requires some type of action, and each has a completion date. They are measurable and verifiable and have specific results that will allow you to determine whether the deliverable was completed. Keep in mind that this list does not contain all the deliverables that you'd have for a project like this. I've listed only a few of them here to give you an idea of what they may look like. An actual deliverables list for a project like this would be much more extensive.

You may be thinking that the deliverables for a project like this look fairly easy to come up with, but what about very large, complex projects? Are they all lumped in together or somehow segmented? I'm glad you asked. That leads us right into the next discussion of project phasing.

Phasing Multiple Deliverables

Suppose the executive management team decides that the upcoming move is the perfect opportunity to reorganize the departments and reporting structures, one of their favorite activities (but don't tell them I said that). They're convinced that this activity is part of the overall project, but you as project manager are convinced that it's a separate project. What should you do? Well, you can compromise.

Consider structuring the project, and the project plans, as a project with two phases. The completion of phase 1, the reorg project, becomes a deliverable and an input into phase 2, the move project. Therefore, phase 1 must be completed prior to the activities beginning in phase 2. (But we're getting ahead of ourselves because these are scheduling issues, and we'll cover them in Chapter 8, "Developing the

Project Plan.") I recommend having two goals in this case — one goal for the reorg phase of the project and another goal for the move phase. Deliverables should be associated with the appropriate goals as well.

Many large, complex projects have phased deliverables. For instance, phased projects are very common in the information technology arena. Users might decide that new programs are needed to capture data that's produced as the result of new business processes and equipment. However, because of resource limitations or budget constraints or both, only the most critical pieces of programming can be completed in phase 1. The users, or stakeholders, and the project manager will work through each deliverable, determining which ones are critical to accomplishing the goals of the project and which ones can be delayed to phase 2. If money and resources were no object, the project could be completed all at once, but this is rarely ever the case.

NOTE

Excellent project management techniques applied to the wrong goal or deliverables will result in an unsuccessful project.

Keep in mind that no matter how good you are at applying project management techniques and managing your team, if you're working toward the wrong goals or the wrong deliverables, your project will not be successful. It's very important that you spend the time to define the project goals, deliverables, and requirements and then get agreement and sign-off. Our goal for the Logan Street Move project would not be successful if employees arrived on Monday morning and found that they had no computers or telephones to work with. The project couldn't be considered successful because the lack of computers and phones would definitely cause an interruption in customer service.

Discovering Requirements

requirements
The specifications or characteristics of the deliverables that must be met in order to satisfy the needs of the project, broken down to their most basic components.

Requirements are different from goals and deliverables. That is, they help define how we know the goal or deliverable was completed successfully. If our project involved building a new car model, for example, one of the requirements might be body style or paint color.

As you might have guessed, requirements are a further breakdown of the deliverables. Requirements describe the characteristics of the deliverable in very specific detail. For example, suppose one of the deliverables for a new car model is bucket seats. The requirements would include the type of fabric, the model number (Are these bucket seats for a coupe or a pick-up truck?), the color of the fabric, whether the seats are manually adjustable or have electronic controls, the type of headrests, and so on.

One deliverable could have multiple requirements, while another may have only one. Typically, you should define requirements for each deliverable. As the project manager, you should determine whether there's enough information in the deliverable and requirements description to produce the product or service. If not, get your group together for another round of requirements definition.

Defining deliverables and requirements should not be done in a vacuum. This is not the sole responsibility of the project manager. In fact, requirements gathering is primarily a user or stakeholder function. The project manager should facilitate the process, but you really need your customer or stakeholder to tell you what you're building. Many organizations today have business analysts on staff to perform this function. Make friends with your business analyst because they will partner with you throughout the project and will not only assist with gathering requirements but can help assure the business team adheres to the project scope; they can also facilitate testing, quality assurance, mediate issues between the project team and business team, and more.

Requirements-Gathering Process

Gathering requirements should be a group effort. Sometime shortly after the project kickoff meeting, set up a meeting or series of meetings to determine and document the project requirements. The primary stakeholders and key team members are the folks who should attend. Reserve a conference room with a whiteboard and give yourselves plenty of room to spread out.

Remember to set an agenda for the meeting. I also recommend sending a copy of the project charter to all the people who will be attending, several days prior to the meeting. This will give them a chance to review the project objective and begin thinking about requirements. At this point, ask whether other stakeholders need to be identified and included in the process. Now is not the time to forget someone important. There's nothing more frustrating than to have progressed a third of the way through your project activities only to discover that you forgot an important stakeholder back in the beginning and now have a new set of deliverables to deal with and squeeze into the project schedule.

Conducting the Meeting

Once the meeting has begun, review the project charter with the group. Ask for questions and clarify any concerns up front. Make certain, to the best of your ability, that everyone has the same understanding of the goals of the project.

Next, examine the deliverables (if they were defined prior to this meeting). Provide everyone with a printed copy of the list you've compiled so far. If deliverables were not identified prior to this meeting, this is your starting point. Ask the participants to name the major deliverables for the project or identify missing deliverables from the current list, and start writing them down. This is a simple brainstorming session where everyone is encouraged to participate and say anything that comes to mind.

You can use several other techniques, in addition to or in place of brainstorming, to get the requirements process rolling. (These techniques are applicable to determining the major deliverables as well.) One technique is to send surveys to the key stakeholders prior to the meeting, asking them to list their requirements. Or you could use an interview process if there are only a few key stakeholders involved. One of my favorite techniques is the sticky-note process. Everyone in the room is supplied with a sticky-note pad and a marker. Ask the participants to place one, and only one, requirement or deliverable per sticky note, being as precise as they can. You'll act as facilitator and gather the sticky notes, placing them on the whiteboard as they're turned in. Eventually, a pattern will emerge, and you can group similar requirements together, eliminate duplicates, and so on. Tell the stakeholders to not hold back anything. They should list everything they could ever want or dream regarding this project at this stage. We'll discuss more information-gathering techniques in Chapter 7, "Assessing Risk."

NOTE

Requirements are the lowest common denominator and cannot be broken down further.

Requirements are the last stop in describing the deliverables and cannot be broken down further. For instance, a requirement for one of the deliverables in the Logan Street Move project might read something like this: "All moving cartons must contain labels on the top and one side."

Some other examples of requirements for the Logan Street Move are as follows:

- All labels must list the owner's last name and room number in the new building.
- All computer equipment must be packed in specialized containers by the IT contractors.
- Managers must indicate office furniture placement on designated forms.
- All employees must update their ID cards by February 22 in order to access the new building.
- Computer cables for each computer must be placed in a plastic bag and marked with the computer's identification number.

business rule
Constraints to the project that are determined by company policy or institutional regulation.

When you're defining requirements, make certain to take into account environmental factors such as the organization's culture, infrastructure, and business rules and policies. A *business rule* is something that must occur in a specific fashion or is a result of a policy or regulation. As an example, a business rule for a financial institution might state that all loan requests over a specific amount must be approved by a vice president. A business rule for the building move project might say that only the IT contract employees may move the computers.

Here's where the lines begin to blur between deliverables and requirements. Deliverables may already be broken down to the lowest level, in which case you could consider them either deliverables or requirements. For example, the deliverable we listed earlier called "Connect and test all telecom and network equipment by 6 a.m. March 4" really can't be broken down any further. The "Provide boxes and labeling instructions to all employees by February 7" deliverable, on the other hand, may have requirements associated with it, including "All labels must list the owner's last name and room number in the new building."

Again, don't get too hung up on deliverables versus requirements. The main point is that you document what needs to be done in order for the project to be successful. Remember that deliverables are the specific items or services that must be produced in order to consider the project successful, and requirements are the specifications of the deliverables or project goals. As long as you've diligently tried to uncover all the deliverables and requirements and then recorded them, you're well on your way to creating better project planning documents. Believe it or not, I've seen projects kicked off and conducted on nothing more than verbal requirements. Should I tell you all the gory details about what happened to those projects and the project managers working on them? No, I didn't think so. Document the deliverables and requirements even if the project is going to take you only a day or two to complete. It eliminates misunderstandings and saves your bacon when the stakeholder comes back and says, "That's not what I wanted." We'll talk more about that in an upcoming section.

Save Good Ideas for Phase 2

You may discover new deliverables during the requirements-gathering phase or requirements that are considered "nice to haves" but not necessary for the completion of the project. You probably do not have an unlimited budget or unlimited resources, so the next and last step in the requirements-gathering process is to determine which requirements are necessary to meet the goal of the project. All others should be weeded out.

But don't throw them out the window. Document these requirements as the phase 2 portion of the project, or ask the stakeholders to keep them on hand and request a new project when this one's completed. You went through a lot of hard work to flesh out everything desired for the project, so don't let those efforts go to waste. You could also consider filing a copy of the additional requirements in an appendix of your project notebook. This is not something I'd necessarily publish on the intranet, but the additional requirements should be kept somewhere for future reference.

Now let's move on to the more critical issues.

Critical Success Factors

critical success factors
The project deliverables or require-ments that absolutely must be completed and must be completed correctly to consider the project a success.

You have one more thing to document regarding your deliverables and require-ments, and those are the project's critical success factors. *Critical success factors* include project deliverables — but not all deliverables are critical success factors. You should gain consensus among your requirements-gathering team and the stakeholders regarding which deliverables and/or requirements are criti-cal success factors and then either document them separately or somehow indi-cate which ones are the critical success factors.

Some of the things I consider critical success factors for *all* projects include the following:

- Understanding of and consensus regarding the project goals by key stake-holders, project team, management team, and project manager
- Well-defined scope statement
- Involvement and buy-in from the stakeholders as evidenced by sign-off of the project charter and scope statement documents
- Well-defined project plan (including all the documents that you'd nor-mally see for projects, such as the project schedule, risk management plan, budget and cost baseline, communications plan, and change control procedures)
- The use of established project management practices

Critical success factors should not be overlooked. If circumstances come up later during the project that are outside of your control, forcing a schedule, scope, or quality change, it's important for you to understand which deliver-ables must be completed and which ones could move to phase 2 if necessary. This is where your critical success factors list comes into play. When you're faced with this circumstance, review the critical success factors with the key stakeholders and project team to make sure that they are still critical to the project, and begin making project plan adjustments and taking corrective action from there.

Some of the critical success factors for the Logan Street Move might include those shown in the following list. Keep in mind that this is not a complete list, just a sample to give you an idea of why these elements were chosen as critical success factors.

- Move telecom equipment, network servers, switches, printers, and desk-tops the evening of March 3 starting at 5:01 p.m. This is a critical suc-cess factor because the goal of the project is to perform the move without disruption to customers. Normal business hours are 8 to 5; therefore, starting at 5:01 prevents disruption. In addition, this activity must start at 5:01, or the team will not have enough time to complete this deliverable and meet the criteria of the next deliverable.

◆ Connect and test all telecom and network equipment by 6 a.m. March 4. This was chosen as a critical success factor to meet the goal of moving the employees without disrupting service to the customer. All equipment must be tested and up and running prior to the employees reporting for work the next morning. Because all company data, customer contact information, customer files, and such reside on the company servers, it's critical that employees have access to the server via their computers. Equally important is the telecom equipment being set up. Customers call in to the company, so the equipment needs to be up and functioning in order to place and receive calls.

◆ Computer cables for each computer must be placed in a plastic bag and marked with the computer's identification number. This critical success factor will ensure that the computers are set up in time for employees to report to work, because all the cables and cords will be kept together with proper identification so that the installers know which cables go with which computers.

The following deliverable is not a critical success factor:

◆ Obtain floor plans from the management team by February 1 showing employee placements. This is not a critical success factor because it doesn't prevent the move from occurring. Furniture and boxes may end up misplaced and on the wrong floors, but since everything that the employees need to access the customer accounts resides on the company servers, access to their books and belongings is not critical to the completion of the project. It may irritate some people if they don't have their things right away, but it isn't critical to providing customer service.

Now, suppose the floor plan mentioned in this noncritical deliverable was also being used by the computer specialists moving and hooking up the computers. In that case, this deliverable now becomes a critical success factor because the specialists are relying on the floor plan to determine where each computer gets placed. I think you're getting the hang of it. Don't, however, make the mistake of assuming that the computer specialists have a network diagram with all the locations marked.

And that brings us to one more piece of documentation for the project scope statement: assumptions and constraints.

Identifying Assumptions and Constraints

Remember the old saying about assumptions? Well, throw it out because in project management, you want to make assumptions, but here's the key. Are you ready? You should document all project assumptions. You'll want to document assumptions regarding people, resources, places, things, or anything that you presume is going to perform in a certain way, be available at a certain time, and so on. This is a critical step that's often missed in the project-planning process. That's too bad because misunderstanding assumptions, or believing something to be true that isn't, can kill your project.

This is an often missed step because we tend to take things for granted, thus *assuming* business as usual. When you leave work for the evening (assuming you're driving a car), you walk out to your car, put the key in the ignition, and assume that the car is going to start. It's not really something you think about because the car starts every day — that is, until the day you put the key in and nothing happens when you turn it. Then the diagnosis process begins...battery, starter, alternator...or crisis mode sets in. "Oh my, little Sweet Pea is at day care, and I have to be there in 20 minutes!"

Project assumptions work the same way. We're so used to operating a certain way or expecting the A-team to drop what they're doing and lend a hand whenever we need it that we don't think about it, until the day they're not available. Don't skip this step — be certain to define and document your assumptions and communicate them to the project team and stakeholders.

Defining Assumptions

assumptions
Events or actions believed to be true. Project assumptions should always be documented.

Assumptions presume that what you're planning or relying on is true, real, or certain. For example, your project might require someone with special programming skills from the IT department. Your assumption is that this person will be available when needed and will exercise their skill on the activity you assign. Document the assumption that this person will be available when needed. (Oh, it's a good idea to check with that person's functional manager ahead of time to make certain that they will be available when needed.)

Discovering and documenting assumptions works just like the requirements-gathering process. Designate one of your project meetings, or a portion of one of the meetings, to discuss and document project assumptions. Use brainstorming techniques in the meeting to get the juices flowing. You could also interview key stakeholders, the project sponsor, and key members to uncover as many assumptions as you can.

We'll revisit these assumptions again when we get to the risk planning process in Chapter 7. Risks are associated with assumptions in many cases, so if you do a good job defining the assumptions, you'll have a good head start on risk identification. Sometimes it's helpful to have someone outside of the project help with this step because they are not as focused on the details as you are. They may see something you wouldn't.

Assumptions might include any of the following:

◆ Key project member's availability

◆ Key project member's performance

- Key project member's skills
- Vendor delivery times
- Vendor performance issues
- Accuracy of the project schedule dates
- Customer involvement on the project
- Customer approvals

OK, let's assume you've documented your assumptions. The next step is to validate and verify them. This means that if you're assuming that a key resource is going to be available to work on the project, you must verify with that person's functional manager that they'll be available at that time.

If you're working with vendors or suppliers on your project, make sure they document and verify their assumptions as well. In fact, if a vendor delivery is one of your critical success factors, make sure they document assumptions concerning that delivery. In the Logan Street Move project, we're relying on a moving contractor to show up on the right day with three trucks at each location and enough workers to load everything and get it moved in one day. Consider putting a clause in the contract that says the moving contractor will pay the cost of hiring temporary laborers or leasing rental trucks if for any reason their own trucks are not available (due to mechanical problems, and so on) or their regular work force is not available (a strike, sick-out, and so on). We'll discuss more situations like this when we talk about risk and risk response plans.

Assumptions should be documented in your project notebook or repository. They will be incorporated into the project scope statement, as you'll see shortly, but it doesn't hurt to copy and paste them into their own document and keep them handy. You should verify and validate these assumptions throughout the course of the Planning process and whenever necessary during the project's Executing and Monitoring and Controlling processes.

Defining Constraints

We talked about constraints in Chapter 1, "Building the Foundation." Remember that constraints are anything that restricts or dictates the actions of the project team. That can cover a lot of territory. The triple constraints — time, scope, and budget — are the big hitters, and every project has one or two, if not all three, of the triple constraints as a project driver. Many projects in the information technology area, for instance, are driven by time. Projects in the pharmaceutical industry are driven by scope but may have time or budget as a secondary constraint. Scope is a constraint that you shouldn't ignore, because you're working within the confines of the project goal and deliverables.

The Logan Street Move project is constrained by time. You must move on March 4. The secondary constraint for this project is budget — there is a limit to how much you can spend. What you want to do now is to document the project constraints. And yes, you can use the same techniques that we've already discussed for deriving project requirements and assumptions.

Besides the triple constraints, don't overlook constraints like these that can cause problems on your project:

◆ Lack of commitment from the executive management team or project sponsor. I would consider passing on the opportunity to lead a project with this constraint. You'll have a hard time getting support or resolution of problems. Watch out for this constraint because it can creep up on you later in the project. The sponsor may lose interest because other things have come along that usurp the priority of this project and so on.

◆ Business interruptions or reorganizations in the midst of the project. This could potentially realign your project resources, leaving you empty-handed.

◆ Stakeholders who have unrealistic expectations of project outcomes. This constraint is overcome through good project communications and requiring sign-off of the project charter and project scope statement.

◆ Stakeholders' unrealistic expectations of the project schedule. This is also overcome through good project communications early in the project.

◆ Lack of skilled resources. This constraint could cause project delays or unfilled deliverables.

◆ Poor communications. This is a potential project killer. Misunderstandings regarding scope, activity assignments, project schedules, risks, or a long list of other project essentials could cause uncorrectable problems.

◆ Uncertain economic times or business conditions. Difficulty obtaining funding for projects, resources for projects, and general economic disturbances could restrict the project team.

◆ Technology. Advances in technology can cause project delays due to lack of knowledge of the new technology, training needs or availability of training, availability of resources with experience in the new technology, and so on.

Constraints, like assumptions, are also documented in the project scope statement. These should be updated as you progress through the project to make adjustments to the constraints you've listed, add new ones that may come up along the way, or delete those that are no longer a constraint. Sometimes you'll find that constraints are also project risks and may need risk response plans. We'll talk more about risks in Chapter 7.

Creating the Project Scope Statement

Everything we've talked about in this chapter so far — goals and objectives, deliverables, requirements, constraints, and assumptions — goes into the *project scope statement*. The purpose of the scope statement is to document these items, particularly the goals, deliverables, and requirements, to use as a baseline for the project. As you proceed through the project, you'll be faced with decisions and changes that you'll need to monitor so that they conform to the original scope of the project. In this way, the project scope statement is your map, or baseline, that you use to determine where you're going. If questions come up or changes are proposed, the scope statement is the first place you're going to check to make certain that what's requested is in keeping with the original request.

Creation of the project scope statement is one of your most important duties as a project manager. Accurately quantifying the deliverables and detailing the requirements of the project and then getting agreement and sign-off on these deliverables helps assure project success. Creating the project schedule, which we'll cover in Chapter 8, probably ties in importance with creating the scope statement.

project scope statement
Documents the project goals and deliverables and serves as a baseline for future project decisions.

Creating the project scope statement and project schedule are two of the most important duties that a project manager performs.

NOTE

The project scope statement establishes a common understanding of the project's purpose among your team members and stakeholders. It contains the criteria you and the stakeholders will use at the end of the project to determine whether the project was completed successfully. The scope statement will assist you later in determining project cost estimates, resource estimates, activity definition, and project schedules.

Contents of the Project Scope Statement

You'll use the project charter and the product description to help you write the project scope statement. It's interesting that this is called a project scope statement when in fact several elements actually make up the project scope statement. It isn't a single statement but several pieces of information contained in one document. If you've followed this chapter in order, most of the work for your project scope statement is already done. You understand the product of the project (from the project charter), you know the goals and deliverables, and you have the assumptions and constraints documented. Now it's a matter of putting it all together in one document.

The components of a well-documented project scope statement include the following:

- Project overview, including a description of the product of the project
- Goals of the project (also known as the project completion criteria — did the project produce what we set out to produce?)
- List of project deliverables
- List of project requirements
- List of exclusions from scope (phase 2 deliverables may be mentioned here)
- High-level time and cost estimates
- Roles and responsibilities
- Product acceptance criteria
- Assumptions
- Constraints

We've covered most of these items in detail. We'll talk about time estimates in Chapter 5, "Breaking Down the Project Activities," and Chapter 8, and we'll cover cost estimates in more detail in Chapter 9, "Budgeting 101." At this point, if you have high-level information regarding time and cost estimates, include it in the project scope statement with a note explaining that the estimates are not final. These will be refined later when you more clearly define the work of the project.

The list of exclusions from scope, roles and responsibilities, and product acceptance criteria needs a little more explanation.

List of Exclusions

Exclusions are the deliverables or requirements that the team identified as not essential to completing this portion of the project. Exclusions from scope for the Logan Street Move project might include setting up the executive management team's office decoration and furnishings, reorganizing the IT department as a centralized service unit, and so on. It's important to note what's not included in the project so that there's no misunderstanding later when those particular deliverables don't show up or don't get done.

Roles and Responsibilities

The roles and responsibilities section in the project scope statement is much more detailed than what you defined in the project charter. In this section, you identify who is responsible for what. You document who has signing authority, who should review, who should create, and so on. Table 4.1 shows a portion of a sample responsibility chart.

Table 4.1   Roles and responsibilities chart

Activity	Assigned	Responsibility/ approval level
Scope statement	Project manager	Create
	Stakeholder	Approve
	Sponsor	Approve
	Project team	Review
	Functional managers	Review
WBS	Project manager	Create
	Stakeholder	Approve
	Sponsor	Approve
	Project team	Review
	Functional managers	Review
Project schedule	Project manager	Create
	Stakeholder	Approve
	Sponsor	Approve
	Project team	Review
	Functional managers	Review

Product Acceptance Criteria

The section on product acceptance criteria describes the process you'll use for determining how the stakeholders will know that the deliverables and products of the project have been completed satisfactorily and how the stakeholders go about indicating their acceptance. This is usually done with a sign-off document or an email indicating acceptance.

Scope Statement Template

The following graphic pulls everything together. You can use or modify this template for your future project scope statements. It contains all the elements we've talked about so far, plus an area for signatures.

Project Scope Statement

I. General Information

Project name:_____ Project number:_____
Project Manager name: _____ Date:_____

II. Project Overview	*Describe the product or service of the project, the reason the project was undertaken, and the purpose of the project*
III. Project Goals and Objectives	*Describe the project goals using the SMART (Specific, Measurable, Accurate and Agreed to, Realistic, Time Bound) formula. These goals will be used to measure and determine the project's success at its conclusion*
IV. Comprehensive List of Project Deliverables	*These are the products or services that must be produced in order to fulfill the goals of the project. Deliverables should have measurable, verifiable results and outcomes. Identify critical success factors.*
V. Comprehensive List of Project Requirements	*Requirements are the specifications of the deliverables.*
VI. Exclusions from Scope	*List all deliverables or requirements that are not part of this project.*
VII. Time and Cost Estimates	*Include initial estimates of time and resources. These are estimates only and will be updated after additional project planning activities are completed.*
VIII. Roles and Responsibilities	*Include a roles-and-responsibilities chart, detailing project responsibilities.*
IX. Assumptions	*List all project assumptions.*
X. Product Acceptance Criteria	
XI. Constraints	*List all project constraints.*
XII. Signatures	*Include signature lines for the project sponsor, project manager, key stakeholders, customers, and vendors.*

NOTE

You can also download a template for the project scope statement from www.sybex.com/go/projectmanagementjumpstart3.

The project scope statement also gets filed in your project notebook or repository and should be published on the project intranet site if you have one.

When your project work is done on contract, the project scope statement can serve as the statement of work (SOW), which was introduced in Chapter 3, "Initiating the Project." The statement of work is part of the contract. The SOW contains the same details as the scope statement and is used to describe the work of the project in clear, concise terms. You'll specify the product or service required here (the goals of the project) and the deliverables and requirements. Consider adding a list of key stakeholders, an organization chart, timeframes or deadlines, and an initial project schedule to this template if you're using it as a SOW.

The contractor will use the SOW to determine whether they're able to produce the product or service of the project, so it should be as detailed and clear as possible. Either the buyer or the seller can prepare the SOW, but both parties must review and approve it.

Obtaining Sign-off

Does there seem to be a recurring theme throughout the project documents so far? Yes, you're right, there is — describe the nature of the project, the goals, what we hope to accomplish, and obtain sign-off.

The project scope statement, like the project charter, should be signed off. This assures that stakeholders, key management team members, and the project sponsor are all in agreement on the deliverables and requirements of the project. I've witnessed many projects (none of them mine, of course) where the project manager failed to obtain sign-off on the scope statement. And, you guessed it, as the project progressed, memories became very fuzzy and stakeholders thought for sure that requirement X was part of the original plan, while the project manager swore up and down it was part of phase 2. If you cannot resolve this situation and end up having to include the new requirement in this project, it usually means you're going to miss the original planned deadline or run over budget or both. Don't let that happen to you. Document the deliverables and requirements. When a stakeholder comes to you and tries the very famous "I thought that *was* included," line (most of them could win an Oscar for their performance delivering this line to you), you can politely point them back to the project scope statement and remind them that, in fact, that requirement is not part of this project.

The next line you'll likely hear is something like, "Well, requirement X has to be included. It's essential to the success of the project." One of two things is happening here — OK, maybe three. First, the project manager didn't do a thorough enough job gathering requirements, and the stakeholders failed to point out the missing requirements when they reviewed and signed the document. Second, the stakeholder is purposely being a troublemaker and withheld the information during requirements gathering...just because. Third, the stakeholder really never thought about this particular requirement until now. This means you now have a scope change on your hands, and that brings us right to the next section — the project scope management plan.

Creating the Project Scope Management Plan

The *project scope management plan* describes several processes, including the process that you'll use to define the project scope; how the work breakdown structure will be defined, maintained, and approved (I'll talk more about this topic in Chapter 5); a process that describes how deliverable verification and

project scope management plan
Describes how the project scope and work breakdown structure will be defined, describes and documents how project scope is managed throughout the project, including how changes to project scope will be managed.

acceptance will occur; and the process requestors must go through to request changes and how the changes will be incorporated into the project. The project scope management plan also tries to determine the probability of scope changes, their frequency, and their impact. This process will get easier as your experience in project management grows. You'll begin to know what types of changes may occur because of the experience you've gained working on projects where change occurred.

Don't forget to file a copy of the project scope management plan in your project notebook or repository. As you progress through the project, changes to project assumptions, scope, schedules, and so on, make it necessary to repeat some project processes, particularly the planning processes. That's not a bad thing; it's part of applying good project management techniques to your project.

One thing that will most certainly occur on your project is change. How you manage and communicate those changes will determine project success. We'll discuss more about scope changes and the change control processes in Chapter 11, "Controlling the Project Outcome."

We have one more document to cover in this chapter, and that's the communications plan. Let's take a look at what that entails.

Creating the Communications Plan

communications plan
Documents the types of information needs the stakeholders have, when the information should be distributed, and how the information will be delivered.

We've done quite a bit of documentation already, so it's probably a good time to talk about the communications plan. The *communications plan* describes who gets what information and when. The *who* includes stakeholders, project team members, customers, management staff, and others who may have a specific interest or role in your project. The *what* includes the project documentation, project plans, status reports, status review meetings, project scope statement and scope statement revisions, performance measures, acceptance criteria, change requests, and more. And, of course, the *when* describes how often the communications are produced, when status review meetings are scheduled, and so on.

The communications plan is documented early in the Planning process. You want to identify all the people who need to know and understand the project progress as early in the project as possible. The communications plan also documents how to collect, file, and archive project communications as well as the distribution methods you'll use to get the information to the stakeholders. This includes how stakeholders can get access to project communication between the established publish dates.

You can create the communications plan in a simple document format listing the who, what, and when, like the example template in the following graphic. Distribute a copy of the plan to everyone listed in the document. This document is a good place to note the location of the intranet site and the types of information that people can access there. This graphic provides a template for the communications plan.

<table>
<tr><td colspan="5" align="center">Communications Plan</td></tr>
</table>

Communication	Recipients	Method	Timing	Prepared By

I. General Information

Project name:_____   Project number:_____
Project Manager name: _____   Date:_____

You can also download the template for the project communications plan from www.sybex.com/go/projectmanagementjumpstart3.

NOTE

List all the project communications on this template such as status reports, minutes, change requests, the project planning documents, and so on. Identify the people who will receive copies of the communication and how the document will be published. Some information might be distributed via email, others posted to the intranet site, and so on. Note how often the information will be distributed and who is responsible for preparing the information. Post the communications plan to the intranet site or file a copy in the project notebook.

Now that you've created the project scope statement, you're off to the next stop in the Planning process, which is the identification of tasks and activities. We'll cover that and related topics in Chapter 5.

Terms to Know

assumptions	deliverables
business rule	project scope management plan
communications plan	project scope statement
critical success factors	requirements

Review Questions

1. What criteria should you use to define project goals?
2. Describe project deliverables.
3. How are requirements different from deliverables or goals?
4. What are critical success factors?
5. Why are assumptions often overlooked in the project planning process?
6. Name three potential constraints for projects other than the triple constraints.
7. What is the purpose of a project scope statement?
8. What is the purpose of the project scope management plan?
9. Why is it important to obtain sign-off of the project scope statement?
10. What does the communications plan document?

Chapter 5

Breaking Down the Project Activities

This chapter continues our journey deeper into the planning recesses of project management. Along the way, we'll define tasks and activities, construct a work breakdown structure (WBS), and discuss how to estimate activity durations.

Creating the overall project plan involves many preliminary and incremental steps. This chapter will get us a little closer to the creation of a project schedule, which is one of the most important Planning process documents you'll create. Paying close attention to creating the work breakdown structure, defining milestones, and activity sequencing will make the job of creating the project schedule much easier.

At the end of this chapter, we'll take a look at some diagramming methods for project activities. As they say, a picture is worth a thousand words, and network diagrams help the stakeholders and project team visualize the workflow of the project.

Constructing the Work Breakdown Structure

work breakdown structure (WBS)
A deliverables-oriented hierarchy that defines all the work of the project. Each succeeding level has more detail than the level above it.

A *work breakdown structure (WBS)* is a tool used to graphically display the deliverables of the project in a hierarchical fashion. It organizes the work of the project into logical groupings and displays the information in a tree form or an outline form.

NOTE

Only the work of the project (including the project management work) is included in the WBS. If the work is not included in the WBS, it's not part of the project. All the work at the lowest levels of the WBS should roll up to the higher levels so that nothing is left out and so that no extra work is included. This is known as the 100 percent rule.

scope creep
A phenomenon where the scope of the project changes over time because of lack of agreement on the original scope statement, not sticking to the original scope statement, or not having a scope statement.

Only the work of the project is included in the WBS. This may seem obvious, but if the work isn't shown in the WBS, it's outside the scope of the project and should be noted as such. (In Chapter 4, "Defining the Project Goals," we included a section in the scope statement to note deliverables that are out of scope for the project.) This is an important distinction to make. Many projects suffer from *scope creep*, whereby the project seems to grow and grow the further you get into it. You no sooner have a list of deliverables and begin working on completing them when more deliverables are "discovered." To top it off, the deliverables you previously defined have been modified or altered from their original description. Thus, the scope of the project grows to a point where the original project estimates are no longer valid because the new requirements have added additional tasks to the project.

If you've done a good job writing your project scope statement and then depicting that work accurately in the WBS, you'll go a long way toward eliminating scope creep on the project. This also implies that you've kept the project team and stakeholders focused on the original scope statement and have not allowed changes that would alter the scope. Legitimate changes that must be made in order to ensure project success are another matter, but we'll take that up in Chapter 11, "Controlling the Project Outcome."

Organizing the WBS Levels

A WBS is similar to a company organization chart or a family tree. It can also be shown in outline form, which we'll get to shortly. It starts out with the big picture, and each successive level gets more and more detailed. Like an org chart, it's a hierarchically oriented view that shows which tasks "report" to which dependencies. There is no set number of levels in a WBS, but I recommend not going more than five or six levels deep, because the WBS will get bogged down in too much detail. If you're working on a large project, you will have subproject managers working with you who will be responsible for developing their own WBS from the project-level WBS. We'll cover this in more detail at the end of this section.

Whether you choose the tree form or the outline form, the levels and organization of the WBS remain the same. The top box of the WBS, level 1, contains the name of the project. The next level of the WBS shows the deliverables or major milestones of the project. (I'll talk more about milestones in the section "Determining Milestones" later in this chapter.) Level 2 may also be depicted as project phases or subprojects. The succeeding levels are further breakdowns of the deliverables that may include tasks or groupings of tasks. All deliverables don't necessarily require the same level of breakdown. What's important is that you get the WBS to a point where the components in the lowest level of the hierarchy are easily estimated, scheduled, and assigned.

TIP

When defining your WBS levels, remember that deliverables are typically described as nouns such as *PCs*, *brochures*, and so on. Tasks, which are developed from the deliverables, are usually described as action words: *create*, *develop*, *establish*, *set up*, *mail*, and so on. (I'll talk more about task identification in the section "Defining Tasks and Activities" later in this chapter.)

Let's look at some examples. The next graphic shows the level-1 and level-2 details for our conference project. Keep in mind that the deliverables in this figure are only a sample. Your project would have many more deliverables than this.

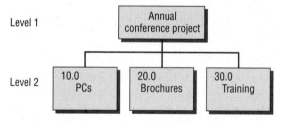

Level 1 shows the project name. This is usually the first level in any WBS. Level 2 for this WBS shows some of the deliverables or milestones for this project.

Now let's take a look at the next two levels:

Level 3 in this WBS shows a grouping of tasks, sometimes called summary tasks. For example, "Obtain PCs" is a summary task under the "PCs" deliverable found at level 2. The "Obtain PCs" summary task at level 3 has tasks under it that must be completed in order to consider the "Obtain PCs" summary task complete. To complete the deliverable called "PCs," the two level-3 summary tasks shown on the WBS, "Obtain PCs" and "Set up PCs," must have all of their tasks completed. The same is true for the other deliverables.

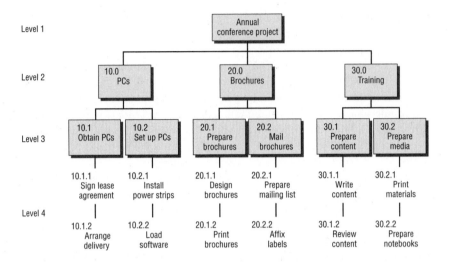

The idea is to start the WBS with the project and then continue to break down the deliverables into smaller, more manageable units in each subsequent level. These levels could include milestones, a grouping of tasks, or individual tasks. The idea is to keep adding levels to the WBS until you've broken the work out to the point where responsibility for each unit of work can be assigned to a specific person or to a team. This is also the level that allows you to easily determine estimates and the skills needed to complete these tasks.

Work Packages

work package
The lowest level in a WBS. Resource assignments and time and cost estimates are established at this level.

A *work package* is the lowest level of a WBS. This is the level where assignments, estimates, and resources are easily determined. It doesn't matter whether the WBS has three levels or five levels; the lowest level in either case is considered the work package level.

In the WBS shown earlier, level 4 is the work package level. In that example, the individual tasks like 10.1.1 ("Sign lease agreement") and 10.1.2 ("Arrange delivery") are the work packages and are assigned to individuals or teams to complete. If we broke off the WBS at level 3 — in other words, if we didn't include level-4 tasks — then level 3 would be the work package level.

NOTE   **The lowest level in any WBS is called a work package. Work packages can be subprojects, milestones, deliverables, or tasks, depending on how the WBS is structured.**

Work packages may include individual tasks, milestones, or subprojects within the project. If you're working on a very large project, the project should be broken down into smaller subprojects rather than individual deliverables.

Level 1 still remains the overall project, level 2 becomes subprojects within the project, and level 3 may also be subprojects within the subprojects, or this level might start the breakout of deliverables. In this case, level 3 is the work package level. Here is an example WBS with projects and subprojects:

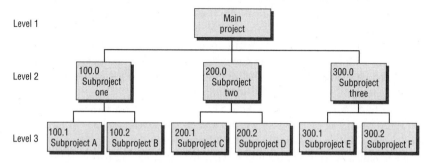

In a structure like this, subproject managers may be assigned to the level-2 subprojects. All subproject managers (also called assistant project managers) report to a single project manager who has responsibility for the overall project. Level-2 subproject managers assign the level-3 subprojects to teams or individual project assistants. At this point, the project assistants create their own WBS for the level-3 subproject they've been assigned.

For large projects, you can see that this could get rather complicated. However, the effort is well worth it in the end, because you have a logical, graphical depiction of the project breakdowns in one place.

Projects that are broken into subprojects, or multiple levels of subprojects, are often called programs. Programs are collections of projects that are managed collectively because of their similarities. The manager of this group of projects is often called a program manager, and the subproject managers are simply called project managers.

NOTE

Once the WBS has been reviewed and approved by the project manager and project sponsor, it's a good idea to hang a copy of it in the project team meeting room. And don't forget, a copy of the WBS should be filed in your project notebook for future reference.

Identification Codes

You may have noticed numbers next to each of the WBS elements. These identifiers, or WBS codes, allow you to uniquely identify each element of the WBS. They're used to track the cost of the work or the cost of each element in the WBS. They also serve as reference numbers to other planning information.

WBS dictionary
A document that contains information about the activities or tasks listed on the WBS. It may include elements such as WBS number, WBS codes, descriptions, and resource names.

As you begin assigning tasks and defining resource needs and such, you'll want to document some of this information (the act of documenting will become contagious over time), and the codes provide you a handy way to tie the information to the WBS. For example, you might want to note that WBS item 10.2 was assigned to the IT department. Maybe there are several costs involved with this summary task that you need to break out. That information can be recorded in the WBS reference document or WBS dictionary. The dictionary is created as a simple Word document or spreadsheet document that lists each WBS reference number down the left side, with comments regarding that WBS element to the right. This document should be filed in the same section of your project notebook as the WBS.

Your budget officer will need these numbers as well to track the cost of the project. Depending on the WBS you've constructed, level-2 and level-1 elements are simply a roll-up of the costs from all the levels beneath them. These codes come in handy when using the outline view for the WBS. We'll look at that next.

Outline View

There's one more version of the WBS that you can use if you don't like the tree form. The outline form works well for small projects or projects that have multiple levels with lots of tasks.

The following list shows a snapshot of the same information we saw in the first WBS graphic but in outline form. The WBS identifiers are especially important in an outline form because they help you easily determine which task goes with which deliverable:

  10.0 PCs -

    10.1 Obtain PCs.

      10.1.1 Sign lease agreement.

      10.1.2 Arrange delivery.

    10.2 Set up PCs.

      10.2.1 Install power strips.

      10.2.2 Load software.

  20.0 Brochures

    20.1 Prepare brochures.

      20.1.1 Design brochures.

      20.1.2 Print brochures.

I think you can see that if you've done a fabulous job of documenting the deliverables in the project scope statement and identifying your tasks, the WBS almost can't miss. If the project scope statement is inadequate or the deliverables were poorly developed, the WBS may also be poorly developed. This will cost you in the end in the form of rework. Rework means you have to go back and redo things you've already done or add tasks that you missed. And remember way back from Chapter 1, "Building the Foundation," that time equals money, so if you're involved in rework or you're adding new deliverables to the WBS after it's been approved, project costs are going to escalate. Take the time to construct your WBS correctly and review it several times with the project team.

Don't be alarmed if you uncover new deliverables as a result of creating the WBS. Updates to the project scope statement may occur two or three times throughout the Planning process.

TIP

Don't forget that as you create the WBS, changes to the project scope statement may result. That's to be expected at this point in the project, so when the WBS is completed, go back through your project scope statement to make sure all the deliverables are reflected there. If not, follow the procedures outlined in the scope management plan, and update the project scope statement to reflect the additions. (Don't forget to get sign-off on the changes.)

Defining Tasks and Activities

Now that you've constructed a working version of the WBS and have your deliverables outlined, your next job involves identifying the tasks or activities for those deliverables. First, you need to decide whether you like the term *tasks* or *activities* to describe the work of the project. Most project managers use these terms interchangeably. This isn't the only controversy you'll run across in project management circles, but it's one of the lighter ones. For the purposes of this book, I'm going to stick with the term *activity* most of the time, but if you see *task* in some places, know that I'm talking about the same thing. We will talk later about activity estimates and network diagramming, which both use the term *activity*, but keep in mind when we get there that *activity* and *task* mean the same thing. Now that we have that out of the way, let's look at what tasks are and explore the purpose of the task definition process.

Activities or tasks are a single piece of work, or units of related work, that must be completed in order to satisfy a project deliverable or the requirement of a deliverable. When you've completed all the tasks of the project, the product or service of the project is complete. And there you have it — define all your tasks, complete them, and your project is complete. Hold on, it's not quite that simple; there's more.

Activities are derived from the project deliverables and from the requirements of the deliverables. You defined those in the project scope statement and then again on the WBS. You'll see as we progress that almost everything we do in the Planning process builds on itself, so it's important to take each process seriously and do the best job you can because you're going to be relying on that information later.

NOTE When working on small projects, you could skip the activity identification process and perform it at the same time you're defining the WBS.

Managing the Work

The purpose of activity definition is to allow you to break down the work of the project into manageable components so that you can easily determine time, resource, and cost estimates. Each activity should be broken down to the point where these estimates are easily derived. Breaking down the deliverables into activities makes the project manager's job easier, because the work is subdivided into small units that are easily assigned to one team member or a group of team members. You can communicate the details of the work to the right team members, manage and track project progress, and provide a way to logically group similar activities together.

NOTE An easy way to differentiate between deliverables and activities is to describe deliverables as nouns (people, places, or things) and use verbs, or action words, for your activities or tasks — words like *define, prepare, program, design, build,* and *research*.

Let's look at an example. You've been assigned as the project manager for your company's upcoming annual conference. Customers from all over the world fly to your city to attend this conference and learn about your company's products, take some training classes, and meet with vendors. One of the deliverables of this project includes connecting and setting up 200 PCs for use at the training seminars held during and after the conference. One of the activities associated with this deliverable might be loading software on each PC. Another activity might be to run two power strips for each table in the ballrooms of the hotel where the training is being held.

At this point, you don't need to worry about in which order the activities appear; just start a list of activities for your project and give yourself room in between each major heading to come back and add to them. You'll find as you start breaking down tasks and activities that you'll think of new activities for some of the deliverables you've already broken down, so if you leave yourself some space, you can add these activities as you think of them.

I recommend using a simple format that lists the deliverables as the main heading with activity breakdowns and comments under the deliverables. If your project is good sized, you might list each deliverable on a separate page (or pages). A small project may have only a few pages of combined deliverables with their activities. Table 5.1 shows an example activity list for some of the activities needed for the "Set up PCs" deliverable. If you're going to use this as a template, add the General Information section to the very top of this form like we had on the project scope statement and charter documents to help identify basic information about the project (project name, project number, date, and so on). You could also consider adding another column that lists the requirements (between the Deliverable and Activities columns) and then define the activities from the requirements. I've kept Table 5.1 simple, but complex deliverables may need further definition than what's shown here before you can start identifying tasks and activities.

Table 5.1 Activity list

WBS #	Deliverable	Activities	Comments
10.0	Set up 200 PCs for training seminars the evening before the conference begins in the designated ballrooms.	Sign lease agreement for PCs.	Coordinate with procurement department.
		Arrange delivery of PCs.	Part of lease agreement.
		Run electric extension cords and power strips.	Coordinate with hotel staff.
		Load software.	Coordinate with IT department.

Activity Sequencing

After you define the activities, you'll want to sequence them in a logical order. This will help you when you're ready to create the project schedule later. For example, you can't load software onto the PCs until they've been delivered and they have a source of electricity, so it makes sense to list the "Load software" activity last in this list. When you're working on small projects, you can easily combine the activity definition with the activity sequencing process. As you list the tasks, group them into a logical order at the same time. Larger projects require a two-step process: First identify the activities and then sequence them.

Activity sequencing also provides a way for you to keep similar types of work together. In our example project, the IT department is in charge of hooking up the PCs and loading the software. They also have the responsibility for setting up the PC connections from the speaker's podium to the overhead projection system. A logical place to include these activities would be in the activity list in Table 5.1. In other words, we've grouped activities that are similar in nature in the same place.

Activity identification and sequencing allows the project manager to define estimates and costs and to determine the skills needed for the work of the project. For instance, the activity called "Load software" tells us what type of skills are needed to complete this activity. Obviously, we need folks who have some understanding of how PCs work and how to troubleshoot problems if the software doesn't load correctly. This means that we're going to have to work with the functional manager of the IT group to assign some resources to these tasks or contract with a vendor to perform these tasks for us.

Your project budget, the project schedule, and resource assignments are determined primarily from the activity identification process and sequencing exercises. As you can see, these are important steps in the project's Planning process, so you want to take the time here to do a thorough job. But don't feel that you're out there all on your own. Hold a team meeting or two and do some brainstorming to come up with all the activities necessary to complete the deliverables. Then, after you've compiled your final list, review the list with the team before moving on to the network diagramming or project schedule process to be sure you haven't missed anything.

Determining Milestones

If you're older than 15, you've experienced some milestones in your life: reaching age 16 (driving!), then 18 (graduation from high school), then 21, and, well, you get the idea. Milestones in projects work the same way. Milestones are markers along the way that let you know that a significant accomplishment has been reached. Milestones are not activities, but they can consist of a grouping of activities. You don't perform actions to complete a milestone; in other words, they aren't work. Instead, they signify that a grouping of work has been completed or a significant accomplishment has been reached.

Milestones might be based on deliverables, a grouping of deliverables, or a grouping of activities. For example, one milestone for our conference project might be "Ballrooms prepped and PCs set up for training."

Some project managers like to use milestone charts as one way to report on project progress. A milestone chart should include a listing of the milestones with their expected completion dates and their actual completion dates. Table 5.2 shows a sample portion of a milestone chart for the annual conference project.

Milestones are a way to help monitor the progress of the project. They are a great tool to use for reporting to executive management because they show at a glance where the project stands and what remains to be completed. Milestone charts work particularly well for smaller projects.

Another way to display milestone charts is in a Gantt chart format (we'll discuss Gantt charts in Chapter 8, "Developing the Project Plan"). You can display the start date of the milestone and its duration. Milestones should be listed in the order in which they'll be accomplished in the project.

Table 5.2   Milestone chart

Milestone	Expected completion date	Actual completion date
Vendor registration complete	5/15	5/15
Website updated with conference info	7/1	7/1
Brochures mailed to prospective attendees	8/1	8/1
Training classes designed and approved	9/15	
Ballrooms prepped and PCs set up for training	11/14	

Constructing the Responsibility Assignment Matrix

We've seen a couple of examples of roles and responsibilities charts in the preceding chapters. The *responsibility assignment matrix (RAM)* is the same idea. After you've constructed your WBS, you're ready to determine the types of skills and resources needed for the project. The RAM will help you do that.

A RAM is usually depicted as a chart, with the types of resources needed listed in each row and the WBS elements as the columns. The intersection of a row and column contains an indicator that shows what level of activity is needed by the resource. This could consist of a simple word like *Approve* or *Review*, or it could contain a code that ties to a legend if you need to be more specific than a one- or two-word description.

Table 5.3 shows an example RAM for the "Set up PCs" summary task.

responsibility assignment matrix (RAM)

A chart that ties roles and responsibilities with the WBS elements.

Table 5.3   Example RAM

Resource	Lease agreement	Install power strips	Load software
Procurement dept.	Create	N/A	N/A
Hotel staff	N/A	Install	N/A
IT dept.	N/A	Review	Install

This example uses three words to indicate the level of involvement of each resource: *Create*, *Install*, and *Review*. Alternatively, you could use the RACI format with the terms *Responsible*, *Accountable*, *Consult*, and *Inform*. Whatever you choose for the key, I recommend limiting the choices to six or fewer to prevent confusion.

You could put actual names in the Resource column if they're known at this time. If you don't yet know the names of the folks responsible for these activities, listing the department name as we did in Table 5.3 will work for the early stages of planning. Later in the Planning process, you will want to associate someone's name with each of these activities so that responsibility for the completion of this activity is assigned to a person. We'll discuss assigning activities in Chapter 6, "Planning and Acquiring Resources."

RAMs can be developed for the project as a whole or for any level in the WBS. When you're working with subprojects within a major project, you might develop RAMs for the level-3 elements in the overall WBS, and your subproject managers can develop RAMs for the elements in the individual work breakdown structures constructed for the subprojects.

Estimating Activity Durations

Estimating activity durations is the next activity you'll undertake after constructing the WBS and RAM. The reasons why you constructed the WBS and the RAM first are so that you know which activities you need estimates for and you know which resources you can ask to help you determine those estimates.

Activity duration estimates determine the number of work periods needed to complete the activities defined in the WBS. Work periods are expressed in hours, days, weeks, or months. Hours and days are the most common work periods used, but you may need to use weeks or months if your project is large or is expected to take a long time to complete.

There are several techniques for determining activity duration estimates. A few of them are interchangeable with the budget estimating techniques we'll discuss in Chapter 9, "Budgeting 101." We'll look at two examples here that are used most often for activity durations, but keep in mind that there are other techniques, described in Chapter 9, that you could use as well.

Expert Judgment

expert judgment
Using individuals or groups of people who have training, specialized knowledge, or skills to help assess information and determine estimates.

Expert judgment is just what it sounds like. When you've determined the type of resource needed to perform the activity, you can ask staff members who are experienced at these types of activities to give you an estimate for those activities. Because of their experience with similar activities in the past, they'll be able to give you a fairly decent estimate. However, this is not a scientific method, and the person giving you the estimate may historically overestimate or underestimate durations based on their biases. To help even out these biases, you could ask more than one expert for an estimate and then combine their results. If possible, combine their expert judgment with historical information from past projects (remember those project notebooks filed away with all that juicy project information waiting for you to use as a reference?) to determine an estimate.

Parametric Estimating

Parametric estimating works with known quantities and calculates estimates based on the quantity of elements needed to complete the activity. For example, you know that it takes six minutes to print the address and postage on 50,000 brochures. If you're going to mail 50,000 brochures, you calculate the duration for this activity by multiplying 6 minutes times 10 to come up with a total duration of 60 minutes to print and seal 50,000 brochures.

These duration estimates are initial estimates right now. You will have a chance to refine these, and you should refine them again when you create the project schedule. At that time, you'll have more information about the activities, and your project team will be in place, so you'll have what you need to fine-tune these estimates.

Establishing Dependencies

When activities are dependent on one another, it means that one activity cannot start or finish until the previous activity has finished or started. To determine dependencies, you have to put the tasks in logical order. We talked about that earlier in this chapter in the section called "Activity Sequencing." Now you'll determine whether the activities are independent activities or activities with dependencies.

Activities with dependencies must be sequenced in the correct order, or you'll end up doing a lot of rework. As an example, the "Load software" activity is dependent on the "Install power strips" activity because if you don't have power, you can't power up the PC and load the software. This is an example of a mandatory dependency because of the nature of the work. One action can be performed only after another action has taken place.

Not all activities have dependencies; some activities may be independent. The "Load software" and "Install power strips" example is what's called a Finish to Start dependency relationship. That is, the "Install power strips" activity must *finish* before the "Load software" activity can *start*.

There are four types of dependency relationships. Let's take a quick look at each.

> **Finish to Start**   The independent activity (the "Install power strips" activity from the earlier example) must finish before the dependent activity (the "Load software" activity) can start. This type of relationship

is the most frequently used dependency. Most of the activities in our annual conference project that have dependencies have Finish to Start dependencies.

Finish to Finish   The independent activity must finish before the dependent activity finishes. There isn't an example of this type of relationship in our annual conference project. But an example from the kitchen will help explain this relationship. When you're making a roast beef with gravy (assuming you're making gravy from the pan drippings), the roast beef must finish cooking before the gravy can finish. You can start the gravy any time by mixing the flour and water together, but you can't add it to the pan drippings until the beef has finished cooking. Therefore, these activities have a Finish to Finish relationship.

Start to Start   The independent activity must start before the dependent activity starts. For example, when preparing the training materials for our annual conference, we might want to review materials as they are written rather than waiting for all the materials to be written and then reviewing them all in one step. Therefore, the "Write content" activity and "Review content" activity have a Start to Start relationship. You cannot start the "Review content" activity until the "Write content" activity has started.

Start to Finish   The independent activity must start before the dependent activity can finish. This logical dependency is a little different from the others we've talked about and is seldom used. This situation exists when the dependent activity drives the completion time of the independent activity. Here is an example. In most states, the Department of Transportation requires trucks hauling hazardous materials to obtain a permit before traveling through the state. The trucking company must notify the department 30 days prior to driving the truck on the state highways. So, the dependent task, entering a new state with the truck, determines when the notice needs to be provided to the Department of Transportation (the finish of the independent activity). Let's say my truck needs to enter the state of Colorado on December 1; therefore, the notice and permit application must be delivered to the Colorado Department of Transportation no later than November 1.

You need to understand the dependency relationship between the activities in order to diagram them, as you'll see in the next section.

Constructing a Network Diagram

A network diagram allows you to show the activities of the project in the order they'll be performed — in other words, in sequential order. A network diagram is a graphical view of the project, starting with initiation as the left-most element followed by all the project activities or deliverables in the order they should be worked. Some activities have dependencies like those discussed in the previous section, and some are independent. The independent activities are often worked at the same time as other independent activities unless, of course, you're the only resource working on the project. Then you have no choice but to work one activity after the other in sequential order. Most projects have more than one resource, though, and that means those independent activities can be worked at the same time by different resources.

The network diagram allows you to visually construct and link the activities the way they should be worked. It's also a great graphic to hang in the project team meeting room to show your progress.

You may be thinking that we did all this with the WBS. Not really. The WBS is in a hierarchical layout, not a sequential layout. For example, if you refer to our WBS example, you'll see that "Prepare content" and "Prepare media" are two different deliverables displayed in a hierarchy. However, based on our previous discussion of dependencies, you can see that the "Print materials" activity cannot (or should not) be done before the "Review content" task is completed. Because these activities are listed under separate deliverables, there isn't a good way on the WBS to show their dependencies. Although all the activities under each of these deliverables are ordered logically, they aren't shown in dependency order. A network diagram allows us to show the flow, or sequence, of activities.

A WBS does a much better job of displaying milestones and deliverables than a network diagram does. A network diagram is better at showing the sequence of activities, so both of these tools have their place in the project's Planning process.

NOTE

A network diagram, like the WBS, can consist of subprojects, deliverables, milestones, or activities. If you're working a large project, the network diagram will likely display the sequential order of all the subprojects. (Each subproject manager is then responsible for developing a network diagram for their individual subprojects.) Small projects will likely show the activities in sequential order. As you've probably guessed, there is more than one way to construct a network diagram, so we'll look at each of them next.

Precedence Diagramming

Precedence diagramming is the method of placing activities in the correct sequential order, taking their dependencies into account. Precedence occurs when one task cannot be started until a previous activity finishes, such as the "Load software" activity we talked about earlier. The "Install power strips" activity has precedence over this activity because it must be finished before the next activity can start.

precedence diagramming
A diagramming method that links project activities according to their dependency, using boxes or nodes to depict project activities and arrows to show dependencies.

Precedence diagramming can also take into account activities that can be worked at the same time and activities with multiple dependencies. Most project management software programs use precedence diagrams. Here is a sample precedence diagram for the activities in our annual conference project:

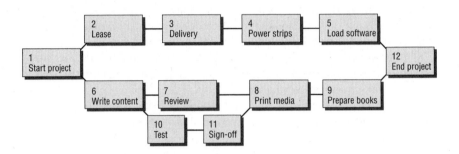

The numbers in the diagram are a way to identify the activities. The numbers are not in sequential order; they're just a way to identify each activity. Here, I've added two new activities: number 10, "Test," and number 11, "Sign-off." For the sake of this example, we'll assume that the "Review" activity, number 7, means a grammatical review of the text, while the "Test" activity, number 10, means that testers must work through each exercise in the manual to make certain they can understand them. The "Print media" activity now has two activities that must be completed before it can begin. Activity number 7, "Review," and activity number 11, "Sign-off," must both be completed before "Print media" can begin. Remember that "Sign-off" also has a dependency. The "Test" activity must be completed before "Sign-off" can be obtained.

You can see how a network diagram is a terrific tool to visualize the progress of the project. You can view the project in one graph (maybe two or three or more if the project is complex), determine how the work of the project must be performed, and see what dependencies exist between the activities. As you progress, you can indicate on the network diagram which activities have been completed by checking them off or coloring them, and so on.

In Chapter 8, "Developing the Project Plan," we'll discuss establishing starting and ending dates for each activity. These can be added to the top corners of the box for a more complete picture.

Activity on Node

Activity on node (AON) is a type of precedence diagramming method that uses circles, called nodes, to depict the tasks and uses arrows to show the dependencies between the activities. AON diagrams can be constructed with boxes as nodes, like we saw in the previous section. In the following example, a sample portion of the activities, or tasks from our annual conference project, are placed on the nodes, and the arrows show the dependency between the tasks:

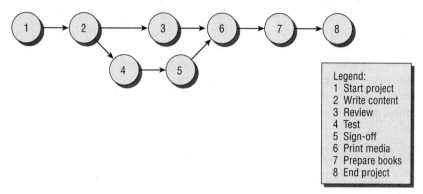

Legend:
1 Start project
2 Write content
3 Review
4 Test
5 Sign-off
6 Print media
7 Prepare books
8 End project

This example shows the "Print media" task dependent on the completion of the "Sign-off" and "Review" tasks. You could add more detail to this diagram by showing the duration estimates on the arrows for a clearer picture of how long each task should take. We'll discuss this technique further in Chapter 8. You should be aware that precedence diagrams are also known as activity-on-node. Both of these methods use nodes to depict the activities and arrows to depict the dependencies between them. Precedence diagrams, or AON, may use boxes as nodes or circles as nodes. You can use either method to construct a precedence diagram.

Arrow Diagramming Method — Activity on Arrow

Activity on arrow (AOA) is the opposite of the AON diagram. It also uses nodes and arrows like the AON, but in this case the arrows depict the activities or tasks, and the nodes indicate milestones or deliverables or simply events between the activities. Here is an example of an AOA:

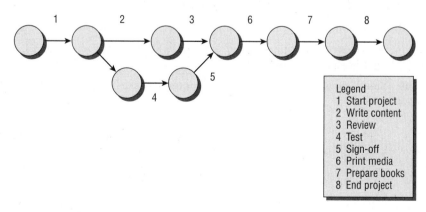

Legend
1 Start project
2 Write content
3 Review
4 Test
5 Sign-off
6 Print media
7 Prepare books
8 End project

Diagramming Method of Choice

Precedence diagrams are the easiest type to construct and the most often used. If you can draw boxes and straight lines or you can draw circles and straight lines, you can assemble a precedence diagram. I encourage you to draw a network diagram for your project and display it, along with the WBS, in the project team meeting room. And as you've heard consistently about other project documentation, put a copy of this diagram in your project notebook. (While I've talked about drawing out these diagrams by hand, keep in mind that most project managers use a tool such as Microsoft Project to do this for them.)

Terms to Know

expert judgment	WBS dictionary
precedence diagramming	work breakdown structure (WBS)
responsibility assignment matrix (RAM)	work package
scope creep	

Review Questions

1. What is the purpose of activity definition?

2. Name some of the purposes of activity sequencing.

3. What are milestones, and what significance do they have to the project?

4. Describe a work breakdown structure.

5. What is a work package?

6. Why are codes used to identify elements in the WBS?

7. Define a RAM and explain how it's used.

8. Name two methods of determining activity duration estimates.

9. Describe the four types of dependency relationships, and indicate which one is used most often.

10. Name two ways to display network diagrams and briefly describe each.

Chapter 6

Planning and Acquiring Resources

In This Chapter
- Planning the project team
- Acquiring materials and supplies
- Contracting for resources

You are well on your way to getting this project in motion. You now understand what the project is expected to produce and what the outcomes will look like, and you have an understanding of the logical order of the project work. You have identified resource types, and you have a high-level idea of how long the project activities will take.

Now it's time to identify and assign the resources that you need to complete the work of the project. This process includes identifying people (those folks who will perform the project tasks to satisfy the requirements of the deliverables) as well as equipment and materials. You may have already named some key team members and even involved them in the project scope statement and activity definition processes. But it's difficult to identify and assign all the team members on a project team without knowing what the activities and tasks of the project are. Equally, you don't really know what resources are needed until you have a full understanding of what the product or service of the project looks like and what types of deliverables, requirements, and tasks are needed to produce it.

This chapter discusses identifying and acquiring resource needs, including human resources, equipment, and materials; and it discusses techniques for negotiating or contracting for these resources if necessary.

Planning the Project Team

One of your most important jobs as a project manager is building the project team. This is probably the most fun activity of all the project processes. But it doesn't end there; you also have to keep everyone working well together. Sometimes you get lucky, and you have a fabulous team that gels right from the beginning and works well together throughout the entire project. It's rare for this to happen without any intervention on your part, however, so don't think you're off the hook. Usually, great teams come about as a result of careful planning and consideration of skills, personalities, knowledge, and so forth. This chapter discusses finding and matching the skills of team members with project tasks, while Chapter 10, "Executing the Project," will deal with team building and motivational issues.

There are several things to consider when thinking about what resources you need for your project. Organizational policies regarding job descriptions and the transfer of employees from one manager to another are some examples. For instance, I work in a government agency that has strict, formal procedures for transferring employees among departments. Job descriptions are also rigid and formal without much room for flexibility. To recruit resources from another area for one of my projects, I need to follow the organizational policies and make certain the job description adequately reflects the work of the project.

Recruitment policies are something else to keep in mind, especially when you know you're going to hire some or all of the resources for your project from outside the organization. Some organizations have policies regarding hiring practices that must be adhered to, or you'll never get the resources on board that you need. Perhaps your organization uses one or two recruiting agencies to assist in the recruitment process. You'll want to get to know those folks so you can describe for them the skills and knowledge needed for the project. Some organizations have policies against recruiting family members, for instance, or even close friends. Others welcome your friends and family with open arms. Be aware of the recruitment policies, and make certain you're following through with all the necessary paperwork. There's nothing like assuming that your new team members will be raring to go on Monday morning, only to find out that the human resources department is still waiting for sign-off from you or your manager on some important document before they can make the offer!

Aside from the organizational and recruiting policies, you should consider several things when planning your project team, including the following:

- Skills needed for each task or group of tasks

- Ability to learn new things

- Knowledge

- Personality
- Availability
- Experience
- Ability to work well with others

We'll explore each of these areas in depth in the next few sections. Before we jump into them, let's look at a department-wide skills assessment.

Skills Assessment

One of the first places you might want to start planning your team resources is with a *skills assessment* of your existing staff. If you know you're going to be using people from your own department or from other functional departments in your company, think about putting together a skills inventory like the one shown in Table 6.1.

skills assessment

A document that details the skills each team member possesses and their experience level in those skills.

Table 6.1   Skills inventory

Employee	Job title	Skills/training	Years	Education
Jason Taylor	Programmer I	Degree		BS in computer science
		Java	3	Java certification
		XML	2	
		.NET	0	Attended training classes
		Payroll system	1	
		Customer-profiling system	2	

Table 6.1 Skills inventory *(continued)*

Employee	Job title	Skills/training	Years	Education
Leah Hutchings	Database administrator	Degree		BS in computer science
		Oracle programming	5	Oracle certification
		Oracle administration	3	
		Payroll system	3	
		Accounting system	3	
		Java	1	Attended training class; some coding
Aziel Rodriguez	Technical writer	Degree	1	BA in English

You can use this table as a template to develop your own skills inventory for your department members. This example is the actual form I use to record my team's skills and training. As you can see, the table lists employees' names, skills, degrees and certifications obtained, and experience in years at the listed skill. Once you gather this information initially, I recommend updating it on a yearly basis. Incorporate an update of this inventory as part of your annual performance review process. Ask team members to update you on training and additional experience in their areas of skill, and then plug it into your skills inventory. This way, you'll know at a glance who has what skills, and it will make assigning internal resources to tasks one step easier.

Now down to specifics — who do we need for what tasks?

Deciding Who's Needed

Imagine that you work for a software development company that specializes in the insurance industry. You have been appointed the project manager over a new product launch for your company. The field representatives have started asking for a new program that allows them to access account information wirelessly from their tablet devices when they're at their client's site. Because you've already defined the work of the project through the project scope statement, WBS, and task identification processes, it's time to find the right people for the right tasks.

Determining Potential Team Members

We know from our skills inventory in Table 6.1 that Jason has programming skills, Leah can help with the database development, and Aziel can do the technical writing that we need for this project. All other potential team member names will be determined from our skills inventory as well. (Our example skills inventory shows only a few of the names available.)

Now we'll use the responsibility assignment matrix (RAM) developed in Chapter 5, "Breaking Down the Project Activities," and the skills inventory of your existing staff from Table 6.1 to construct a chart like the one in Table 6.2 to help match skills to people. The first column shows the task or work package detail, followed by the type of skills needed to complete this task, the level of experience necessary, and, finally, the team member assigned to this task.

Table 6.2   Skills definition by task

Task or work package	Skills needed	Level of experience	Potential team member
Define program requirements	Web programming	2 years	Jason Taylor
	Database	2 years	
	Good communication skills	Experience writing requirements on previous project	
Determine platform and languages	Senior programming skills	5 years	Paul Garcia, Ross Moore
Design program modules	Senior programming skills	5 years	Kathy Tan, Lance Tschida
Write help screens and manual	Technical writing	1 year	Aziel Rodriguez

This is another template that you can use or modify to suit your needs. Remember, add the General Information section at the top of all these templates so that the name of the project, date, and so on, are associated with the chart.

You may have more than one person who fits the qualifications for each task. If so, list their names in the "Potential team member" column. At this point, you don't know their availability, so if you're requesting Paul to work on the "Determine platform and languages" task and it turns out Paul is not available, you know that Ross also meets the qualifications for this task. You don't have to backtrack and figure out who else is available since you've defined all the potential candidates here.

Don't forget to list all the resources you'll need for the project on your skills definition chart. The example in Table 6.2 focuses on one type of resource, but you'll need resources from other areas of the organization such as finance, procurement (to assist with vendors and contract work), training, marketing, human resources, customer service, and so on.

NOTE   **If you're working on a medium to large project, you may want to consider adding a column to this chart that indicates the number of resources you need for each task. A project of this size will likely require five or six programmers with similar skills and varying levels of experience.**

You may find that you don't have enough resources in your own department to perform all the tasks of the project or that specific skills are needed from resources that don't report to you or your manager. That means you'll have to either hire those resources or meet with other functional managers in your organization and discuss the possibility of using folks from their departments on your project.

Part of this discussion should also include the team member's availability. It sounds like it's time for the negotiations to begin.

Negotiating for Team Members

Unless you work in a projectized environment and have control over all the resources in the company, which few of us do, you'll have to negotiate with other managers for resources. This can include negotiating for folks from the finance department to help determine and track the budget for programmers, for customer service personnel, and more. The types of people you will negotiate for depend on the skills you identified in the previous section. Once you've identified the skills, the next step is a visit to the functional managers.

Send a copy of the project charter to the person you're meeting with to review before the meeting. This gives the manager the opportunity to see what the project is all about, informs them that the executive management team is behind the project, and helps them begin figuring out who from their department might be the best fit for the project.

Meeting with the Functional Managers

Depending on the culture of your organization, you may need to set up a face-to-face meeting with each manager, or you might be able to send email detailing your request for resources. I recommend face-to-face meetings whenever possible so that you can answer questions and address concerns right away. This also gives you the ability to read body language and drive out underlying concerns the functional manager may not freely talk about without a probing question or two. In either case, you'll want to have completed the WBS and identified the tasks that you need the resources to work on. The functional managers will want to know what types of work you have for their employees and how long you'll need them. That's one place where the activity duration estimates come in handy.

TIP

Come prepared to the meeting with the functional managers. They'll want to know what types of resources are needed, when, and for how long.

Buyer beware! Functional managers may see this as their opportunity to hand off a less-than-ideal employee. You're not interested in inheriting problems; you want folks who are willing and able to do the job. Ask the functional manager specific questions about the people they're recommending for the team, such as the following:

◆ Does this person have experience at this activity?

◆ Is their experience in keeping with the level of complexity of this project? Ask for some examples of their past work.

◆ What kind of training and/or certifications does this employee have?

◆ What are their career goals and interests?

◆ What about personal characteristics?

◆ Is this person interested in working on this project?

◆ Has this person worked successfully with a variety of team members in the past without complaints from the other team members?

◆ Are there any outstanding personnel actions against this employee that you should know about?

◆ Are there any personal issues that may prevent the employee from working a standard work schedule or that will require regular absences for a period of time?

The answers to these questions will help you determine whether the folks they're recommending are the right people for the job. Although you aren't always going to get all the star employees, you surely don't want to be stuck with all those "retired on the job" types either.

Team members who are needed from the beginning of the project should be assigned to the project now. People with specific skills who are needed intermittently on the project, or maybe aren't needed until close to the end of the project, can be assigned as they are needed. However, at this point, you don't yet have the project schedule completed (Chapter 8, "Developing the Project Plan," talks about creating the project schedule), so you don't have specific dates and times when the special resources are needed. Tell the functional managers what you do know — tasks, estimated durations, types of resources, and an estimate of when you think you'll need the resources to be available. Let the functional managers know that you'll give them the specific details regarding the need for people with those unique skills when the project schedule is completed. In the meantime, the functional managers should keep those resources available within the estimated timeframes you think you're going to need them.

Staffing Assignments

Now you're ready to assign names to the tasks. Like most everything we've done so far, you'll want to document this information. You could simply update Table 6.2 to reflect the actual team member name in the last column or construct a new sheet with the tasks down the left and resource names listed next to them. In the case of those highly specialized folks with unknown availability, you can put their manager's name next to the task temporarily until you have an actual resource identified.

Experience and ability are only part of the picture when making staff assignments. Personal interests and characteristics should be considered when making team assignments as well. Unfortunately, some employees are picky about who they work with. If someone has made mortal enemies out of some of the team members on the last project they worked on, you probably don't want this person on your team. However, you may not have a choice if this person is the only person available with the specific skills you need. If that's the case, try to manage their time and assignments so that their exposure to other team members is minimal.

Another factor to watch out for is team members who don't want to work on the project. They may be terrific at the job they came from but have little interest in your project; therefore, their performance will be less than stellar. As the project manager, it's up to you to motivate them and rally the team around the project's purpose. We'll talk more about how to motivate, reward, and recognize team members in Chapter 10.

Defining Training Needs

What happens when your resources don't quite measure up to the skills needed and you don't have the money to hire consultants? You can deal with this in a couple of ways. Encourage the senior project team members to act as mentors to the junior members, allowing the junior members to learn and ask questions of the senior team members.

NOTE Don't forget to account for additional time on the project activity estimates for those activities assigned to the senior team members if you plan to use them in a mentoring role.

Formal training is another option, depending on the skill you need the team member to acquire. You'll have to weigh this option to determine whether the investment in training is worth the payoff. For example, if you're working on a small project of a short duration, it would probably make more sense to lengthen the project schedule to give an experienced team member the time to complete that task rather than training someone else to perform the task. In the case of our software project for the field reps' handheld PCs, suppose we have senior-level programmers with lots of experience writing programs for regular desktop PCs but no experience writing software for wireless devices. You could hire a consultant with expertise in this area to come in and work with your senior programmers to show them the ins and outs of wireless communication. Because the senior programmers are seasoned professionals, all they need is a little boost in this one area of expertise, so the benefits of hiring a consultant outweigh the costs.

Creating the Project Team Directory

This is a good time to construct a *project team directory*. The directory lists the names and contact information for all the stakeholders, the project sponsor, all the team members, and any vendor contacts working on the project. It should also describe their roles on the project and could include communication needs and information. (You captured communication needs when you created the communications plan described in Chapter 4, "Defining the Project Goals.") I recommend posting the team directory to the project site on the network or including it as an appendix in the project notebook.

project team directory
Directory of contact information for everyone involved in the project, their roles, and communication needs.

If most of the folks you're assigning to the project are from your own department, you're probably ready to hold a team kickoff meeting. If you've recruited folks from other departments and they aren't scheduled to start on the project until after the work begins, invite them to the team kickoff meeting so that they have the benefit of hearing the project overview and goals with all the team members present. We'll discuss the project kickoff meeting in more detail in Chapter 10, including what information you should cover with the team in this meeting.

Acquiring Materials, Supplies, and Equipment

Now that you know the tasks required to complete the deliverables for your project, you're ready to fill out your supplies list. As we discussed in the resources section earlier, you can't really know all the materials and supplies you're going to need for the project without having first defined the tasks. If one of your tasks involves calibrating some machinery, for example, how will you know what kind of equipment you'll need to perform the calibrations until you've defined the tasks?

Defining the materials and supplies, along with the human resources we've already outlined, will help you estimate the costs of the project and determine a budget. After defining the materials list, you'll also be able to decide where the resources will come from — will you buy them, lease them, or contract them? First, though, you should ask some questions.

Questions to Ask

Pull out your copy of the WBS. This is the first place you're going to look to start compiling your materials list. The tasks defined on the WBS dictate the kinds of materials, supplies, and equipment you're going to need for the project. Let's go back to our example project at the beginning of this chapter. You're heading up the development and implementation of a new software program for the field representatives for an insurance company. Some of your WBS tasks include "Define program requirements," "Determine languages and platform," and "Design programming modules."

Starting with these requirements, you can begin to ask some questions:

◆ What hardware and software will you need in order to write the program code?

◆ What hardware and software will you need in order to test the programs?

◆ Will the field reps be receiving new tablet devices or using their existing devices?

◆ If they are using their existing equipment, are they, or should they be, upgrading it prior to implementation of the new programs?

◆ What other software is needed to assist with design, coding, and testing?

Don't forget to also explore questions regarding facilities, new technologies, and services you might need. Because this particular project involves wireless communications, ask questions such as these:

◆ Are there field staff stationed in locations where commercial wireless services are not available? If so, are there alternative possibilities such as satellite services?

What about facilities? Make sure to ask the following questions:

◆ Does the project team work at the same location? If not, do you need a common meeting place to kick off the project and meet on a periodic basis?

◆ Should the team work at the same location? If so, what types of resources are needed to make that happen?

Spend some time brainstorming with your team and some of the key stakeholders to determine the resource needs of the project. And as you've probably already guessed, you'll want to document these needs. You can construct a simple document like the example shown here, noting the amount of resources you're going to need, whether the resource is available or must be procured, and so on.

NOTE   You can also download the template for the resource needs document at www.sybex.com/go/projectmanagementjumpstart3.

Task	Materials Needed	Quantity	Available/Procure	Approximate Cost
Design program modules	New PCs	4	Procure	$2,100 each
	Software licenses	6	Procure	$42,000 total
Write programs	Programming software	6	Procure	$62,000 total
	Sample handhelds	2	Procure	$1,900 total
	Training	10	Procure	$2,500 each

Materials, Supplies, and Equipment List

I. General Information

Project name:_____   Project number:_____

Project Manager name:_____   Date:_____

II. Materials, Supplies, and Equipment Needed

You could consider adding another column to this template that identifies potential vendors or suppliers and a column for cost per unit. In this example, all of the resources listed are going to be procured from a vendor, so listing possible vendors or contractors on this table would make sense. Modify this template to suit your project needs, and file a copy in the project notebook for future reference.

Make or Buy

This question won't always apply to your projects, but it could apply to certain aspects of your project. The question is, should you make or buy the products or services needed for the project?

Make-or-buy decisions involve determining whether it's more cost-effective for the organization to make or buy the products or services of the project. This decision can be made at the individual resource level, for an entire deliverable, or even for the project itself. Some projects are too cost-prohibitive for the organization to take on internally, and it makes the most economic sense to out-source the project. Make-or-buy decisions regarding the entire project usually happen back at the Initiating stage of the project.

There are several things to consider regarding make-or-buy decisions. Obviously, the biggest factor is cost. You should take into account the costs to produce the product or service — goods, materials, equipment, facilities, employee salaries — as well as the indirect costs. Indirect costs include such things as train-ing costs, management costs, administrative overhead, and ongoing maintenance. Compile all the costs associated with producing the product or service before you compare it to the cost to outsource it or buy it. Ongoing maintenance and change-order costs are costs that are often overlooked in make-or-buy decisions, so be sure to include those in your analysis.

TIP

Cost is not the only consideration in make-or-buy decisions. Skills, training, capacity issues, and availability are some of the other issues that should be examined before a decision is made.

Other things you should consider that aren't necessarily driven by cost alone are issues like capacity — can the organization take on a product of this mag-nitude? What about the skill level of the folks who'll work on the product or service? Do they require extensive training, or can they produce the product or service without much forethought? Consider things like process controls and trade secrets. If you can't divulge the secret ingredients of the magic formula, you probably can't outsource the production of the magic formula to a vendor. Also consider the availability of your staff and the existing workload. If your staff is buried in a backlog of top-priority projects, it isn't likely that they can take on the production of a new product or service at this time, so buying the products or services needed might be the most beneficial solution.

The goal of this process is to decide whether making or buying the products or services of the project is the most cost-effective and efficient for the organiza-tion. Remember, this can involve only one product or deliverable or the entire project. When it is necessary to procure goods and services, you'll need to pre-pare a procurement plan.

Procurement Plan

Some organizations have departments that handle the procurement process and have long lists of established policies regarding purchasing goods and services. They may have lists of vendors for you to choose from, or they may require an extensive bidding process to take place (depending on what you're buying). And, depending on the amount you're spending, there may be certain procedures in place that require multiple signatures and/or multiple reviews of the requests. Other organizations may have simple guidelines regarding their purchasing policies. These might include signing authority limits that depend on your title or function in the organization.

As the project manager, it's important for you to know and understand the procurement process for your organization. If there are extensive rules to follow and you miss crossing a *t* somewhere along the way, the holdup could cost you time on the project schedule and potentially money as well.

No matter what your procurement policies might be, you should create a *procurement plan* for the items you're purchasing for your project. The procurement plan can be as simple as listing the service or resources needed, the quantity, the price, and the vendor who'll be supplying the services in a spreadsheet format similar to the graphic shown previously. Or the plan can be very detailed, including deliverables, requirements, dates, and so on.

The contract statement of work (CSOW) could be prepared in conjunction with the procurement plan or in place of the procurement plan if you're purchasing all your goods and services from one vendor. Remember that the project scope statement we talked about in Chapter 4 can also be used as the CSOW or as input to the CSOW. The project scope statement is usually used for the CSOW when you're outsourcing the entire project. Keep in mind that the project scope statement is usually written by the project team members, whereas a CSOW should be written by the customer. You'll want to make certain the appropriate stakeholders are involved in developing the CSOW.

procurement plan
Describes the resources or services to be purchased from an outside vendor and how procurements will be managed.

Just to keep us honest, we talked about the project SOW in Chapter 3, "Initiating the Project," as one of the inputs to the project charter. The project SOW in that case describes the products or services the project intends to create, which isn't any different from the CSOW here. The CSOW can also be prepared in conjunction with the procurement plan when you're purchasing from a vendor, and it contains the same information as it does as an input to the project charter.

NOTE

Resource Plan

Resources include people, equipment, supplies, and software — anything that's required to complete the work of the project. We've now defined all the resources of the project including the skills assessment, skills definition by task, staff assignments, and physical resources needed for the project.

All of this information collectively is known as the *resource plan*. As stated, the resource plan covers all the resources you need for the project. You should devote a section of the project notebook to the resource plan. I recommend including the procurement plan as a subset of the resource plan. You're probably beginning to see how the project notebook is going to help you in the future. When you're assigned to a new project that's similar in scope to a project you've already completed, you'll be able to use the information you filed

resource plan
Describes all the resources needed for the project, including human resources and goods and materials.

in the project notebook as a reference for the new project. Why reinvent the wheel? You can use the resource plan from this project to help you document a resource plan for the new project. At the very least, reviewing this information will trigger questions or ideas for the project plans on the new project.

The resource plan might include purchasing some or all of your products or services from an external party, which may require the use of a contract. We'll wrap up this chapter with a discussion of the contracting process.

Contracting for Resources

Project managers often purchase goods or services on contract. Many organizations have departments that handle contract negotiation and fulfillment, but this doesn't mean you can sit back on your heels and let someone else do the work. As the project manager, you should have an understanding of the contracting process. You're the one who will be communicating with the vendor regarding the work of the project, and you are also the one who will report the status of the work to the procurement department or the contract manager so that payment can be made to the vendor. Many times, contracts are paid incrementally according to the milestones or deliverables listed in the contract. Payment is authorized when the milestones are reached and sign-off is obtained. The project manager is the one who notifies the procurement department when the milestones have been reached.

The contract manager is not the project manager, so they'll be looking to you to make certain that the items outlined in the contract are completed satisfactorily. That means you'll monitor the vendor's performance to make sure it measures up to the terms of the contract. When it doesn't, you'll have to work with your procurement department to document the problems, notify the vendor, and then take corrective action or terminate the contract. If you're administering the contract, these duties will fall to you.

NOTE **Contracts are a way to ensure that the parties who have agreed to exchange goods and services for money (technically this is called *consideration*, which almost always means money) fulfill their end of the bargain. The contract is enforceable in a court of law and ensures that the goods are delivered and that the money is paid.**

As the buyer of the goods or services, you'll want to create the CSOW to make certain the requirements are defined accurately and that no important deliverables are missing. The vendor or supplier will use the CSOW to determine whether they can fulfill the terms of the contract (they'll do this during the next cycle, which we'll get to in a moment). The WBS is developed at this time as well, cost estimates are determined, and the make-or-buy analysis is performed.

Contracts have a lifecycle of their own, just as projects do. The four *contract lifecycles* are requirement, requisition, solicitation, and award. We've already covered the things that occur in the requirements cycle. This is where the CSOW is created and both parties agree to the requirements and deliverables of the project. If you follow the guidelines for writing the project scope statement, you'll end up with a clear and concise CSOW that accurately describes the work of the project. I'll cover the requisition process next.

contract lifecycle
Contracts progress through specific phases, similar to a project lifecycle. The phases of a contract lifecycle include requirement, requisition, solicitation, and award.

Request for Proposal and More

Requisition is the next contract lifecycle. In this process, you'll reconfirm that the project objectives are accurate and make any necessary corrections. The primary purpose of this process is to prepare requests for information regarding your project objectives and deliverables for the vendors who will be bidding on the project work. You'll actually distribute this information to the potential vendors in the next cycle — the solicitation process.

You'll use the project objectives and the CSOW to help you prepare requests for information from vendors. These requests are called *requests for proposals (RFPs)*, *requests for information (RFIs)*, and *requests for quotations (RFQs)*. The idea here is to outline the project objectives in a way that allows the vendors to determine whether they can perform the work accurately and satisfactorily. Again, check your organization's policies regarding RFPs and such. They may require you to use predesigned forms and follow specific steps in order to complete and post the RFP.

request for proposal (RFP)
Procurement document used to solicit input from vendors when purchasing goods or services or outsourcing project work.

Here's another controversy you'll likely find yourself in the midst of during the RFP process. Some project managers believe that the RFP should outline every detail of the project. For example, if you're contracting a new software program, the RFP would dictate the programming language to use, the operating system, the database to use, and so on. Other project managers might say that this boxes the vendor in and doesn't give them any flexibility to offer creative solutions. In addition, the organization doesn't have the chance to approach the project from a new or different perspective because the project specifics have already been dictated.

Still other project managers use both of these approaches depending on the project — I think this is the best approach. If you have a solid idea of the way the project should go and you do have specific requirements regarding operating systems or other details, then put that in the RFP. If you're not certain how the project should come together and prefer to rely on the vendor for input or want to examine alternative approaches, go heavy on the requirements and objectives of the project and let the vendor detail their alternative solutions in the response to the RFP.

If your project dictates that you spell out detailed requirements or specifications in the RFP, make certain that these get included in the final contract.

TIP

One thing to keep in mind regarding RFPs, particularly for technology projects, is that technology changes so quickly in some areas (such as telephony, for example) that you might require certain equipment or software in the RFP that is actually outdated by the time the vendor completes the project. Be choosy about the types of requirements that must meet certain specifications, and give the vendor a little room to come up with some interesting alternatives.

Soliciting Bids

The soliciting bids contract lifecycle process is where the vendors respond to the RFP, RFI, and so on. This process is also known as Conduct Procurements. Essentially, vendors are competing for your business in this process and are putting their best foot forward by addressing all the requirements you outlined in the RFP. Most of the work in this process falls on the vendors.

Some organizations require vendors to register with them on a vendors list before they can participate in the RFP process. The vendor is required to provide information regarding their experience, the services or goods their company offers, prices for standard offerings where appropriate, a list of the officers in the company, and so on. The procurement department then reviews the vendor's qualifications and determines whether to put that vendor's name on the organization's qualified vendors list. Vendors lists are usually updated on a yearly basis, and typically only vendors on the qualified vendors list are allowed to participate in the bidding process.

The RFP is posted or released, and a deadline for responding is announced at the same time. Vendors obtain copies of the RFP, read over your requirements, and set about writing their responses. Before they submit their responses, however, they'll want to ask some clarifying questions.

Sometime after the RFP has been released, you should hold a bidders conference or meeting that allows the vendors to ask questions about the RFP in an open forum. Depending on your organizational policies, you and others on your team might be restricted from speaking with the potential bidders until after the RFP process has been closed. The exception to this is the bidders conference, where all participants have a chance to ask questions and hear your responses all at the same time, so no favoritism is shown.

WARNING   **Check the organizational or procurement policies regarding your contact with vendors during the RFP process. You could jeopardize or disqualify a vendor if you violate the policy.**

Make certain to use a method of advertising that gives every bidder the opportunity to know about the conference ahead of time. The bidders conference could be announced on your company's website, in professional journals, or in newspapers, depending on your procurement policies. Another alternative is to advertise the bidders conference at the same time you release the RFP. If you don't have the bidders conference scheduled yet, let them know where and when you'll be advertising that information.

Choosing a Supplier

The last contract lifecycle process is the award cycle. This is where you'll review the responses to the RFPs, choose a vendor, and award a contract.

You can use several methods to help you choose among the RFP responses and make a final award. Usually a selection committee is assembled for this purpose, and together the committee reviews and ranks the responses using one of the following methods.

Weighted Systems

A *weighted scoring model* or weighting system is a great tool to use for scoring RFP responses. It's an objective tool and assures that all the selection committee members are using the same criteria to evaluate the responses.

weighted scoring model
Used in the procurement process and the project selection process to weight and rank various criteria and make a final selection.

Typically, the project selection committee decides on the criteria they'll use for the scoring model prior to receiving the RFP responses; often this is provided in the RFP itself so the vendors understand what they will be judged on. Suppose our example wireless project is going to be outsourced. In the RFP, we've specified certain development environments that the vendor must work within because of compatibility issues with other programs. Because of the importance of the new program's compatibility with existing systems and programs, the selection committee has determined that this should be one of the criteria that are weighed in the decision process. Other criteria are determined based on their importance to the project and the selection committee.

Each of the criteria is assigned a weight, depending on the importance of the criteria to the committee — the higher the importance, the higher the weight. Each vendor's response is then read and scored according to the criteria detailed on the scoring system. Here, individual judgment comes into play as each selection committee member scores the vendor response to each criterion based on their own perception of how well the RFP addressed that particular issue.

Table 6.3 shows a sample portion of a weighted scoring model, with the criteria listed in the left column and the weight for each criterion in the next column, followed by the rating and scores for each vendor.

Table 6.3 Weighted scoring model

Criteria	Weight	Vendor A rating	Vendor A score	Vendor B rating	Vendor B score
Development environment proposed to create programs	5	4	20	4	20
Technical skills of proposed team members	3	5	15	3	9
Ease to produce and support	2	4	8	5	10
Weighted score			**43**		**39**

The rating for each criterion is multiplied by the weight to come up with a score for that criterion. All the scores for a vendor are added together to come up with a total weighted score. The highest scoring vendor receives the award. In the example in Table 6.3, Vendor A is the winner of the bid.

Screening Systems

screening systems
Used in the procurement process to outline criteria that must be met in order for a proposal to make it to the next level in the selection process.

Screening systems are used to screen out proposals that don't meet predetermined criteria. For example, our wireless software project requires a specific platform because of compatibility issues with existing hardware and software. The platform requirement could be used as a screening criterion. If Vendor A submits a proposal that outlines a different platform than what we specified in the RFP, they are immediately disqualified from the selection process.

The selection committee determines the screening criteria before the proposals are received. Screening systems are often used in conjunction with weighted scoring models to make an award. For instance, the screening system criteria must be met before the proposal can proceed to the weighted scoring model process.

Awarding the Contract

The last step in this process is actually awarding the contract. Your procurement department will likely draw up the contract, but you should be part of this process. Make certain that the requirements listed in the RFP make it into the contract. Review the timelines, deliverables, requirements, and so on, and request a copy for your records when it's signed.

You'll use the contract and the SOW to monitor the vendor's performance and assure that the agreed-upon deliverables are met. If they're not, you'll have to document the violations and assist the procurement department with enforcing the terms of the contract or terminating the contract when the vendor is in violation or refuses to correct their errors.

Terms to Know

contract lifecycle

procurement plan

project team directory

request for proposal (RFP)

resource plan

screening systems

skills assessment

weighted scoring model

Review Questions

1. What policies should you consult before putting together your project team?

2. Name at least four things you should consider when choosing project team members.

3. What tools can you use to help determine human resource needs for the project?

4. What document should you look at first to help you determine the supplies, materials, and equipment needed for the work of the project?

5. What is the purpose of the project team directory?

6. What is the purpose of a make-or-buy decision?

7. Describe the resource plan and its purpose.

8. Why is it important for project managers to understand contracts?

9. What is the purpose of the requisition process in the contract lifecycle?

10. Name two processes used in the selection or award process of the contract lifecycle.

Chapter 7

Assessing Risk

Each of us takes risks every day. For most of us, reasonable risks don't prevent us from doing our daily tasks and routines. The same is true for our projects. But you must identify the risks and analyze their potential impacts and the possibility that the risk will happen during the course of your project in order to know how to handle the risk should it occur.

The goal of this chapter is to show you how to create the risk management plan and the risk response plan. The risk management plan documents how the risk management processes will be implemented and monitored throughout the project. The risk response plan consists of risks you've identified that could impact the project, an analysis of the risks and their impacts, and planned responses for the risks should they occur.

One thing is certain — risk does exist on your project, and it poses either a potential threat or a potential opportunity. It's your job to document the risks and determine which ones need response plans.

Identifying Risks

A *risk* is the possibility of a problem occurring on the project, thereby threatening the project's outcome in some way. However, not all risks are bad, and not all risks have negative impacts. Some risks are actually opportunities in disguise. For example, agreeing to take on and complete a new project is a risk. Since one of the definitions of a project is creating a unique product, service, or result, the project itself is a risk that's taken on to exploit an opportunity.

It doesn't matter whether the risk is a threat or an opportunity; if you don't take the time to identify it, you won't know that either exists. Failing to document risks and develop plans for those with the greatest probability for impact can cause your project to fail.

Why should you identify risks, and how do they cause projects to fail if you don't plan for them? Risk can cause rework, which means you have to go back and repeat some activities you've already completed. Rework almost always means that there will be schedule delays or additional costs or both. If you've completed one of the deliverables of the project only to have a risk event wreak havoc with the results, you'll have to perform additional steps to correct the impact of the event, or perhaps you'll even need to scrap the work that's been done and start over. None of that will come without a cost. You'll likely need to retain resources longer than you had planned, which could jeopardize other projects as well as cost you more money. If all your resources are internal to the organization, you will still incur additional costs. The extra time they are spending on your project prevents them from doing work on other projects, thereby increasing the cost. Additional supplies and materials, extended lease times for equipment you're using on the project, and the replacement of resources that were scrapped all cost money as well.

NOTE   **Risk management is a multistep process. First you identify the risks. Then you analyze the risks and determine the impact of the risk event should it occur. Next you determine the probability of the risk occurring. Finally you combine the impact analysis with the probability analysis to determine which of the identified risks needs a risk response plan.**

Remember that your goal as the project manager is to complete the project to the satisfaction of the stakeholders. To do that, you'll need to know what obstacles can spring up along the way to prevent you from completing the deliverables on time and on budget. It isn't possible to know every risk in advance, but the more risks you identify and plan for, the less impact they'll have on the project outcomes. When you plan for risk events, the consequences of those risk events are reduced or perhaps avoided altogether. Take the time in the planning stage to identify risks and come up with action plans even for those risks you cannot avoid or reduce. You'll save yourself precious time figuring out what to do when they do occur if you've planned ahead of time.

Risk management is an activity that occurs throughout the life of the project. It begins in the Planning process and continues until the Closing process is completed. Good risk management practices help you bring your project to a successful ending because you'll have plans in place to deal with potential threats before they occur and you'll have identified potential opportunities that may bring your organization more business, an increase in efficiency, or new ways of performing the work of the project. The advantages of practicing good risk management include the following:

◆ It helps you identify potential project showstoppers early in the process and develop plans and strategies to reduce or avoid their impacts.

◆ It helps you identify potential opportunities and take advantage of them, maybe even creating whole new projects out of the opportunities that come about through the risk management process.

◆ It enables you to reduce rework and keep the project budget on track.

◆ It allows you to be proactive instead of reactive, which increases your credibility and reputation among the stakeholders.

◆ It increases the likelihood of project success.

Project risk is greatest at the beginning of the project because the potential for unsuccessful outcomes or incomplete projects is most likely to occur at the beginning of the project. At this point, so many aspects of the project are yet to be completed and thus have unknown outcomes. This risk decreases as the project nears completion. Careful attention to risk events during the Planning, Executing, and Monitoring and Controlling processes helps ensure project success. Let's take a look at some of the risks that all projects have in common.

Types of Project Risks

All projects have risk, and several risks are common to all projects no matter how easy or complicated the project appears.

Most risks fall into three categories: known risks, known risks with uncertain outcomes, and unknown risks. Obviously, there isn't much to say about the unknown risks category. By nature of the fact that they're unknown, you can't identify them up front or create specific plans in the event they'll occur. You can plan for them in nonspecific ways, however. We'll talk more about those plans in a later section.

Known risks are events that you (or the project team) know have the potential to occur, and they have predictable outcomes. For example, let's say you've been asked to head up your company's annual all-employee meeting. Your company employs 500 people, and all employees plus one guest of their choice are invited to attend the meeting. The owner of your company is a generous person and believes in sharing the wealth because, after all, the employees helped her get to where she is today. The meeting is going to be held at a famous resort in the mountains near your city, and each employee and their guest are encouraged to stay at the resort for one evening (at the company's expense). The meeting itself will consist of a formal dinner and an awards ceremony. Every employee in the company will receive something. You've been sworn to secrecy regarding the awards and will have to handle these arrangements yourself with no help from the project team.

Known risks with predictable outcomes are fairly easy to spot. An example of a known risk for this project would be the weather — the meeting is being held in November, which means there's a potential for a snowstorm that will prevent folks from getting to the resort.

An example of a known risk with an uncertain result in this case is the number of attendees. Even though you're limiting the employees to one guest each, there's the potential that some may bring more than one guest or that employees say they will attend with a guest but won't show up. Now let's take this one step further and find out how to identify specific risks for your project.

Common Project Risks – Where Are They Hiding?

Risks can come from internal or external sources. Internal risks come about because of the nature of the project itself, organizational issues, employee or resource problems, and so on. External sources of risk include political issues, legal concerns, environmental issues, and social issues.

One of the first places to start identifying risks is with the project itself, looking at internal, known risks. Some of the planning processes you've already completed can help you with this task. The project constraints, WBS, task list, and critical success factors can help you uncover risks regarding the project itself.

Business risks are another area to consider when identifying risks. These include marketing concerns, timing of the product release, and public perception.

This section examines some of the common risks you may encounter on your projects. I'll conclude this section with a checklist that you can use as a template for identifying your project risks.

Constraint-Related Risks

Project constraints limit the project team in some way, and you usually know about them at the start of the project. Risks, on the other hand, are generally unknown at the beginning of the project. However, looking closer at the constraints can help you identify project risks. Remember that the triple constraints of schedule, scope, and cost generally have the biggest risk impact on the project. Resource and quality constraints are also attention getters in the risk arena. Whatever the primary constraints are on the project, you can be certain that risks are usually lurking in each of them.

If time (or schedule) is your primary constraint, risks associated with this constraint could include loss of key personnel, lack of training opportunities in time for critical project activities, vendor delays, equipment failure, weather or other forces of nature, and so on. Each of these potential risks has an impact on the project schedule. Risks that occur to the project schedule also have the potential to impact the project budget. If vendor delays or equipment failure occur, for example, it may require additional budget to hire another vendor (or replace the existing one) or purchase new equipment and expedite the shipment. These risks may also impact the project scope. For example, if the equipment you need is highly specialized but continues to cause problems, you may need to modify the project scope to accommodate a different type or version of the equipment you originally required for the project. So, not only is the project schedule, or time, a constraint, it's also a key area for us to examine in the risk-identification process. We should examine resource and quality constraints in the same way.

A risk that involves one of the triple constraints will more than likely involve at least one, if not both, of the other constraints. For example, the loss of a key employee during the project is not only a project schedule (or time) risk but a potential cost risk as well. If the employee leaves and you haven't devised a plan to deal with this risk, the project schedule will be impacted, and it may cost you megabucks to bring in a contractor with the skills needed to finish the tasks, and therefore that impacts the project budget.

TIP

For risk-identification purposes, it really doesn't matter which of the constraints is the primary constraint, because each of them has associated risks. Exploring schedule, scope, and cost will almost always turn up risks on the project. Taking a closer look at each of the constraints is a good way to kick off the risk-identification process.

Identifying Risks in the WBS and Task List

Other great tools you can use to help in the risk-identification process are the WBS and the task list. You can see how these planning tools begin to build on themselves and why it's important to document all the project plans. Not only can you use this information as a reference on future projects, you can use it now in the risk-identification process to help you identify potential threats and opportunities. (Hint: You'll use all these documents again in the Executing and Monitoring and Controlling processes of the project.)

Using the WBS, examine the deliverables and the work package levels for risks. One of the deliverables for our employee meeting project is setting up the speaking area of the meeting room with a laptop, projector, and microphone. Some of the risks associated with this deliverable are equipment malfunction, lack of power, and delayed delivery of equipment.

Use the task list in the same manner. Examine each task from the perspective of what can go wrong. Add those risks, or things that could go wrong, to your risk-identification list. We'll talk more about the list shortly.

Critical Success Factors

We talked about critical success factors in Chapter 4, "Defining the Project Goals." They are usually deliverables or milestones that absolutely must be completed, and completed correctly, to consider the project a success. Again, look over your critical success factors to see what risks you can uncover that might be associated with them.

In Chapter 4, I gave you a list of some of the things that I consider critical success factors for all projects. Let's look at a few of them again in light of the risks that could be associated with them:

Understanding of and Consensus Regarding the Project Goals by Key Stakeholders, Project Team, Management Team, and Project Manager Risk: If understanding and consensus are not reached, the project will not produce the results expected by the stakeholders, and therefore the project will be unsuccessful. This could result in the loss of business for your company or contractual issues that require legal intervention. Your own job or personal reputation could suffer as a result.

Well-Defined Scope Statement   Risk: Poorly defined scope will result in misdirection for the project team, leading to missed deadlines, continual scope changes, rework, inaccurate results, and/or increased costs.

Well-Defined Project Plan   Risk: The risks here are similar to what was outlined in the scope statement risk, including rework, incorrect results, poor quality, increased cost, and missed deadlines.

The Use of Established Project Management Practices   Risk: Not using a standard project management process could result in a lack of communication and organization regarding the project activities, ultimately resulting in an unsuccessful project.

The theme is consistent regarding these critical success factors — if you don't take the time to adequately plan your project activities and communicate well with the project team and stakeholders, your entire project is likely in jeopardy. Planning is an important step in any established project management methodology. I can't emphasize enough the importance of planning, so don't skip these processes.

Business Risks

Depending on the type of project you're working on, business risks may not have as much probability of occurring as risks associated with the triple constraints or critical success factors, but you should be aware of them and identify them because their impacts pack a big punch. If you're caught by surprise and don't have a plan to respond to any of these risks that may affect your project, it could spell disaster. Let's look at some of the most common business risks:

Marketability   If your project is the launch of a new product, marketability is a business risk. One concern regarding marketability is the question, Will customers really pay for this product? This project may build a product or service that everyone inside the company thinks is the next greatest blockbuster hit, but if customers don't perceive the product to have the same value as the company does, they won't buy it.

Timing   Timing of the project is another business-related risk. For instance, maybe your project involves creating the perfect holiday bakeware for home chefs, but because of schedule delays, the product didn't hit the retail shelves until January. Or maybe your project concerns creating a documentary of the world's greatest ice cream parlors, only to have the FDA issue a ban on all ice cream production for health reasons (heaven forbid!). Be aware of timing issues or impacts to timing like these because they could also cause an otherwise successful project to fall flat.

Management Issues   Management risks are related to business risks. Management issues that may pose risks to your project include changes in corporate strategic direction, reorganization of the business units, layoffs and cutbacks, mergers and acquisitions, and budget restrictions (after budgets have been approved for your project) to name a few. If you're aware of these issues lurking behind the scenes, take them into consideration, and evaluate the impacts they could have on the project.

Business and management risks have a small bark and a big bite, so don't overlook their potential impacts to your project.

NOTE

Vendor Delays   Vendor delays and contract issues are another type of business risk. If you're relying on a vendor to deliver critical components or equipment at specific times during the project, you should note the failure to deliver these items on time as a risk. Contract issues can also delay project schedules or impact the project budget. If the vendor does not live up to the terms of the contract, you'll either need to take action to force them to comply or find another vendor. Either way, it will likely cause schedule delays and impact the project budget.

External Project Risks

External project risks include things that are outside the control of the project team and the organization itself. Political issues, legal issues, environmental issues, and social issues are a few examples. Don't overlook obvious things such as the weather, earthquakes, fires, sunspots, alien invasions, and so on.

Technical concerns can also be an external project risk. If you're relying on new technology for a project you're working on but the release of the new technology is delayed, your project will also be delayed — unless you have alternatives to deal with this risk event. The opposite of this situation can occur as well. Aging technology can be a risk to the project if you're relying on specific technology for your project, but that technology is outdated by the time you're ready to launch the product of the project. Your product may not have a long shelf life as a result, or, more likely, it will be canceled before completion.

Other Risks

There are a couple of other issues to think about when identifying risk. One risk that you should be aware of is the complexity of the project itself. Ask the team or project sponsor whether the project team has ever taken on a project of this magnitude before. If the answer is no, then you should document this as a risk and be aware that the project team may require additional training or you may need consulting services to assist the project team, and so on.

Also, examine your own skills and ability as a project manager. Are you prepared to take on a project of this size? Have you had sufficient experience with other similar projects to lead this project to a successful conclusion?

Along these same lines, be sure to examine the skills and abilities of the project team members. If the project involves writing a new software program in a language that project team members are not familiar with, document this as a risk. Keep in mind that senior or experienced team members can help identify and mitigate risks more easily than junior team members with less experience.

Identification Techniques

The process of identifying risks is something the project manager should do together with the project team, the stakeholders, the project sponsor, and others you think are helpful to the process. In this section, we'll look at a few techniques you can use to get the team's creative thinking processes going to uncover as many risks as possible.

The first attempt at risk identification is more easily accomplished with a small group consisting of key project team members and key stakeholders. Using some of the techniques described shortly, document the risks the team comes up with during this initial meeting in a spreadsheet or word-processing document. List each risk, assign it a number for tracking purposes, and identify its impacts or characteristics.

After you've compiled an initial list, hold another meeting (or set of meetings depending on the size of the project), expanding the number of participants to include more of the project team members and stakeholders. Again, use some of the techniques outlined later in this section to identify more risks with this bigger group, and add those to the risk list.

Some of the participants you should consider including in your risk-identification meetings are as follows. The project manager should always attend these meetings.

- Project team members
- Project sponsor
- Stakeholders
- Technical experts
- People who have experience on previous projects of similar size and scope
- Customers or end users
- Vendors (when appropriate)

Historical Information

One of the first places you should look for risks is past projects. Here's where those project notebooks you've been putting together and past project documentation come in handy. If you're working on a project that's similar in nature, scope, and complexity to past projects, you can review the previous project as a starting point for documenting risks in this project.

Brainstorming

You are probably already familiar with this technique. *Brainstorming* is a process in which the project team members, subject-matter experts, stakeholders, and anyone else who might have information or knowledge about this project meet in a single location and name the risks they see for the project.

A facilitator documents the items on a list or a whiteboard, while the participants keep calling out the risks as they occur to them. The dynamics at work here are interesting. The old saying that two heads are better than one applies to brainstorming. Each of the participants will come to the meeting thinking about the risks that may impact their particular function or area. When you bring all these folks together, one group of stakeholders or functional managers will hear the risks the other groups are naming, which will bring to light new risks they might not have thought about if they were doing this individually.

The rules for brainstorming are simple. The group should not look down on anyone's ideas; in other words, no one is allowed to pass judgment. List all the risks identified, using one or two words whenever possible. Try to manage the group so that only one person is speaking at a time, but I'll warn you, once they start rolling with the ideas, it will be hard to keep them from speaking over one another. Keep the enthusiasm going, but do try to maintain order at the same time. Don't assume that one of the risks someone mentions is the same as a risk that was identified earlier.

brainstorming
A method of discovering risk events, alternatives, requirements, or other project information with a group of people who have knowledge of the project, product, or processes used during the project. This process is intended to produce free-form ideas, and no restrictions are placed on the participants.

Delphi Technique

The *Delphi technique* uses a questionnaire method often designed with forced choices that require the expert to select between various options. Delphi is typically used as a project selection method, but I've also used this technique to help identify potential project risks. The questionnaire asks participants about risks associated with the project, the business process, and the product of the project, and it asks the readers to rank their answers in regard to the potential impacts of the risks. If you're acting as the facilitator, you can assemble your participants via email or an Internet or intranet site, or you can use a online tool that participants can log onto on their own time. Experts from inside and outside the company are asked to identify potential risks for the project using a questionnaire that the facilitator created ahead of time. The participants complete the questionnaire and send it back to you, the facilitator. You will then compile all the responses and organize them in some logical manner — by content or risk type, for example. After you've compiled the responses, you send this list to each of the Delphi members and ask them for further input, additions, and comments. The participants send their comments and additions back to you, and then you compile a final list. As you can see, this is a labor-intensive process. If you have a small group of participants, it's probably manageable, but if you have a large group, you'll want to consider using an online questionnaire or using a software program designed to compile and summarize the responses. The Delphi technique removes bias from the process. Because the team members completing the questionnaire are not meeting together as a group, one member is not unduly influenced by others, and each one is free to state what they're really thinking.

Nominal Group Technique

The *Nominal Group technique* is similar to brainstorming, but it's more like brainstorming by secret ballot.

One approach to this technique requires all the participants to be in the same room together. Everyone is given a marker and a pad of sticky notes. You, the facilitator, then ask everyone to write one risk, and only one risk, on a note. You might consider starting out each round by telling the group to think of the most important risk or the risk with the greatest impact to the project and write that risk on a note.

You then collect the notes, post them on a whiteboard or flip chart, and ask the group to think of the risk with the next-greatest impact to the project and write it down. Continue asking them to write down risks in this manner until they can't think of any more.

After all the risks have been identified and posted on the board, ask the group to rank them and prioritize them. They should perform this first ranking and prioritization in writing, and each of them should submit their rankings to the facilitator. You then assemble and prioritize the risks in order according to the consensus of the written rankings. At this point, you can ask for input or clarification from the group. When you've finished, you'll have a complete list of risks in their order of importance or impact.

The rules for this approach to the Nominal Group technique are also simple. Only one risk can be written per note. Once the notes are posted and all the participants can see them, risks should not be duplicated in subsequent rounds. And the participants should not pass judgment on the risks submitted by others. Keep the group size to a manageable number when using these techniques, or you might end up stalling the process.

The Nominal Group technique is also a great technique to use for determining project requirements.

TIP

Interviewing

An interview is a question-and-answer session held with key stakeholders, team members, functional managers, subject-matter experts, and others who have an interest in the project or who have previous experience on projects similar to yours. These folks can tell you what risks are likely to occur on the project, based on their experiences with similar projects.

Ask them about risks they've experienced on previous projects or what they think may happen on this project. Ask them about their industry expertise or specialized knowledge regarding the product of the project and its outcomes. Show them the WBS, the task list, and the list of constraints and assumptions to help them think of risks that might occur on this project.

Checklist of Common Project Risks

As you saw earlier, the most common project risks are those risks associated with the triple constraints: time, scope, and budget. If you focus on these areas as well as other common constraints such as quality and resources, you'll probably discover a great many of the risks that could affect your project. In a later section, we'll discuss how to determine and weigh the impacts of these risks.

Table 7.1 is a checklist of risks that you can use to help you begin to identify risks for your projects. I've listed the risks we talked about in the preceding sections in the first column and added a few new ones. You can add new risks to this list that consistently apply to the types of projects you work on. The next column on the checklist is an area for you to briefly note the impact of the risk or to note its characteristics. The last column is a check-off area where you can indicate that you've examined this risk category and documented the risks associated with it.

Table 7.1   Checklist of common project risks

Project name:		
Project number:		
Project Manager's name:		
Type of risk	**Describe the impact or characteristics**	**Examined**
Project schedule	Increased project time	❏
Budgets/funding	Increased cost	❏
Personnel issues	Loss of key team member, not enough team members assigned to project	❏
Quality	Doesn't meet standards	❏
Key stakeholder consensus	Conflicts and project delays	❏
Scope changes	Increased project time and costs	❏
Project plans	Increased project time and costs, impact on quality, poor direction and communication	❏
Project management methodology	Increased project time and costs	❏
Business risk	Poor public image	❏
Management risk	Reorganization resulting in loss of team members	❏
Vendor issues	Delivery delays	❏
Contract risks	Project delays, increased costs	❏
Legal issues	Increased costs, poor public image	❏
Political issues	Poor public image	❏
Environmental risk	Increased costs, delays to schedule, poor public image	❏
Weather or natural disasters	Schedule delays, delivery delays, increased costs	❏
Technology risks	Not available when needed	❏
Project complexity	Inexperience of project team	❏
Project manager skills	Inexperience of project manager	❏
Team skills and abilities	Inexperience of team members, lack of training	❏

This checklist is intended to be a guideline to start you thinking about risks and their impacts. The risks and impacts you list for your projects should be more specific than what this example shows. When identifying risks for your project, it's important to be specific. For example, simply listing "weather" in your list may not be specific enough. In our annual conference project, snow is much more difficult to deal with than rain and requires different planning. Keep this in mind when identifying your risks.

You can also download the Checklist of Common Project Risks at www.sybex .com/go/projectmanagementjumpstart3.

NOTE

Checklists like the one in Table 7.1 can be developed based on historical information or on the previous experience of the project team members. If you work on projects on a consistent basis that are similar in nature and scope, construct a checklist like the one in Table 7.1 to help you identify risks on future projects. Don't use checklists as your only form of risk identification, however, because every project is different and you might miss an important risk. Combine the use of checklists with some of the other techniques outlined here to find all the risks for your project.

Risk is something that good project managers plan for ahead of time and monitor throughout the course of the project. All project risks should be identified and documented. This checklist is a way to get your thought processes charged up to start identifying risks on your project. You should also check with your organization or industry associations for checklists. Many industries have checklists that are very specific and will help offset inexperience in the risk identification process or help make certain you've identified all the risks for complex projects.

As with all the other project documents so far, you'll file your list of risks in the project notebook, but you don't want to file them there and then forget about them. As you get further into the project, you'll want to reevaluate the risk list and make any adjustments needed based on new information you have at the time. So, keep your risk list handy or make a mental note to yourself to check the list periodically.

Once you've identified and documented the risks and their potential impact, you're ready to perform some risk analysis and rank and prioritize the risks. You'll want to know which risks carry the greatest threat so that you can then develop response plans for those risks. First, let's take a look at some analysis techniques.

Risk Analysis Techniques

The potential for serious risk can bring about a couple of reactions — we avoid the risk altogether, we take steps to minimize the risk, or we make plans to deal with the risk event in case it occurs. The potential that a risk will happen during the course of your project depends on the nature of the risk. If your project involves constructing a highway overpass in North Carolina, the probability of an earthquake is very low, so you wouldn't even bother coming up with a plan to deal with this risk event. However, the probability of a hurricane is very high, so you may want to take this into consideration as a project risk.

Risk analysis takes into consideration the probability that the risk will occur and its impact if it does. The end result of this process is a prioritized list of risks that you can use to determine which risks need response plans.

One of the easiest ways to rank the risks is using the Nominal Group technique that we talked about in the previous section. After identifying the risks, ask the group to rank them in their order of importance. This technique will work for very small projects, but I recommend going a step further for all other projects and examining probability and impact.

Risk Probability and Impact

probability
The likelihood that an event will occur.

Probability can be assigned using a simple high-medium-low scale that ranks the probability for each risk. For instance, our fictitious annual employee meeting project is scheduled to occur in November. There's a high probability of snow in November, which could prevent employees from getting to the event or getting there on time. So, you would assign this risk event a high probability.

Examine the remaining risks on the risk list, and assign a probability to each. Table 7.2 shows an example of a risk probability chart. The risk number is used to track the risk throughout the project and to tie it to a response plan a little later in this process.

Table 7.2   Risk probability chart

Risk number	Risk event	Probability
1	Snow on the night of the event	High
2	Not all the employees show up	Med
3	Employees get food poisoning at the dinner	Low
4	Banquet hall not set up properly for awards presentation	Med

Risk 1 has a high probability rank, which means this risk should have a risk response plan developed to avoid the risk or reduce its impact if it occurs. Risks 2 and 4 probably need risk response plans as well. You may want to combine the probability score with an impact score to help you further determine the need for risk response plans for these two. We'll cover impact scores shortly. Risk 3 doesn't need any further attention, but it should remain on the risk list.

Probability can also be expressed as a value. The classic example is the coin flip. There is a 50 percent probability that you'll get heads and a 50 percent probability that you'll get tails on the flip. The probability that the event will occur plus the probability that the event will not occur always equals 100 percent, or 1.0. For example, if there is a 60 percent probability of snow on the evening of the event, there is a 40 percent chance it will not snow, and the total of both probabilities equals 1.0. The closer the probability of the event occurring is to 1.0, the higher the risk.

Assigning Risk Impacts

Impact values can be assigned to risk in the same way that the probability scores are assigned. You can use a high-medium-low value to indicate the impact the risk event has on the project if it should occur. For example, the snow risk event has a high probability of occurring, and the impact is also high should this event occur. Any risk event with a combination of high probability and high impact should have a risk response plan developed to deal with the risk should it occur.

You can also develop predefined measurements that will qualify the risk event and tell you what value to place on the impacts of the risk event. For example, you can rate the impact using a high-medium-low scale like the one shown next. Depending on where the risk impact falls on the scale, it's assigned a value from .05 to .80. The ranks and values are as follows:

Rank	Value
Very Low	.05
Low	.20
Medium	.40
High	.60
Very High	.80

The snow event is assigned a rank of high, which means the impact's value or weight is .60. You'll want to assign a value to the probability of the risk event and to the impact of the risk event so that an overall risk score can be determined. The overall risk score, which we'll calculate next, will determine what type of risk response should be developed for the risk.

Probability Impact Matrix

Now we'll put this altogether in a probability impact matrix. The idea here is to multiply the probability score by the impact value to come up with an overall risk score. The higher the overall risk score, the higher the risk to the project. Table 7.3 shows an example of a probability impact matrix.

Table 7.3 Probability impact matrix

Risk number	Risk	Probability	Impact	Risk score
1	Snow on the night of the event	.80	.60	.48
2	Not all the employees show up	.40	.40	.16
3	Not enough food prepared for employees and guests at the dinner	.05	.20	.01
4	Banquet hall not set up properly for awards presentation	.40	.80	.32

The risk management policies that your organization has in place (or that you establish) may dictate that all risks with overall risk scores greater than or equal to .30 need risk response plans. This means that both the snow risk event and the banquet hall risk event need risk response plans. The risk response plans are documented in the risk management plan that we'll discuss later in this chapter.

How to Assign the Ratings

Assessing the probability and risk impact and assigning values to each are accomplished using some of the same techniques you used to identify the risks. You can consult subject-matter experts, use interviewing techniques, or use the Delphi or Nominal Group technique to determine probability and impact values. Once you have the values, you can calculate the overall risk score as we did in the previous section. The risk score then tells you what you should do about the risk.

Your organization may have policies already established regarding how to rank risks and what actions need to be taken to plan for the risk events depending on their scores. Some organizations have specialized teams that are devoted to risk analysis and risk management. But if your organization does not have any predetermined policies regarding risk management, you should spend some time developing them yourself by working with a few key team members, subject-matter experts, and stakeholders to determine the criteria for risk responses based on the risk scores.

Risk Tolerance

Risk tolerance is the comfort level that you have for particular risk events. For instance, driving to work every morning carries some level of risk. Your car may not function properly, you could have a fender bender at the corner stoplight, or road crews could have set up a detour on your regular route that adds significant drive time to your commute. None of these risks keeps you from coming into work, however. The benefits of going to work and generating revenue for the company, gaining satisfaction from a job well done, and earning a paycheck for yourself outweigh the risks of driving to work. That means you're willing to take the risk of driving to work to get the benefits.

Organizations, like individuals, also have risk-tolerance levels. Some are more risk averse (that is, they avoid risk at all costs) than others. Stakeholders also have risk-tolerance levels that you should consider when planning for risks. One organization may think nothing of taking on a project that has a high likelihood of failure because of the information they'll gain in the process, while another organization wouldn't even allow the project to make it to the project selection committee's attention.

Be certain you're aware of the risk-tolerance levels of your organization and key stakeholders when you're the one responsible for developing the risk management plans.

risk tolerance
The amount of risk a person or organization is willing to tolerate in exchange for the perceived or actual benefits of partaking in the activity.

Planning for Risks

Planning for project risks is an activity that you should undertake for all projects. The better prepared you are going into the Executing processes, the more likely you'll be able to respond to risk events with a cool, level head. In Chapter 2, "Developing Project Management Skills," we talked about operating in fire-fighting mode. When you're in fire-fighting mode, the object is to put the fire out — fast. That usually means you deal with things in the quickest, easiest way you can just to put the fire out. And putting the fire out doesn't necessarily solve the problem in the long run. Planning for risks by identifying them, analyzing their impact, and preparing response plans where appropriate will help you avoid risks altogether in some cases and minimize their impact in others and keep you out of fire-fighting mode.

Project risk is highest early in the project and lessens as the project progresses.

TIP

Project risk is higher during the Initiating and Planning processes than later in the project. More factors are unknown at the beginning of the project, and the work of the project hasn't begun. As the work of the project is completed, project risk lessens. However, it's important to keep in mind that the potential impact of unidentified risk is much greater as the project progresses because time and money have been expended on the project. That's why it's important to identify risks and develop plans to deal with them early on in the project.

Risks are often ignored and the risk-identification and analysis process is often skipped because of a lack of understanding of the risk management process. Risks aren't something to fear. Risks should be identified and documented, and their impacts should be examined to determine opportunities that may spring from the risk events or to develop risk response plans. Sometimes the process of risk identification itself will minimize risk impacts and allow you to come up with plans to avoid the risk altogether.

Risk response plans involve detailed actions of how the organization will deal with the risk should it occur. They include descriptions of the risk events and where or when in the project the risk events could occur. They should also include a description of the causes of risk and how the risks impact the project objectives or deliverables.

In our example project, we identified the possibility of a snowstorm on the day of the employee meeting as a risk that needs a risk response plan. The plan should include what's described in the previous paragraph, and it should also include the alternatives available to deal with the risk event. Perhaps you can avoid the risk altogether by holding the meeting at a hotel in town instead of the mountain resort; the company could consider hiring drivers with four-wheel-drive vehicles to transport people to the event; and so on. There are some specific responses you should consider when writing your risk response plan that we'll cover in the next section.

Responding to Risks

The amount of effort you'll put into the development of risk response plans depends on the nature of the risk. Some risks require extensive plans, some may need only to be noted and accounted for in an overall plan, and others need only to be listed on the risk list.

Risk response planning is a matter of deciding what steps to take should the risk event occur or look like it's about to occur. It also includes assigning individuals (or departments) the responsibility of carrying out the risk response plan if the risk event occurs. Be sure to note the individuals or department that's responsible for enacting the response plan in the plan documentation.

As we discussed in the previous sections, the organization's risk management policies contain the guidelines you should follow for determining which risks need response plans. Generally speaking, those risks with a high probability of occurring that also have a medium-to-high impact should have a plan.

You can use several recognized strategies to reduce or control negative risks: accepting, avoiding, transferring, and mitigating. It's important to use the right strategy for each risk so that each risk impact is dealt with adequately and in the most efficient way possible. It's not a bad idea to designate a secondary strategy for the highest impact risks. Let's look at each of the strategies in more depth.

Accepting

This first strategy is straightforward. Accepting the risk means you're willing to accept the consequences of the risk should it occur. There are two alternatives with the acceptance strategy; you can simply let nature take its course and see what happens. If and when the risk does occur, you can implement an unplanned response (known as a workaround) to deal with the risk. The second strategy is to create a contingency plan. We'll talk about this in the next section. If we used this strategy when dealing with the snow risk event, for example, we would leave all the existing arrangements in place, we wouldn't investigate alternative locations for the event, and we would either do nothing if snow occurred on the evening of the event or implement a workaround.

Avoiding

Risk avoidance involves taking steps to avoid the impact of the risk event or eliminating the cause of the risk altogether. This is different from the acceptance strategy because plans are developed to avoid the risk or its impact before it occurs, whereas the acceptance strategy either waits for the risk to occur and implements a workaround after the fact or implements a contingency plan.

Back to the snow example. The avoidance strategy for this risk event would be moving the employee meeting to a location in town so that the effects of bad weather are eliminated. Because it doesn't snow in the month of November in the city, the impact of the snow event is eliminated. This assures that all the employees will be able to attend the meeting.

Transferring

Risk transference doesn't eliminate the risk or its impacts — it transfers the responsibility for the management of the risk event to a third party. The classic example of risk transference is insurance. Your own car insurance policy is a perfect example. The insurance company takes on the risk of paying for damages caused by an accident in exchange for money. Keep this in mind because risk transference almost always involves the exchange of money. You'll want to account for transference costs in the project estimates and the project budget.

Contracting is another form of risk transference. The vendor takes on the responsibility for the work as outlined in the contract and accepts the responsibility for the cost of failure. They're going to charge you for the work they perform and will build in a margin for the amount of risk they think they're taking on. Obviously, this impacts the project budget, so you'll want to take contract costs into consideration when determining project estimates.

Watch out when using contracting as a risk strategy because sometimes you're simply swapping one risk for another.

Keep in mind that contracting as a risk strategy doesn't always mean you won't experience the impact of the risk. One way to transfer the impact of the snow risk event is to contract with a shuttle service to transport employees from the office to the meeting location should it snow. However, if all the drivers go on strike the morning of your event, the four-wheel-drive vehicles won't show up at the designated time to take everyone to the meeting. You've simply traded one risk for another. Closely weigh your options in cases like this to determine which risk your organization is more likely to accept. In addition, make certain that the party you're transferring the risk to is able to assume the risk.

Mitigating

The last technique involves risk mitigation. This strategy attempts to reduce the impact of the risk event by reducing the probability of the risk occurrence or reducing the impact of the risk event to an acceptable level. If it's important to hold your employee meeting at the resort location and changing locations isn't an option, you could consider moving the meeting to another date when there is no chance of snow in the resort area to mitigate the impact of the risk. You could also reduce the impact of the risk by requiring all employees to be at the meeting location two hours prior to the start of the meeting, which gives everyone time to deal with bad weather conditions should they occur and still get the meeting started on time.

There are three additional strategies you can use to take advantage of positive risks: exploit, share, and enhance. Let's examine each of these strategies next.

Exploit

When you *exploit* a risk event, you're looking for opportunities for positive impacts. This is the strategy of choice when you've identified positive risks that you want to make certain will occur on the project. Examples of exploiting a risk include reducing the amount of time to complete the project by bringing on more qualified resources or by providing even better quality than originally planned.

Share

The *share* strategy is similar to transferring because you'll assign the risk to a third-party owner who is best able to bring about the opportunity the risk event presents. For example, perhaps what your organization does best is investing. However, it isn't so good at marketing. Forming a joint venture with a marketing firm to capitalize on a positive risk will make the most of the opportunities.

Enhance

The *enhance* strategy closely watches the probability or impact of the risk event to assure that the organization realizes the benefits. This entails watching for and emphasizing risk triggers and identifying the root causes of the risk to help enhance impacts or probability.

Contingency Planning

Have you ever worked on a project where one of the project team members was so critical to the project that if they left the company the project would fail? More than likely, you or one of your managers took steps to protect the project and the organization should this occur. For example, you may have required this employee to document their knowledge and train one or two others so that the other employees understood and knew what the critical employee knew. This is an example of *contingency planning*.

Contingency planning is similar to risk avoidance and mitigation in that you outline alternatives to deal with the risk events should they occur. Contingency plans can be developed for individual risks or for groups of risks. In our annual employee meeting project, we defined some risks that have a medium probability and low impact. These risks may not need detailed plans of their own, but they can be incorporated into a contingency plan that briefly details each of these risks and the strategies to deal with their impacts.

Contingency planning should occur after you've identified the risks and performed risk analysis to determine the extent of their impacts. These plans should be filed in the project notebook and be available at all times for reference when a risk event occurs.

contingency planning
A process of planning for known risks to help ensure project success if a risk event occurs.

The contingency reserve is a cushion of funds to help absorb the impact of risks on the project scope, schedule, cost, and quality.

NOTE

Most project managers also account for contingencies in the project budget. Contingency allowances or reserves are built into the budget, and the funds are set aside for the specific purpose of dealing with risks as they occur. These funds are typically for the risk events you've identified with medium or low impacts and probabilities or for risks that occur where the strategies we talked about previously don't address the risk event. Risk plans and strategies that were developed for individual risks should also be accounted for in the project budget.

Residual and Secondary Risks

Two types of risks may occur on the project that the contingency plan should take into consideration. They are residual risks and secondary risks.

Residual risks are the leftover impacts or minor risks that remain after the primary risk event has occurred and responses have been implemented. If you've used the mitigation risk strategy when defining your risk response plan, the impacts of the risk event are reduced, but some minor leftover effects may still occur. The contingency reserves are set up for situations like this.

Secondary risk is risk that occurs as the result of implementing a risk response plan. The example given earlier of hiring four-wheel-drive vehicles to transport employees to the meeting, but then the drivers declaring a strike the morning of the employee meeting is an example of a secondary risk.

Risk Management Plan

The primary goal of the risk management process is to identify risks, document their impacts, and develop plans to reduce their impacts or take advantage of the opportunities presented. The process you'll use to go about performing these functions is documented in the risk management plan.

The following list is a recap of the steps you'll take to assemble the risk management plan. The risk management plan encompasses all the elements of risk identification, analysis, and response planning that we've talked about in this chapter. You can use this as a checklist or reminder of how to complete the risk management process for your next project:

1. Identify the risks.

2. Analyze risks to determine the probability of the event occurring.

3. Analyze risks to determine the impact on the project if a risk event occurs.

4. Calculate an overall risk score and determine which risk events need detailed response plans.

5. Create detailed response plans and assign resources to carry out the plan in the event a risk occurs.

6. Create a contingency plan.

7. Document everything in the risk management plan section of the project notebook or on the project's intranet site.

The risk management plan should make up one section of your project directory or notebook. You may want to consider creating a spreadsheet or a chart, similar to the one shown in Table 7.4. This directory lists the risk by number and name, indicates whether a plan exists for the risk, shows where the risk plan can be found (references a page number in the notebook or a website), and tells who the responsible party is for carrying out the risk response. Use the following chart as a template for your risk directory, and make this one of the first pages in the risk management section.

Table 7.4 Risk directory

Risk number	Risk name	Risk plan created	Plan location	Responsible party
1	Snow on the night of the event	Y	Risk management section pgs. 12–14	Noelle Butler
2	Not all employees show up	N	See contingency plan	
3	Employees get food poisoning	N		
4	Banquet hall not set up properly	Y	Risk management section pg. 15	Kate Newman

As the project manager, it's your responsibility to make certain that risk events are monitored throughout the life of the project and that the risk response plans are carried out when necessary. Always be on the lookout for risk events ready to occur.

One way to do that is to pay attention to *risk triggers*. Risk triggers warn you that the risk event is getting ready to happen. If dark-gray, snow-laden clouds start gathering over the mountains the morning of the meeting, it's likely that the snow is going to fly. This risk trigger signals you that the risk event is about to occur. You could add a column to your risk list table and/or risk response plan that describes the risk triggers to watch for.

risk triggers
Signs that a risk event is about to occur.

Risks exist on all projects. Don't skip the risk management process, because not taking the time to identify and document the risks could end up killing the project, not to mention your reputation as a project manager.

Terms to Know

brainstorming	probability
contingency planning	risk
Delphi technique	risk tolerance
Nominal Group technique	risk triggers

Review Questions

1. What is a risk?

2. Name some of the planning documents or elements of the planning documents that you can use to start identifying risk.

3. Name three of the most common project risks.

4. Name five types of participants who should assist in the risk-identification process.

5. Which risk-identification technique places all the participants together in the same room with a facilitator, has each participant record risks on sticky notes, one per round, and then posts the notes to a white board?

6. What are three other techniques, in addition to the Nominal Group technique, that you can use to identify risks?

7. Briefly describe a probability impact matrix and the purpose it serves.

8. What is risk tolerance?

9. Name the seven risk response strategies.

10. What are contingency reserves used for?

Chapter 8

Developing the Project Plan

The main focus of this chapter is the creation of the project schedule, which is the next-to-the-last document you'll create in the overall project plan. Creating the budget is the last task you'll do in the Planning process, and I'll cover that in Chapter 9, "Budgeting 101."

In this chapter, you'll look at some methods for determining accurate project scheduling estimates and discover the critical path for the project. You'll then look at some examples of project schedules and ways to balance the resources needed for the activities of the project. In addition to covering scheduling, I'll discuss the quality plan.

Creating the Project Schedule

The project schedule is a culmination of many of the project planning activities you've undertaken up to this point. Many of the things I've talked about, including the project scope statement, WBS, the activity list, activity estimates, network diagrams (these show the activity dependencies), and resource needs, are either linked to the project schedule or used to help develop it.

NOTE   **The project schedule is *not* the project plan — it's part of the project plan. The project plan may include but is not limited to elements such as the project scope statement, the communications plan, the budget, the risk management plan, the resource requirements plan, *and* the project schedule.**

The project plan is everything you've done up to this point plus the quality plan (I'll cover that later in this chapter) and the budget (which I'll cover in the next chapter). The project schedule is part of the project plan and should not stand in as a substitute for a project plan. The project schedule is an important part of the plan, but it does not list project risks, quality requirements, or critical success factors, and it does not tell you how and when to best communicate with the stakeholders. Substituting the schedule for the entire plan could lead to an unsuccessful outcome because you're seeing only part of the picture.

Most project managers prefer to create the budget after the project schedule is completed. Since you don't yet know what the final schedule looks like, it's difficult to come up with a project budget, particularly for those elements dependent on specific timeframes, resources, or predecessor activities. Say you're contracting resources to complete a particular activity. Until you finish the project schedule, you don't know exactly when the resources are needed, what other activities these resources may be dependent on, or how long you'll need the services of those resources.

Project Schedule Components

The project schedule details the activities and work of the project in a format that outlines the work from start to finish. The schedule is usually displayed in some type of graph or chart form. We'll look at different ways to display the schedule itself in a later section.

The project schedule is built primarily from the WBS work package level. From the work packages, you'll develop an activity list, activity estimates, resource requirements, and a network diagram. Each activity is plugged into the project schedule according to the dependencies shown on the network diagram. Start and stop dates are entered for each activity, and resource assignments may be noted on the project schedule as well, depending on the format you're using for the project schedule.

In Chapter 5, "Breaking Down the Project Activities," I talked about estimating activity durations and came up with the number of work periods it takes to complete each activity. We derived these initial estimates by asking team members, subject-matter experts, and so on. There are two more closely related techniques you can use to derive activity estimates that I'll talk about in the next section, called the PERT method and three-point estimates. (You can also use PERT to calculate total project duration.)

Typically, the project duration is calculated by plotting all the activities on the project schedule. Most project schedule software programs automatically calculate the duration of the project based on the difference between the start date of the first activity and the end date of the last activity. However, don't just simply go through your activity list and add up the number of work periods for each to come up with the total duration. That method would apply only if you were the sole resource on the project, and even then it still might not be accurate.

Some activities can be completed simultaneously, which means that the project schedule is not lengthened by the duration of the lesser activity. For example, if Activity A takes five days and Activity B takes three days, the total duration is five days because Activity B can be completed at the same time Activity A is being worked on. If Activity B were dependent on Activity A to finish before it could start, then the project schedule would be eight days. Let's look at one more method for making activity and project duration estimates.

Program Evaluation and Review Technique

The *Program Evaluation and Review Technique (PERT)* was developed by the United States Navy to help determine estimates for a complex engineering project called the Polaris Missile Program. The project team needed a way to estimate the project schedule and forecast it with a high degree of reliability. PERT was developed as a result and is widely used today.

You'll look at PERT in its simplest form here. Keep in mind that PERT is typically used for highly complex projects, but I think you'll find that the simplified technique described here can be used for any size project. It's a reliable and accurate technique for determining estimates.

The Big Three

PERT relies on three estimates for activity durations instead of one. The three estimates are used to calculate the weighted average, which then becomes the final activity duration. PERT calls this weighted average value the *expected value*.

The three estimates you'll use to calculate PERT are the optimistic estimate, the pessimistic estimate, and the most likely estimate. Here's an explanation of each:

> **Optimistic Estimate**   The optimistic estimate is the ideal. It assumes that everything goes according to plan, that no risks interfere with the

Program Evaluation and Review Technique (PERT)
Uses the expected value, or weighted average, of critical path tasks to determine project duration by establishing three estimates: most likely, pessimistic, and optimistic.

expected value
The weighted average of PERT's three estimates: most likely, pessimistic, and optimistic.

activity, and that everything regarding this activity falls into place almost effortlessly.

Most Likely Estimate   This estimate is a balance between the optimistic and pessimistic estimates. It is the most likely duration of the activity.

Pessimistic Estimate   The pessimistic estimate is the opposite of the optimistic estimate. It assumes that almost everything that can go wrong will go wrong, that problems will come up, that resources won't cooperate, and so on. The pessimistic estimate determines how long it will take to finish the activity, assuming that problems will appear on the project.

The PERT Formula

Now that you have those three estimates, what do you do with them? You guessed it — plug them into the formula. As stated earlier, expected value is the weighted average of the three time estimates. The formula to calculate expected value is as follows:

Expected Value = (Optimistic + (4 × Most Likely) + Pessimistic) / 6

Now let's look at an example. Suppose you're heading up a project to write a new software program for your company that automates the employee leave system. The employees will now enter their leave requests online via a form on the intranet. This system also allows the management team to access leave reports and leave balances through one of the programs available on the system. You interviewed the lead programmer in the engineering department and asked for the three estimates you need to calculate expected value for this programming activity.

The lead programmer has given you these three estimates: optimistic is 45 days, most likely is 60 days, and pessimistic is 120 days. Let's plug them into the formula and see what we get:

(45 + (4 × 60) + 120) / 6 = 67.5

The expected value for the programming activity is 67.5 days. Repeat this process for the remaining activities on your project to determine an expected value for each activity.

NOTE   **Consider using this technique for those activities with the greatest risk, and use other estimating methods, like expert judgment or the three-point estimate (described in the section called "Three-Point Estimate") for those activities that are not critical to the project.**

To calculate the total project duration, add up the expected value for each activity that has a Finish to Start dependency. The activities that do not have dependencies do not influence the project schedule, as I talked about in a previous section, so don't include them in your sum.

When you use PERT estimates as described here, you have a 50 percent chance of finishing the project on schedule. Roughly half of the activities will finish sooner than scheduled, and roughly half of the activities will finish later than estimated. If you don't like those odds, read on.

How Confident Are You?

Confidence levels state how strongly you believe in the estimates you've derived. Suppose you're very confident that the programming activity for your project will take 67.5 days. You know the lead programmer who gave you the values for this estimate and have worked with her for several years. She's reliable and has consistently given you good estimates that have been met in the past. As a result, you might assign this estimate a 95 percent *confidence factor*, indicating that you (or the person you got the estimates from) are very confident that this activity will be completed in that amount of time. The confidence factor in this case is based on the experience level of the lead programmer who gave you the estimate. In this example, the lead programmer has performed similar activities to this one many times in the past and is confident in the estimates given for this activity.

As you may have suspected, there is a mathematical way to calculate a confidence factor if you don't like using the experience (or seat-of-your-pants) method. This method gives even finer detail to the project estimates. This gets a little complicated, and you do not have to go to this extreme for small projects, but it's good information to know. Showing that you've calculated the confidence factor for your key project activities will also impress your boss at your next project meeting.

PERT calculations follow a bell curve. This means that most of the time the work will finish within plus or minus three standard deviations of the PERT calculation. Without getting too deep into mathematical and probability analysis, keep the following in mind:

- 99.73 percent of the time the work will finish within plus or minus three standard deviations.

- 95.44 percent of the time the work will finish within plus or minus two standard deviations.

- 68.26 percent of the time the work will finish within plus or minus one standard deviation.

confidence factor
The level of confidence you have in the estimate that has been calculated.

Calculating Standard Deviation

Where does the standard deviation figure come from? I'm glad you asked. We'll calculate the standard deviation for our programming activity to plug into the confidence factors in the preceding section. This will give us a range of days for each of the confidence factors to work from. Remember that in this example we're using days to calculate estimates. If we were using hours, minutes, months, and so on, for estimates, the results of the calculation would be in the same increments of time we're using for estimates. The formula for standard deviation is as follows:

(Pessimistic – Optimistic) / 6

Let's plug in our estimates:

(120 – 45) / 6 = 12.5

Now we'll calculate the range of date estimates for the 95.44 percent confidence factor for this programming activity. Add two times the standard deviation (12.5 × 2 = 25) to the expected value, and then subtract two times the standard deviation from the expected value to determine the estimate ranges. The expected value is 87.5 days. Here is the formula to determine a 95.44 confidence factor for this activity:

87.5 + (2 × 12.5) = 112.5
87.5 – (2 × 12.5) = 62.5

Now we can say with 95.44 percent certainty that the programming activity will finish between 62.5 and 112.5 days.

The remaining confidence factors are calculated the same way. Use the number of standard deviations shown in the other confidence factors, adding and subtracting from the expected value to determine the confidence level.

Be aware that the higher the standard deviation for an activity, the higher the risk. The confidence measurement calculates the difference between the pessimistic and optimistic times, so the greater the spread, the higher the number. And of course the opposite is true — the lower the standard deviation, the lower the risk.

Three-Point Estimate

three-point estimate
An estimating technique that uses the average of the pessimistic, optimistic, and most likely estimates.

Three-point estimates are a simpler version of PERT. You simply average the three values (optimistic, most likely, and pessimistic). The formula looks like this:

(Optimistic + Most Likely + Pessimistic) / 3

The PERT calculation weights the most likely estimate (it's multiplied by four), whereas the three-point calculation gives equal weight to all the estimates. Remember that PERT is generally used for highly complex, lengthy, or multiphased projects. Three-point estimates are great for small to medium projects, as well as large projects that are similar in size and scope to other projects your team has performed. Either estimate will work; it's just a matter of the confidence you have in the folks who gave you the estimates.

Getting to the Estimates

You will have to enlist the help of some other folks to get at the estimates you're going to use. There's no getting around it; when you work on projects, you're going to be involving people at all levels. None of what you've done or will do throughout the remainder of this book can be accomplished without the assistance and cooperation of a team of folks. Brush off those communication skills, and get to know the team members and stakeholders. Their opinions are valuable, and you're much more likely to gain their cooperation throughout the life of the project when you involve them in important project activities and decisions.

NOTE

PERT and the three-point method are good estimating techniques, but you'll still rely on other people's judgment to come up with the initial estimates you need in order to use these formulas. Consider interviewing subject-matter experts, vendors, experienced team members, experienced managers, and others for estimates. And don't forget to look at historical information such as previous projects of similar size and scope.

Unfortunately, there are no magic formulas for determining estimates. Many industries do have tools they use to help determine estimates, but these tools are usually based on predetermined criteria. If the project fits those criteria, the estimates are probably reliable. Generally speaking, rely on your subject-matter experts to determine the estimates the way they are most comfortable, whether it's with an established tool or based on their own experience.

Calculating the Critical Path

The *critical path* is the longest full path on the project. This means that when the durations for each of the tasks or activities in one sequence (those that have dependencies) are added up from the beginning to the ending of the project, the path with the longest duration is the critical path. Any task on the critical path is called a *critical path task*.

critical path
The longest path through the project made up of activities with zero float.

The following graphic shows an example critical path diagram for our software project:

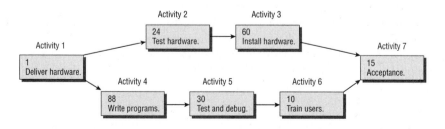

Each task shown in this diagram has the duration of the task in the upper-left corner. The topmost path with activity numbers 1-2-3-7 has a duration of 100 days, and path 1-4-5-6-7 has a duration of 144 days. Path 1-4-5-6-7 is the longest full path on the project, so it is the critical path.

<table>
<tr><td>═════ WARNING ═════</td><td>**When you change the duration of a critical path task, it always changes the project duration. Noncritical path tasks will not change the duration of the project because they can be completed at the same time as the tasks on the critical path.**</td></tr>
</table>

Float Time

float time
There are two types of float time. Total float is the amount of time you can delay the early start of a task without delaying the finish date of the project. Free float is the amount of time you can delay the start of a task without delaying the earliest start date of a successor task.

You may be wondering how to determine which tasks are on the critical path. All tasks with zero *float time* are considered critical path tasks. Keep in mind that tasks with float time need to be completed in order to consider the project complete. The project wouldn't be considered complete if you finished all the critical path tasks but left the tasks with float time uncompleted. But tasks with float time are flexible. Their starting and ending dates do not influence the other project tasks as long as they are completed within the available float time, so you can schedule them when it's most convenient for the project team.

Now let's look at how to calculate float time for the project tasks.

Critical Path Method

Critical Path Method (CPM)
Determines a single early and late start date and an early and late finish date for each activity on the project.

The *Critical Path Method (CPM)* was originally developed by DuPont in the 1950s and is used to calculate the duration of the project. It calculates several dates for each task, including the following:

- ◆ Earliest start date
- ◆ Earliest finish date
- ◆ Latest start date
- ◆ Latest finish date

Once these dates are known for each task, float time can be calculated by subtracting the earliest start date from the latest start date. If the float time is equal to zero, the task is a critical path task.

Here are the steps we're going to use to complete the CPM calculation for our project, as shown in Table 8.1. Please note that these calculations do not take weekends or holidays into consideration. Assume all the dates given in the example are workdays.

1. List the tasks on the worksheet, referencing the task number, or WBS number, and task description.

2. List the dependencies of each task.

3. Record the duration of each task.

4. Calculate the early start date and early finish date for each task. The first task is the "Deliver hardware" task, and it's also where the project starts. The early start date for this task is the first day work can begin on the project.

   This project is scheduled to begin March 1. The first day is always considered day zero. To calculate the early finish date, take day zero plus the duration of the task (one day) to come up with an early finish date for the first activity, March 1. Because task 2 is dependent on task 1, the early start date for task 2 is the day after task 1 finishes, or March 2. The early finish date for task 2 is 24 days after March 2. Counting March 2 as day zero makes the early finish date March 25, and so on, for the other tasks. Watch out for task 4 because its dependency is task 1, not task 3. That means the "Write programs" task (task 4) can start the day after task 1 finishes.

   Keep dependencies in mind when calculating the early start dates because tasks without dependencies can start anytime after the project has started. Tasks without dependencies are known as *danglers*, and you could end up with an incomplete schedule if you have too many of them. Typically, the first task in a project schedule is the one without dependencies.

5. Calculate the late start and late finish dates for each task. To calculate these dates, start with the last task listed. In this example, it's task 7, acceptance. The early finish date for that task is July 22. This date now also becomes the latest finish date for the project. Subtract the task duration from the latest finish date to calculate the late start date, remembering that the first day is day zero. This is the reverse of what you did to calculate the early dates. Continue in reverse order through the tasks, calculating the late finish and late start dates.

   Keep dependencies in mind when making these calculations. Task 3 is a dependency to task 7, which means the latest finish date for task 3, "Install hardware," must be one day prior (July 7) to the latest start date for task 7 (July 8). Task 3 is dependent on task 2, so task 2's latest finish date must occur one day prior (May 8) to the latest start date for task 3 (May 9).

6. Calculate float for each task by subtracting the early start date from the late start date. If float time equals zero, the activity is on the critical path. Both task 2 and 3 have float time, so they are not critical path tasks.

7. Determine the critical path for the project by adding up the duration of every activity with zero float. Do not add the duration times for activities with float since they are not critical path tasks.

The total duration for this project is calculated by adding up the duration for all tasks with zero float. Task numbers 1, 4, 5, 6, and 7 are the critical path tasks, and their durations total 144 days. This calculation matches the network diagram constructed previously. Either of these methods can be used to calculate the critical path.

Most computer software programs designed to perform project scheduling calculate the critical path automatically. But it's important for you to understand what makes up the critical path, including the start and finish dates and float times. If you don't understand the basics behind the critical path, you won't be able to make schedule adjustments where needed, and you may not focus the team on the right tasks at the right times.

Working with the Project Schedule

You've calculated the start and finish dates, you know the critical path, and now it's time to assign resources to each of the tasks. At this point, you'll put individual names with each task. You could add a column to the spreadsheet in Table 8.1 showing the resource name, and you'd have all the information together in one place.

Now you have the perfect schedule for the project. The problem is, you don't work in a perfect world. Some resources are not going to be available when the schedule says they're needed. Most folks don't like working through vacations and holidays, so you have to take business schedules and personal schedules into account. Or the project duration may not be acceptable to management (99 percent of the time they think the project duration is too lengthy).

Let's look at some of the ways you can work with the project schedule to accommodate these situations. First you'll look at resource issues.

Resources

When creating the project plan, you'll need to know some basic information about the organization and about each of the resources you're planning to assign to the tasks in order to make adjustments to the schedule.

First, you need a calendar or list of all the company holidays. As you calculate the task start and end dates, take the company holidays into consideration by adding the additional days into the start and finish date calculations.

Next, you must determine the normal working hours for the organization. Do most employees work eight hours a day, or do most employees work flexible schedules? Are all the resources full-time employees, or are some part-time? You'll need the answers to these questions in order to adjust the schedule tasks according to your resource schedules.

Then, you need to determine individual vacation schedules. If one of your key team members is planning a wedding or taking some maternity leave, for instance, you'll need to adjust the schedule to accommodate these times.

Table 8.1   Critical path calculation

#	Task description	Dependency	Duration	Early start	Early finish	Late start	Late finish	Float time
1	Deliver hardware.	–	1	March 1	March 1	March 1	March 1	0
2	Test hardware.	1	24	March 2	March 25	April 15	May 8	44
3	Install hardware.	2	60	March 26	May 24	May 9	July 7	44
4	Write programs.	1	88	March 2	May 28	March 2	May 28	0
5	Test and debug.	4	30	May 29	June 27	May 29	June 27	0
6	Train users.	5	10	June 28	July 7	June 28	July 7	0
7	Acceptance.	6, 3	15	July 8	July 22	July 8	July 22	0

If your project calls for the use of certain types of equipment at different times on the project, make certain you and the vendor are aware of the times the equipment is needed so that the schedule can stay on track. Don't forget to consider all the resources that could have a potential impact on the schedule. For example, your project may be dependent on the release of a new version of software or a new product release. You'll have to account for the release dates when building your project schedule.

Contingency Time

One of the things you should consider when constructing the project schedule is adding time to the tasks for unforeseen circumstances. Especially if your project has a lengthy duration, you should consider that employees sometimes get ill, have family emergencies, and so on, that will require unscheduled time off from the project. Projects that fall into this category should also have contingency plans in place for key employees who may leave the project.

TIP **Projects with long durations need contingency time added into the schedule for unforeseen events.**

Even though most of us follow a regular eight-hour workday schedule (I know, many times it's more like 10 or 12 hours, but stay with me on this one), we aren't working the full eight hours on the project. There's email to answer, phone calls to make, the recent ball game scores to discuss, and those vacation pictures to share with our teammates. Typically, you can count on people being productive about 75 to 80 percent of the time. Given a 40-hour workweek, you'll likely get 30 to 32 hours of productive work on the project. Don't forget to account for this time in the project schedule.

Administrative time is another time killer that many project managers don't think about. For example, you'll require the team members to fill out status reports on a periodic basis, show up at team meetings, meet with users or stakeholders when appropriate, and meet with you one-on-one.

Keep in mind when calculating activity estimates and start and finish dates that personal and administrative time should be accounted for in the schedule. Many project managers add a percentage to the project schedule to account for this kind of time. The percentage used depends on the project manager and the type of project. My area of project management expertise is information technology, and I typically add an additional 10 percent of the total project duration to the project schedule to account for administrative activities such as status reports, meetings, and unforeseen circumstances.

Be careful with this tactic. You can be accused of "padding" the schedule if your percentage is off and you consistently bring projects in ahead of schedule. The stakeholders will come to expect that your estimates are incorrect from the get-go and will be looking for the projects to complete sooner than you've promised. This can haunt you when you're working on a project that is going to need that additional time. After you've gained some experience with the projects and the project team, you'll be able to determine percentages fairly accurately.

━━━ ━━━ ***WARNING*** ━━━

Adjusting Project Schedules

Remember that you have some flexibility regarding the start and stop dates for the noncritical path tasks. They can be scheduled when it's most convenient. This might be early in the project or late in the project, depending on when you have the resources available.

Critical path tasks can't be changed without impacting the project duration. If you lengthen a critical path task, you'll lengthen the project schedule. Sometimes you'll find that because of resource constraints or resource schedules you have no choice but to lengthen the project duration. This will require approval from the project sponsor and key project stakeholders.

After you've determined an initial schedule, the chances are high that you'll have to make adjustments to it. Here are some tips to help you when adjusting the project schedule:

Estimates   Stay within the most likely range duration estimates for your tasks. As you gain experience at this, you'll learn when you can use the optimistic estimate and when you should use the pessimistic estimate.

Task Estimates and Duration   Task estimates and duration are not always the same. If you have more than one resource working on the task, the duration of the task is usually shortened, so determine the number of resources you have available to perform the task and adjust the schedule accordingly. For example, the duration for the "Write programs" task is 88 days. The expert who gave you the estimates assumed that only one person would be writing the code. If two people who have equal experience work on this task, the task can be shortened to 44 days.

Adding more resources to a task will not always solve your problems. Sometimes too many resources actually lengthen the task because they're stepping all over each other instead of being productive. And it's not always possible to add more resources. When stakeholders on projects at my office start insisting that we add more resources, the team members start reciting one of their favorite project management sayings: "Nine women cannot have a baby in one month." Adding resources is not always the answer.

━━━ ━━━ ***WARNING*** ━━━

Another situation to consider is tasks taking much longer to complete than what the estimate says. For example, the "Train users" task has a task estimate of 10 days. However, the users are over a three-state area, and one of your trainers will have to fly to each location to perform the training. That means the duration of this task is actually longer than the 10 days stated on the schedule.

Shortening the Project Duration

"Is it really going to take that long?" is a question you're going to hear many times throughout your project management career. Sometimes the answer is, "Yes, it's going to take that long." When stakeholders or sponsors insist that the project duration be shortened, you can consider doing several things:

◆ Adding more resources. This may include hiring consultants, bringing in folks from other areas of the organization, or outsourcing some or all of the project tasks.

◆ Changing the scope of the project by breaking the deliverables into phases or paring down some of the deliverables.

◆ Rescheduling the tasks in a different order. Sometimes this will free up resources or better utilize the resources already assigned.

◆ Bringing in different resources. Perhaps you can find people who are more qualified, more experienced, or better trained to work on the critical path tasks than the team members from the original plan.

◆ Asking for more time. This is another example of when you'll need to use those communication skills and negotiating techniques. Sometimes it's a matter of communicating the complexity of the project or explaining the processes the team must use in order to bring the project in according to the quality plan and stakeholder expectations. This option really doesn't shorten the project duration, but it might be the only choice you have.

◆ Start two tasks at the same time that you previously scheduled to start independently. (I'll talk more about this technique in Chapter 11, "Controlling the Project Outcomes.")

Resource Leveling

One more set of adjustments you might need to make to the schedule involves resources. Once you've assigned names to the tasks, you may discover that some resources are used too much and some not enough. Still others may not be available when the schedule calls for them.

Resource leveling is a fancy term for distributing the workload among the team members. You'll smooth out the task assignments so that those folks who are overloaded have some of their work assigned to other members of the team who are underutilized.

Mentoring is good technique to use when you're faced with this situation. I've had lead programmers on many different projects tell me that they are the only one in the whole wide world who can do the particular task you've

resource leveling
Attempts to smooth out the resource assignments so that tasks are completed without overloading individuals and without negatively impacting the project schedule.

assigned to them. Don't always fall for that line. You'll find many times that this is a great opportunity for a senior programmer to mentor a junior programmer. By assigning the task to the junior team member (with the senior team member acting as mentor), the senior team member still has oversight control so they don't feel as though you've completely cut them off, and the junior member has an opportunity to learn something new. In the process, you've successfully leveled the tasks.

You can use this technique for partial tasks also. Consider splitting tasks so that the easier portions of the task can be assigned to a junior team member, leaving the more complicated portion for the senior team member. Use your judgment when using this technique, and do consider the validity of the senior team member's comments about the experience level needed to complete the task.

Schedule Display Options

You can use several different methods to display your project schedule. You can draw the schedule yourself using software tools or even pen and paper. However, most software scheduling programs give you all the display options I'll talk about here, so get familiar with your project scheduling tool and the different ways to display the schedule. The Gantt chart view and the calendar view were produced using Microsoft Project. Keep in mind that these schedules do not take weekends or holidays into account, and I used the early start dates in the samples you'll see in the coming sections.

Gantt Chart

Gantt charts are easy-to-read charts that display the project schedule in task sequence and by the task start and finish dates. This image shows the tasks from the programming project plotted on a Gantt chart.

		Task Name	Duration	Start	Finish	Predecessors	February	March	April	May	June	July
1		− Software Project	144 days	Sat 3/1/03	Tue 7/22/03							
2		Deliver Hardware	1 day	Sat 3/1/03	Sat 3/1/03							
3		Test Hardware	24 days	Sun 3/2/03	Tue 3/25/03	2						
4		Install Hardware	60 days	Wed 3/26/03	Sat 5/24/03	3						
5		Write Programs	88 days	Sun 3/2/03	Wed 5/28/03	2						
6		Test & Debug	30 days	Thu 5/29/03	Fri 6/27/03	5						
7		Train Users	10 days	Sat 6/28/03	Mon 7/7/03	6,4						
8		Acceptance	15 days	Tue 7/8/03	Tue 7/22/03	7						

The black bar displayed on the first item, Software Project, indicates the duration of the entire project. The Duration column for this entry shows 144 days, which is the total duration for the project. All the tasks listed under the summary bar show their duration, and because these tasks are related to the summary task, all of their durations are summed to show the total duration.

It's also possible to add resource names to this view so that the name of the resource assigned to a task appears at the end of the bar. That's a good first check you can perform when resource leveling because you can see at a glance whether certain resources are overloaded. Most software programs also have resource reports that will allow you to view, determine, and adjust resource loads.

You have several display options for the Gantt chart, including hours, days, weeks, and so on. Choose the appropriate view depending on the length and complexity of the project. If your project has a lengthy duration and you choose to display the Gantt chart in the week view, for example, you'll end up with pages and pages of printouts for the chart. Try to keep the Gantt chart printout to one or two pages for easy viewing by the stakeholders and sponsor. The project team may want a more detailed view, in which case you could print out all the pages and tape them together on a wall in the project team meeting room.

Calendar View

Calendar views are useful for small projects or as a high-level view for larger projects. Record the task start dates on the calendar, noting the resource assigned to the task and the expected duration. I like to note the finish date on the calendar as well.

You can also use calendar views to manage multiple small projects and to easily track resource usage among the projects or on an individual project. Use different colors to track the projects or resources.

The next image shows a sample portion of a calendar view of our project tasks. You can see that the "Deliver hardware" task begins on March 1 and is the only task on that day. March 2 shows two tasks beginning on that day, "Test hardware" and "Write programs."

Network Diagram

A precedence network diagram like the one in the following graphic is another alternative to displaying the project schedule. This diagram typically shows the task number, the task descriptions, the duration, and the start and stop dates. The dependencies are shown as well.

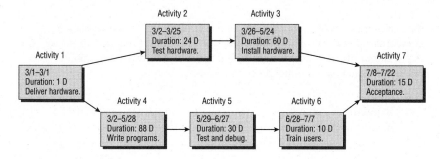

Milestone Chart

Milestone charts can be used to display the project milestone and due dates. This is a good reporting tool to use in the project status meetings to show stakeholders the progress of the project. If you need a refresher on milestone charts, look at Table 5.2 in Chapter 5.

Quality Management Plan

Quality is another one of the primary constraints on a project. It's important to the success of the project and helps determine whether the stakeholder expectations were met. Quality can be defined by the stakeholders, project team, project sponsor, industry standards, or a combination of these and more. If your project involves manufacturing a new instrument for heart surgeries, for example, there will likely be several quality standards you'll have to meet. The parts should measure a certain size or shape, the instrument must be constructed of a certain material at a certain grade or specification, and so on.

The quality plan describes in detail the quality standards for the project and the quality criteria that are used to determine whether the deliverable is complete and correct. The next step is creating and documenting a plan to meet those standards. Some of the elements you should consider before documenting the quality standards for your policy include the following:

> **Quality Policy**   Your organization may have a quality policy guideline already established for projects the company undertakes. The quality policy is usually published by the executive management team, and it contains predetermined guidelines regarding quality standards for projects. Be certain to review your organization's quality policy so that you can incorporate important information from the policy into the project.

Standards Standards are guidelines, rules, or characteristics that should be followed. The organization itself may have quality standards you should know about, and the industry you're working in may also have standards that should be followed. Most industries do have standards, and it's up to the project manager to perform any research necessary to find out what those standards are.

NOTE As an example, the Project Management Institute (PMI) has established standards for project management practices. You aren't required to follow these standards, but they're a good idea because PMI has spent untold hours researching and documenting best practices.

Regulations Regulations are mandatory and usually result from governments, institutions, or organizations with the power to establish regulations within their own industry. Regulations require adherence, and you could face penalties, lawsuits, or fines if you do not comply. Be certain you're aware of any regulations that may impact your project.

Documenting the Plan

After you've determined any organizational standards or regulations that apply, it's time to document the quality criteria. The quality criteria are used to determine whether the deliverable is considered complete and correct according to the documented quality criteria. The example given earlier of manufacturing surgical equipment has several quality criteria, including size, type of material, shape, and weight. If these criteria are met, the deliverable is considered complete and correct.

The last piece of information that should go into your quality plan is the quality assurance process the project team will follow to assure that quality standards and criteria are being met. This includes processes used by the project manager, the project team, or vendors acting in an oversight capacity to assure that quality criteria are met. Our surgical equipment example may require inspection by an outside source to assure that the measurements and other quality factors are correct. I'll talk more about quality control, which works hand in hand with quality assurance, in Chapter 11.

When writing the quality plan, note any standards or regulations that may impact the project in the quality plan. If the regulations are lengthy or complicated, you could also reference where readers can find a copy of the standards without retyping all of them into the plan itself. You should also make the stakeholders and project team aware of any standards or regulations that impact the project. A sample quality management plan template is shown in the following graphic. Depending on the size of the project, you may choose to recap the project overview as shown in the first section or note where this information can be found.

Quality Management Plan

I. General Information

Project name:_____   Project number:_____

Project Manager name:_____   Date:_____

II. Project Overview	*Provide an overview of the project, including its primary goals.*

III. Quality Standards and Regulations	*Note any quality policies, standards, or regulations the project team will be required to follow.*

IV. Quality Criteria	*Provide a detailed list of the quality criteria needed to consider the deliverables complete and correct. Include each deliverable and its quality criteria.*

V. Quality Assurance Procedures	*List the activities and processes that will be used to monitor adherence to the quality criteria.*

VI. Quality Management Roles and Responsibilities	*Include a roles and responsibility chart detailing who's responsible for which quality activities.*

VII. Signatures	*Include signature lines for the project sponsor, project manager, and those responsible for quality assurance and review.*

You can also download a template for the quality management plan at
www.sybex.com/go/projectmanagementjumpstart3.

NOTE

Although you don't really need approval of this plan, unless your organization requires it, it's a good idea to make certain that the project sponsor, the key stakeholders, and those responsible for the quality assurance process have reviewed the quality plan and agree to the criteria.

Cost of Quality

There's usually a trade-off where quality is concerned. It's going to cost you something — time or resources — to meet the quality standards for the project. This is known as the cost of conformance. There is also a cost associated when the quality standards are not met and you must spend time or money to correct the mistakes and bring the product or service into conformance. This is the cost of nonconformance. Conforming and nonconforming costs are known as the *cost of quality.*

The benefits of conforming to the quality standards include the following:

◆ Customer and stakeholder satisfaction is increased because the final product or service of the project will meet or exceed their expectations as a result of taking the time to measure and meet quality standards.

◆ Project teams will experience higher levels of productivity because the quality standards cause them to examine the methods and processes they're using to complete the work of the project for efficiency and effectiveness.

◆ The costs to produce the product of the project and administer project processes may be lower because of adherence to quality policies and standards. However, there are times when these costs may be higher during the life of the project and then lower when the final product, service, or result is transitioned to ongoing operations.

◆ The project team will perform less rework because the quality results have been identified ahead of time and are being measured and monitored throughout the remaining project processes.

Determining the Cost of Quality

Cost-benefit analysis is one of the techniques you can use to determine whether the cost of quality associated with conforming costs is worth the benefits received. The cost of rework alone can sometimes drive the need to adhere to the quality plan. Rework, as I've discussed previously, isn't much fun and is generally a demotivator, not to mention costly in terms of salary, equipment rentals, and so on.

Benchmarking is another technique used to determine the cost of quality. As an example, if the project team was able to write programming code for the print functions in a similar program on a previous project in three days, then three days becomes your benchmark measurement for this project.

Four costs are associated with the cost of quality. Appraisal costs and prevention costs are related to the cost of conformance, while internal and external failure costs are related to the cost of nonconformance.

Appraisal Costs   These include costs to examine the product or the process to make certain the requirements are being met. Inspection and testing costs are typical appraisal costs.

Prevention Costs   These are costs associated with keeping defects out of the final product. These costs are usually seen early on in the process and include such things as quality planning, training, and design review.

Internal Failure Costs   These are the costs you'll incur when things don't go according to plan. When customer requirements are not satisfied while the product is still in the control of the organization, the expenses incurred are considered internal failure costs.

External Failure Costs   External failure costs occur when the product has reached the customer and they let you know that the requirements have not been met. Internal failure costs aren't ideal, but it's much better to discover quality problems while the product is still in your control. I'll talk more about issues like these in Chapter 11.

You've heard this many times by now, but it's worth repeating. Document the quality plan, and file it in a section of the project notebook devoted to the quality plan. The quality plan, as with all the other Planning documents, becomes part of the overall project plan, which I'll cover in the next chapter.

Terms to Know

benchmarking	expected value
confidence factor	float time
cost of quality	Program Evaluation and Review Technique (PERT)
critical path	resource leveling
Critical Path Method (CPM)	three-point estimate

Review Questions

1. Name three items completed previously in the project's Planning process that will assist you in building the project schedule.

2. What three estimates does the PERT calculation use to determine duration?

3. What is expected value?

4. What is the formula for determining the expected value of PERT estimates?

5. What is a confidence factor?

6. Describe the critical path.

7. Describe the two types of float time.

8. Name two things you can do to shorten a project's duration.

9. What is resource leveling, and why do you use it?

10. What is the cost of quality?

Chapter 9

Budgeting 101

This chapter concludes the coverage of the Planning processes. You've reached a major milestone in the project's Planning process; the budget is the last Planning document you'll create.

If you're lucky enough to be working on a project where "money is no object" (very doubtful), you still should read this chapter. I'll talk about what makes up a budget, tracking the budget, and establishing a cost baseline. Stakeholders want to know the project costs and whether what you're spending on the project is on track with what you estimated. Stakeholders will use this information to determine future project budgets, so you'll want to do the best job you can estimating, tracking, and reporting on the project budget.

Then you'll pull together everything you've done so far and document this as the official project plan.

What Makes Up a Budget?

budget
An itemized list of estimated expenses needed to complete the work of the project.

The project *budget* will be used throughout the remainder of the project to track project expenses and measure the money actually spent on project activities against the estimates given for those activities. The final budget figures are based on estimates provided by the project team, key stakeholders, vendors, and others after careful review of the Planning documents.

NOTE — Depending on the structure of the organization you're working in, the project manager may write the budget, or the finance manager may take on this responsibility.

Project Costs

Most of the costs expended on the project, known as *project costs*, are fairly obvious and apply to most projects you'll work on. For example, salaries, office supplies, and telephone charges will apply to almost all projects. These project costs and most others fall into one of three categories: human resource costs, administrative costs, or resource costs. Let's take a look at each of them in more detail.

Human Resource Costs

These are the costs associated with the personnel on the project. They include salaries and the cost of benefits (such as vacation time and health insurance) if they apply. When you are calculating salary expense and including benefits such as health insurance, vacation time, life insurance, disability insurance, and so on, this is often known as a *loaded salary* or *fully loaded salary*.

Salaries, or contracting fees for human resources, can be one of the project's largest expenses if you're working on a labor-intensive project. For example, information technology projects typically require folks with very specific skills. These skills come with a price — usually a high price — and you'll find a large portion of your project budget allocated to them. If you happen to be working for a nonprofit company that is using all volunteers to complete the project work, your salary expenses may be smaller, but you'll still probably have expenses for subject-matter expertise, contractors, the project manager's salary, and so on.

TIP — Employee or contractor salaries and expenses can be one of the biggest budget items on any project.

Administrative Costs

Administrative costs are the everyday costs that support the work of the project but are not necessarily directly related to a specific activity on the project. Utilities, phone expenses, copier paper, and support personnel are examples of administrative costs. Project teams have to work and meet somewhere, so that means there is some sort of facilities expense in the form of rent, lease, or mortgage payments. The facilities expense in this example should be proportionate to the amount of building space that's dedicated to the project. If the building or facility was leased or purchased specifically for the project, it would be classified as a project cost instead of an administrative cost.

Resource Costs

Resource costs include things such as materials needed for specific activities, equipment leases, long-distance telephone expense, travel expenses, and so on. These expenses are specific to the project. For example, if the project consists of building a new set of luxury condos in a prime downtown location, you'll need the use of a crane during the early phases of the construction to lift the steel beams and other needed items several stories in the air. Resource costs are typically the largest expense for construction projects, and estimating these costs will require research on your part.

Examining each of these categories of resource costs will help you identify your initial budget items. If you think about the human resources, the administrative support, and the project resources needed for each activity, you'll have a list of budget items started in no time.

Direct Costs versus Indirect Costs

In addition to the three categories of project costs, there are also two types of costs: direct and indirect costs. *Direct costs* include costs such as salaries, equipment rentals, software, and training for team members. Any cost that can be directly attributed to project work is a direct cost.

Indirect costs are not specific to the project. For example, your project team probably works with other members of the organization (who are not working on the project) in the same building. The lease cost for the building is an example of an indirect cost because it is not specifically related to the project since all the company employees work there. Another example of an indirect cost is administrative staff, managers, or other functional members who will be assisting you with project tasks (such as someone from the procurement department) but aren't assigned activities themselves.

You'll need to find out from the accounting or finance department how indirect costs should be accounted for in the project budget. Each organization has its own procedures for accounting for indirect costs, so you'll want to check with them before finalizing the budget.

direct costs
Costs specifically related to the work of the project.

indirect costs
Costs associated with the project but not directly related to the work of the project.

Gathering the Docs

I'm not talking about a gathering of doctors here, although some budgets are so sick they need budget doctors to make them healthy. I'm talking about the Planning documents you've diligently created.

The first step in creating the project budget is to gather all the Planning documents for reference. You should start with a review of the project goals and deliverables for obvious budget expenses, which you can find in the project scope statement. Next, take a look at the activity list, the WBS, and the network diagram. Record activities or items that will have costs associated with them on your budget list. In addition, look over the project schedule, resource list, and roles and responsibilities chart for expenses you may need to account for. Don't forget to include equipment rentals, facilities, and material expenses associated with activities and WBS elements. Keep in mind that you can capture all of these costs in most project management software programs, and you can also include fully loaded salaries and resources right on the project schedule in most programs.

Start your budget list on a piece of paper or an electronic spreadsheet, and record the items needed in one column and estimated costs in another column (if you know them at this point; otherwise, leave that column blank). If you want to be really organized, you could use the project schedule and start recording initial costs right on the activities listed on the schedule. You'll look at some sample budgets later in this chapter.

Budgeting Process

The process for creating the budget is similar to identifying the resource requirements and creating the project schedule. Review the Planning documents to uncover all the materials and resources you'll need, estimate their costs, record them in the budget, and finally get approval of the budget.

Here are the steps you'll follow to get your budget process rolling:

1. Review the Planning documents.

2. Create cost estimates, and integrate them with the project schedule (I'll cover this shortly).

3. Submit the budget for approval to the project sponsor or project committee.

4. Notify the appropriate project team members and stakeholders when the budget is approved.

5. Assign the code of accounts to the WBS elements if this hasn't been done previously. The code of accounts is a unique numbering or lettering system used by the organization's accounting department. These unique numbers or letters (codes) should be assigned to the WBS work packages.

6. Publish the project budget on the project's intranet site.

As the project manager, you should go into the project fully equipped to execute the project based on the resources available. To accomplish this, you need an accurate budget to use as your guideline.

Now let's take a closer look at some of things you'll want to include in the budget.

Budget Items

Regardless of the type of expense, you need to identify everything needed for the project and document its estimated cost.

You can use the same techniques for identifying budget items as you did for identifying deliverables and activities. Examine the budget from previous projects of similar size and scope, interview stakeholders, ask project team members who have worked on similar projects in the past, interview vendors, or hold a meeting with key team members and stakeholders to brainstorm on the budget items. To save time, you could consider starting a list of budget items yourself before meeting with stakeholders or interviewing team members, especially if the project is small. You'll be able to identify many of the items simply by reviewing the Planning documents. Then let others look over what you've done and give you estimates for the things you've identified or add new items of their own.

Ask stakeholders or team members who have experience working on similar projects to help you create the budget for this project. Their experience will help ensure that you don't miss anything important and will make the process go faster.

TIP

Here is a list of some of the common budget items to help you get started identifying them for your project. You could use this list as a checklist for future projects, adding your own commonly used items that require budget allocation and deleting the ones that don't occur on the types of projects you typically work on:

- Project team salaries
- Equipment and materials expense
- Rent or lease costs for facilities
- Marketing costs, including focus group and market research costs
- Legal costs
- Travel expenses
- Advertising costs
- Research costs
- Feasibility study costs
- Consulting services for subject-matter expertise or as project participants
- Phone, fax, and long-distance charges

◆ Office supplies (remember all those sticky notes we used!)

◆ Internet access charges or website-hosting fees

◆ Software

◆ Hardware

◆ Training

Budget Woes

Budgets, like project schedules, can be the cause of conflict. Project schedules, particularly the resource assignments associated with the schedules, are typically the biggest source of conflict on any project, and budgets probably run a close second. Be prepared to defend the budget items to the project sponsor or senior managers. Be ready to explain why the items are needed to successfully complete the project and the impact on the project if those items are not funded. You will likely put a heavy dose of negotiation skills to use during the budget process.

NOTE   **Senior managers who want to cut the budget are easily spotted because they're usually the second cousin of the senior manager who wants to cut the project schedule.**

For some reason, senior managers seem to think it's politically beneficial to cut the project budget (and/or the schedule) just so they look good in front of the big boss. They may have no other motivation than to appear as though they're saving the company money, even though it negatively impacts the project. Or they may have projects of their own competing for the same funds, and cutting your budget helps ensure that their own project budgets won't get cut. Although cutting the budget might make them look good to the big boss, it will definitely impact the project, which may not make you look so good at the end of it all.

Your best defense against this happening is to communicate with the project sponsor and make certain they understand the importance of the items included in the budget. At that point, they'll have to go head to head with the other executive managers and fight to secure the funding for the project. But they can't do that if you haven't first communicated the importance of the things you'll need to successfully complete the project and why. The important thing to keep in mind in this case is for you to know the reason the items are needed and their impact on the project if they are not obtained, and you need to be able to communicate this information when senior managers start wielding their big scissors at your budget.

TIP   **Never underestimate the importance of communicating with the project sponsor and stakeholders during all phases of the project.**

If the project is not successful as a result of an inadequate budget from the get-go, no one is going to come out looking good. If your project budget is woefully inadequate because of cuts made before you reach the Executing process, I recommend you pass on the opportunity to lead the project if you can, because it's highly probable that it will end up as an unsuccessful project.

Following the Processes

Many organizations have a procurement department that will help you purchase the items needed for your project. They may also help you create the budget. Always check with the procurement department to determine whether there are procedures you should follow when preparing your budget. Also be certain to work with the procurement department when purchasing services from vendors or contractors. You may need to follow a specific process, for example the RFP process, to the letter so as not to hold up the project schedule (and ultimately cost you more money).

Your organization may have a finance manager in addition to the procurement manager, or the finance manager may act in both roles. In large organizations, the responsibility for determining project costs will likely rest with you and the finance manager. And sometimes the finance manager is the one who works up the budget and gets approval from senior management, and you're simply told what the final budget is and are expected to work with it. If this is the case, use your communication and negotiating skills to work with the finance manager and ask them whether you can contribute to the budget process.

Estimating Techniques

The WBS has been a handy tool so far in the creation of Planning documents, and it's indispensable in the budget process. The WBS is used to identify, estimate, and assign costs to each element of the project. The work package level is where you'll see individual costs and estimates for each activity (provided the work package level shows activities), whereas the higher levels in the WBS will show rolled-up costs.

Before I get into the details of each estimate, let's look at the most common estimating techniques you can use during the budget process.

Analogous Estimating

The *analogous estimating* technique determines estimates for the current project based on the actual costs of previous projects that are similar in size and scope to the project you're working on. The key here is that the project you're using to base this project's estimates on should be very similar in all respects: size, complexity, scope, quantity of resources needed, quality criteria, and so

analogous estimating
Establishes an estimate for the project based on the actual costs of previous projects similar in size and scope to the project being estimated.

on. Sometimes projects may look alike on the surface, so make certain you analyze the two projects side-by-side before using this technique.

Analogous estimating is easy to perform and doesn't cost a lot of money. However, it's also a less accurate form of estimating than the other techniques you'll look at. This technique works best when you're trying to establish estimates early on in the project before a lot of information is known or for small projects or for individual deliverables on small projects. It's best to use this technique in combination with the next one I'll discuss — bottom-up estimating.

Bottom-Up Estimating

bottom-up estimating
Establishes individual estimates for each activity and adds them all together to determine a total estimate for the project.

Bottom-up estimating is the opposite of top-down estimating. This involves estimating each activity or work item individually and then rolling up those estimates to come up with an overall project estimate. For example, each activity included in the work package level is estimated, and then these estimates are added together with other work package–level estimates to come up with WBS level-3 and level-2 estimates. Then these can be added together for an overall project estimate.

NOTE Bottom-up estimating used in combination with analogous estimating techniques is especially useful for large projects. Analogous estimates are given for the individual activities or work package levels, and then these estimates are rolled up to come up with one estimate for the entire project.

Resource Cost Rates

Resource cost estimates usually involve obtaining quotes on the work to be performed (or resources to be procured). For example, perhaps your project requires the purchase of two new servers. You can jump on the Internet, obtain a quote from a supplier for the equipment, and, *voilà*, you have your budget estimate. Apply the same principle for other resources needed for the project such as contract labor, equipment and supplies, services, and so on.

Some vendors have published price lists that you can use for this activity. Along those lines, some organizations require vendors to supply an updated price list to their procurement department on a yearly basis for just this purpose. Check with your procurement department first to see whether such a list exists. If your organization does a lot of procurement throughout the year, chances are you'll get a better price off the price list than from the vendor's website.

Parametric Estimating

We discussed parametric estimating in Chapter 5, "Breaking Down the Project Activities." This method of estimating is quantitatively based and multiplies the number of units times the cost to determine the estimate. For example, if you know your project requires 100 hours of contract staff assistance at an hourly rate of $65 per hour, then the estimate for this activity is $6,500.

Computerized Tools

Most project management software packages allow you to put cost estimates on the activities listed on the project schedule. The software will then automatically calculate the total project costs for you. You could use a spreadsheet program to accomplish this as well by listing all the budget items in one column with their associated costs in another.

Ask the Experts

Interviewing techniques work well for estimating activities. Ask stakeholders, subject-matter experts, vendors, and project team members with previous experience on projects like the one you're working on for estimates. Many times functional managers who've loaned out resources on similar projects in the past have fairly accurate estimates ready. Never be afraid to ask.

Another useful technique in this category is to peruse historical documents. Past project documentation can be referenced to determine how much was actually spent on activities that are similar to the ones on the current project. This is a great technique if the past project was completed fairly recently because you have actual costs to use as a base instead of estimates. Don't forget to adjust your historical estimates to account for inflation or increases in salaries if the data is old.

Ask the Vendors

Vendor bid analysis is a good source for estimate information. This technique is especially useful when contracting out the work of the project. Start first with your procurement department. They may have lists of vendors who've provided pricing guides that you can reference and use as initial estimates for your project activities.

It's a good idea to get input from more than one vendor when asking them for estimates because they can vary widely. Ask different vendors to give you estimates so that you can check one against the other. Be aware that some vendors hope to get future business from you, so they will purposely provide a low initial estimate. They also may be using this project as a pilot project in the hope of getting business from other companies similar to yours. Keep these things in mind when comparing estimates from different vendors. Also make certain that all the vendors providing estimates on the project have the same understanding of the requirements, assumptions, and delivery dates.

If the estimates are coming in high and the budget is tight, ask the vendors for a discount. I've used this technique with vendors, especially with the vendors I work with all the time. This isn't something you should do for every project, however; be judicious about when to use this tactic.

Last, always ask vendors to put their estimates in writing. This will help ensure you're getting estimates you can rely on throughout the project and will help you avoid setbacks later.

Estimating Costs and Finalizing the Budget

The question you'll hear most often from executive managers is, "How much is this going to cost?" Now that you've learned what makes up a budget and how to derive the estimates, you're ready to answer that question. Let's look at an example project to pull all this together.

Your project involves opening a computer retail store in a new strip mall being constructed in your city. One of the deliverables involves building out the store space. This includes things such as signing the lease, installing counters and shelves, installing display cases, assembling a workspace area in the back room, and building five checkout counter lanes. The partial WBS for this one deliverable looks something like this:

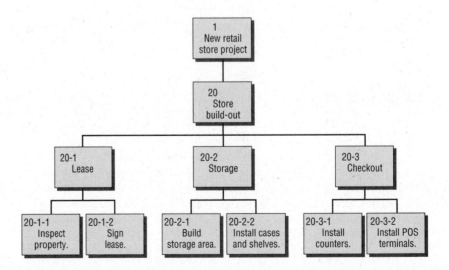

Using a combination of analogous and bottom-up techniques, your team has identified the costs in Table 9.1.

Table 9.1　Cost estimates

ID	WBS element	Cost estimate	Comments
20-1	**Lease**	**$300**	**Total cost of lease**
20-1-1	Inspect property.	$300	Contract inspector
20-1-2	Sign lease.	$0	No additional costs for this item
20-2	**Storage**	**$35,000**	**Total materials expense**
20-2-1	Build storage area.	$25,000	Materials expense
20-2-2	Install cases and shelves.	$10,000	Materials expense
20-3	**Checkout**	**$28,500**	**Total materials and contract labor expense**
20-3-1	Install counters.	$5,000	Materials expense
20-3-2	Install POS terminals.	$23,500	$18,500 materials, $5,000 contract labor

The deliverables level (which is level 2 on the WBS) shows item numbers 20-1, 20-2, and 20-3. These are in bold in Table 9.1. Each of these items is the total cost of all the individual activities below it. These costs have been rolled up, using the bottom-up estimating technique, to give a total for each level-2 item. Each of the level-2 estimates can be added together to come up with a total budget for this level-1 element titled "Store Build-Out," for a total of $63,800. When you've established the cost of the other level-1 elements, you can add all of those together for an overall project estimate.

Questions to Ask

Once you've plugged in some initial numbers and created the first draft of the budget, you'll want to sharpen up the estimates by asking some questions. You want to be certain you've identified all the budget items and that the estimates you've recorded are accurate. Here are some questions to help you with this activity:

1. Are the budget estimates for salaries and contractor expense realistic? How do these compare to past projects of similar scope and size?

2. Have all materials and supplies estimates been checked by the procurement department or another subject-matter expert? Letting a second pair of eyes double-check the estimates is a good idea to see whether something looks out of place or to uncover estimates that seem too high or too low.

3. Have you identified the potential risk to the project if the requested budget item is not purchased? Identifying the risk will help you justify the expense if this is an item you must have. If it's an item you can compromise on, identifying the risk is the first step in helping you examine the alternatives.

4. Ask whether the budget item requested is absolutely necessary in order to deliver the product or service of the project. Will this item be needed in order to complete a task or deliverable that is required to consider the project a success?

5. Are there other costs associated with the purchase of this item? For example, software programs often have ongoing maintenance expenses in order to get support for the product or upgrades. Depending on the length of the project, these may or may not be considered project expenses, but the end customer will have to pick up these costs when the project is delivered, so you'll want to tell them about them.

Finalizing the Budget

Now you're ready to finalize the budget and submit it for approval. You've established estimates and double-checked your work. Before you submit the final budget for approval, though, there a couple more things you should do to make sure the budget is accurate. (P.S. Taking the time to triple-check your estimates is not a bad idea.)

TIP   It's very difficult to go back to the well and ask for more money once the budget is submitted and approved. You're usually stuck with the budget that was approved, so you want to be certain you've included everything and that the estimates are accurate.

Contingency Reserves

Way back in ancient times (as my children call it) when I was a teenager, I remember asking my dad for money to go to the movies with my friends. My dad wasn't a big movie-goer himself, so he never knew exactly how much the movie cost. I confess that I used this to my advantage and padded my request to include enough money for popcorn and soda. (Don't tell him, though; I don't think he suspects a thing!) This usually worked well. Sometimes I could save up enough change from several movie trips to buy sodas for my friends. That was a really big hit. Or I could stash some so that if Dad didn't have enough cash on hand, I could pull out my reserves and still go to the show.

Project budgets work the same way. You'll want to build *contingency reserves* into the budget for unexpected items that are bound to pop up — I only recommend that you be honest about what you're doing. Movie money is one thing; a few million dollars added to the project budget for your spending pleasure can land you in the unemployment line or maybe even in jail!

contingency reserves
Money added to the project budget to pay for unexpected events.

In Chapter 7, "Assessing Risk," I talked about contingency plans and contingency reserves. Contingency reserves give you a buffer zone to absorb unexpected costs or deal with unanticipated risks as they arise. You can't know everything, and your team can't predict everything that will occur on the project, so having a contingency reserve in place will help you out of those tight spots as they arise.

One method for calculating reserves is to add an additional percentage of the total budget back into the budget for contingency. This percentage is going to vary depending on the project. The risk identification and planning process can help you zero in on a reasonable contingency number, and the risk response plans will help justify your need for a contingency reserve. Or you could research historical project documents to see how much reserve was used on projects in the past and then adjust it as necessary for your project.

Be careful with contingency reserves, though, as they can backfire. If you consistently add too much into the budget, stakeholders will always be leery of your estimates. If you don't add enough, you're going to be stuck figuring out how to solve problems within the budget you have because you aren't likely to get more. Make certain that the contingency amount you're using is reasonable and accurate. Document how you came up with the reserve amount, and be certain to control the use of these reserves. Again, ask the experts to take a look at your reserve estimate and see whether it sounds reasonable based on their past experience with similar projects.

One More Time

Ask the key stakeholders on the project to give the budget a thorough examination. Experienced project team members are also a good source for giving the final budget a good look before submitting it for approval. Ask them to think about some of the questions I talked about earlier and to identify anything that was missed or looks miscalculated.

If stakeholders question your contingency reserve, ask them to tell you why it should be adjusted. Don't let them convince you that a contingency reserve is unnecessary. All good project managers build in contingencies to the project budget; it's a common practice.

Down Memory Lane

Sometimes you'll find that funds are short and project budgets are not going to adequately cover the expenses of the project because of cuts or lack of approval for certain expenditures. If this leaves you high and dry, you'll have to go back through the Planning process and make adjustments. Start examining some of the Planning documents to find ways to either cut or reduce activities to accommodate the decreased budget. You'll also need to revisit the project's Planning processes when others tell you that your estimates are off or need adjustment.

Here are some of the first things you should look at to help reduce or adjust budget estimates:

◆ Reduce the project scope.

◆ Reduce features or functionality of the deliverables.

◆ Reduce the number of team members.

◆ Perform activities in-house that were originally scheduled to be completed by contractors.

Planning and tracking the budget will allow you to make adjustments to the project schedule, scope, or deliverables as needed. Revisiting the Planning processes will happen often during Planning, so don't be dismayed when you have to pull out the project schedule for the fourth or even fifth time to make adjustments. It's part of the project management process, and going back through Planning processes is to be expected.

Are You in Control?

Who has signing authority for budget item purchases? This is a question you'll want answered up front in the Planning process. Some organizations have strict controls over budget expenditures requiring management signatures, the finance officer's signature, and the project manager's signature. If this is the case, you'll need to make a note to build in the lead time needed to get all those signatures, or you could have team members sitting around twiddling their thumbs waiting for important deliveries to arrive.

The ideal situation is for the project manager to have control over the budget. This doesn't mean you should have unlimited signing authority, but you should be able to sign for normal supplies, contractor invoices, and so on. Work with the finance manager and your project sponsor to establish some level of signing authority for yourself so that you don't have to get signatures every time you need another box of screws or need to place a support call to a software vendor.

Project managers who have no control over the budget should not be held responsible for budget mishaps or for the results of budget and cost measurements taken during the Monitoring and Controlling process of the project.

NOTE

The organization may be set up such that finance managers have all the control over the budget. They approve budget item purchases, sign for them, and see that payment is made. If at all possible, you should negotiate with the finance manager for some signing authority so that there isn't a delay in the delivery of day-to-day needs. If the finance manager is the only one allowed to purchase and sign for items, you should not be held responsible for the condition of the budget. Also make certain that the adherence to the budget is not part of your performance evaluation for the project.

What's the Cost?

Some projects seem to have a life of their own. Information technology projects are a perfect example. I can't tell you how many projects I've witnessed in this industry where the project estimate conversation goes something like this:

> The project manager says, "Well, Ms. Sponsor, I've completed the estimates. This project is going to take 18 months and $700,000 to complete."
>
> To which Ms. Sponsor replies, "You're wrong. It's going to take 12 months and $350,000."
>
> The End.

Can you guess what happens next? The project manager agrees to this unrealistic schedule and decreased budget, but, miraculously, they deliver the project on time. So, how did that happen?

The real question here is, at what cost did that happen? Although the project may have been delivered on time and on budget, that isn't the end of the story. To accomplish this feat, many of the deliverables were postponed to the second phase, and the programming team had to cut out several important steps to meet the unrealistic deadlines. Your project team likely worked extraordinary hours to accomplish their activities, and even though the overtime didn't cost the project in terms of dollars, you now have a lot of unhappy team members on your hands.

In the end, the extended support costs because of lack of design and proper planning, coupled with all the extra hours needed by the programming staff to fix the problems, cost much more than the initial project budget. If Ms. Sponsor would have taken the time to examine the project's Planning documents, the critical deliverables, and the critical activities needed to complete the project successfully, she might have approved the original budget. Instead, the costs to fix the problems far surpassed the approved budget, making not only the sponsor look bad for sponsoring an unsuccessful project but the project manager as well.

Budget Approvals

The last step in the budget process is getting the budget approved. The project sponsor, key stakeholders, and the finance manager are the folks most likely to approve the budget, but every organization is different. Check your organizational procedures to determine how to go about getting the approvals for the budget. Whatever the process is, you cannot proceed without approval of the budget.

Establishing a Cost Baseline

cost baseline
The expected cost of the project. It's used to measure actual project expenses against the budgeted expenses.

The budget is used to allocate costs and resources to the project activities. As such, the finalized budget becomes the *cost baseline*. The project's actual costs are measured against the cost baseline throughout the Monitoring and Controlling process to ensure that actual costs are in line with the budgeted costs.

Depending on the project, the budget could be very small with only one or two items, or it could be a large budget with several layers of detail. You may also have a case where the project is so large, the budget is divided up at the work package level so that the subproject managers are responsible for their own portion of the budget. You'll want a copy of each of the individual budgets from the subproject managers to keep with the project documentation. You can then create an overall project budget that shows the total budgets for each of the WBS elements.

There are several ways to record your budget. You can use a spreadsheet format like the one in Table 9.2 to track the activities, the budgeted amount, and actual amounts. Table 9.2 shows the partial budget for the Store Build-Out deliverable for the new retail store project.

Table 9.2   Budget spreadsheet

ID	Activity	Cost Estimate	Actual Cost
20-1-1	Inspect property.	$300	$300
20-2-1	Build storage area.	$25,000	$26,225
20-2-2	Install cases and shelves.	$10,000	$9,315
20-3-1	Install counters.	$15,000	$15,475
20-3-2	Install POS terminals.	$23,500	$23,500

Another good method of tracking the budget is to record the budgeted costs along with project information in a spreadsheet, such as the one shown in Table 9.3.

Table 9.3   Project schedule with budget estimates

ID	Activity	Duration	Start date	End date	Cost
20-1-1	Inspect property.	3 D	June 1	June 3	$300
20-1-2	Sign lease.	1 D	June 4	June 4	$0
20-2-1	Build storage area.	10 D	June 5	June 14	$25,000
20-2-2	Install cases and shelves.	10 D	June 5	June 14	$10,000
20-3-1	Install counters.	4 D	June 15	June 18	$15,000
20-3-2	Install POS terminals.	5 D	June 19	June 23	$23,500
Totals:		**23 D**			**$73,800**

Most project management software packages allow you to put cost information at the activity detail level of the project schedule. You can run reports on the cost information right from the software and track budgeted versus actual expenses. When it comes time to report on project progress, you can simply print the budget report or print the spreadsheets shown previously in Tables 9.2 and 9.3, depending on how you're tracking and recording the budget.

How you display and track the project budget is a matter of personal preference, unless your finance department has specific guidelines you should follow. At a minimum, you must include the activity number, the activity description, and the estimated cost.

Call It a Plan

Congratulations! You've made it all the way through the project's Planning process. I warned you early on that Planning was a lengthy process. But it's a process that's well worth the effort because this process is critical to the success of the project. It's your map throughout the course of the project, and it needs to be updated on a regular basis.

Table 9.4 recaps the major planning activities you should complete for all projects. Take a look at the following processes to see how everything you've done interrelates.

Table 9.4 Project planning processes

Project name:		
Project number:		
Project Manager's name:		
Project planning activity	Inputs	Outputs
Project scope management plan	Project scope statement	Scope management plan that outlines how scope will be defined and how changes to scope will be handled
Project scope statement	Project charter	Project goals and objectives, assumptions and constraints, critical success factors
WBS	Project scope statement, project scope management plan	Deliverables-oriented breakdown of the work of the project
Activity identification	Project scope statement, WBS	WBS, activity list
Communication planning	Project charter, project scope statement	Communication plan
Resource identification	Project scope statement, WBS, activity list	Resource plan that identifies physical and human resources needed for the project
Task dependencies	WBS, activity list	Logical dependencies of activity
Network diagram	WBS, activity list, dependencies	Graphical picture of activity in dependency order
Activity duration estimates	WBS, activity list, resource plan, network diagram	Time needed to complete each task

Table 9.4   Project planning processes *(continued)*

Procurement planning	WBS, activity list, network diagram, resource plan	Procurement plan
Risk planning	Project scope statement, WBS, activity list, network diagram, resource plan	Risk plan
Quality planning	Project scope statement, project scope management plan, WBS, activity list, network diagram	Quality plan
Project scheduling	Project scope statement, WBS, activity list, network diagram, resource plan	Project schedule
Budgeting	Project scope statement, WBS, activity list, network diagram, resource plan, procurement plan, risk plan, project schedule	Project budget

All of these documents together make up the project plan. Remember that the goals and objectives and the assumptions and constraints are contained within the project scope statement. The roles and responsibilities chart is also part of the project scope statement, and this outlines everyone's responsibilities on the project. If your plan is lengthy, you could add a table of contents in the front to direct readers to the pages they're interested in, for example the roles and responsibilities chart. Don't forget to include the project team directory discussed in Chapter 6, "Planning and Acquiring Resources," as part of the project plan.

How Big Is It?

So how big is the project plan, you may be wondering. That depends on the project. If your project is small in scope and duration, all of this information can be captured in just a few pages. If the project is lengthy in duration and large in scope, it's probably going to take several pages per Planning activity to complete the project plan. You should keep the plan as concise as you can, and experience will tell you how much detail you should include in each plan. It's always a good idea to add some narrative description with these documents to help the stakeholders and management team understand the information that's being presented.

I also recommend adding an executive summary at the front of the project plan. An executive summary gives casual readers a high-level overview of the project, the project goals, and what the product or service of the project will look like when completed.

The better the project plan, the better prepared you and the project team will be to carry out the work of the project and deal with unexpected events. Reviewing and keeping the plan up-to-date is as important as writing the plan in the first place. Doing so lets you effectively judge new situations that come up and make the necessary corrections to get the project back on track.

Large Projects

Large project plans consist of several subproject plans that roll up to a master project plan. Subproject managers are the ones responsible for creating the project plans for their deliverable. The project manager oversees the preparation of the subproject plans and consolidates them to form the master plan. Each subproject manager follows all the Planning processes I've talked about to come up with their subproject plan.

The following graphic contains a sample portion of a WBS for a large project. Each of the deliverables at level 1, "Information technology," "Store build-out," and "Retail products," requires its own project plan.

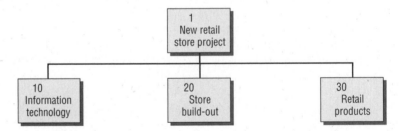

It's possible that this project is so large that each level-2 WBS element requires a subproject plan that is in turn rolled up to a level-1 subproject plan. All the level-1 plans are then consolidated into the overall project plan.

Obtaining Approvals

The project sponsor and key stakeholders should approve the final project plan. At this point, approval is really a formality because they've seen and approved each of the documents that make up the plan. But this gives them one last chance to look over the plan as a whole and make recommendations before approving the project plan.

Don't assume because you've made it to this point that the project is automatically going forward to the next phase. Things can change between the time the project was first selected, the time the project plans were completed, and now. For example, you might be preparing the plans for a high-profile project that the entire organization is excited about only to have the CEO or some other top executive resign at the conclusion of the Planning process. You guessed it — a new CEO comes on board and wants to know what the heck everyone thought was so great about that old project when their new project is much more important!

Fortunately, that doesn't happen often. But be aware that projects can get killed in the Planning process. Don't take it personally (unless of course it was poor planning or incomplete planning on your part that killed the project). Business changes over time; organizational goals change; personnel turnover occurs, changing the dynamics of the team; and even the risk tolerance of the stakeholders can change, given economic indicators or new marketing data or a host of other reasons, ultimately giving executives reason to kill the project.

Once the final plan is approved, you're ready to execute the project...er... progress to the Executing process, that is. That's where the work of the project happens. You'll kick off that process in the next chapter.

Terms to Know

analogous estimating	cost baseline
bottom-up estimating	direct costs
budget	indirect costs
contingency reserves	

Review Questions

1. What is a project budget?

2. Name the three categories of project costs.

3. Describe the two types of project costs and give an example of each.

4. Describe the analogous estimating technique.

5. Describe the bottom-up estimating technique.

6. What is a contingency reserve used for?

7. Your project budget has been approved, but it's been approved at a lower amount than the original request. What are some of the things you can do to deal with this situation?

8. What is a cost baseline and what is it used for?

9. Changes in project scope typically require changes to what other two project's Planning processes?

10. Does approval of each of the Planning documents guarantee overall project plan approval? Why or why not?

Chapter 10

Executing the Project

This chapter opens the Executing process of the project life cycle. Executing is where the work of the project gets done. We've talked about the work, planned for the work, and described what the work will look like, and now it's time to do the work.

You can't complete a project without people, so we'll spend considerable time in this chapter talking about project team development, negotiating and problem solving, and your roles and responsibilities as the project manager, including motivation techniques.

We'll also talk about progress reporting and who gets what types of information. The chapter concludes with a discussion of taking corrective actions to keep the project on track.

Assembling the Team

One of the most important activities you'll perform as a project manager is managing and leading the team. You've created the Planning documents and gotten approval for the budget, but you will have difficulty keeping the project on task and on time without a smoothly running team. And guess who's responsible for putting the team together and keeping team members motivated? You guessed it — the project manager.

Projects exist to create a unique product or service, and they require the cooperation of a team of folks to do the work accurately and completely. Aside from the robots in *Star Wars* and those found on some factory floors, most project teams will be made up of people. And here's the tricky part: Team members are people, and all people come preloaded with personalities, biases, work ethics, abilities, and so on. It's your job as the project manager to manage these folks and channel their energy into getting the work of the project completed.

One of the activities that will help your team function effectively is team building. Team building starts in the project's Planning process when you begin to assemble some of the key team players, and it continues throughout the life of the project. Team-building activities help improve your team's performance and keep team members motivated. Team-building activities can be elaborate or simple. You could consider throwing pizza parties as team-building activities or taking the team out to a ball game one afternoon. You could hire consultants to come in and host team-building activities, or you could take the entire team off-site to a ropes course or similar activities. Many books are available on team-building activities, and it's beyond the scope of this one to go into all the possibilities. I encourage you to engage the help of consultants who are specialists in this area or read some books on the topic. Engage your team, encourage participation and open communication, and find out what motivates them to perform at their best. (We'll discuss motivation a little later in this chapter.)

We've already identified the types of skills needed to complete the work of the project in Chapter 6, "Planning and Acquiring Resources." We've also assigned some of the key individuals to the project team and used their expertise to help create the project schedule, determine estimates, and so on. Now it's time to identify all the other team members and bring those folks together and get them started on the work of the project. We've already covered how to negotiate for team members and the importance of assuring their availability for the time you've scheduled them on the project schedule. Let's take a look at what happens when you get all these people together in the same place.

Project Team Kickoff Meeting

Now it's time to get everyone together in a room and get the work of the project started. The kickoff meeting with the project team includes those folks who are going to do the work of the project. This is a different meeting from the project kickoff meeting we talked about after the charter was signed. That meeting included the stakeholders, the project sponsors, and so on. This meeting is for your project team.

The purpose of this meeting is to lay the groundwork for the project. Not only will you inform the group of the goals of the project at this meeting (among other things), but you'll be setting the example for what's to come in future meetings. Start this meeting by sending out an agenda ahead of time. Let everyone know you intend to start promptly, that you'll be requesting them to participate in the meeting, and that you're sticking to the agenda.

At the first meeting, allow time for all the team members to introduce themselves and spend a minute or two describing their role on the project. You will take it from there and discuss the following information:

◆ Project goals and objectives

◆ Critical success factors

◆ Deliverable due dates

◆ Project schedule

◆ Task assignments

◆ Task due dates

◆ How to alert the project manager of problems or issues

◆ How and when to turn in status reports

◆ Dates of future team meetings

It's critical that this first meeting convey the information in the preceding list and that the team members understand what you've told them. Ask them for feedback, and ask them to confirm that they understand the project goals.

It's also important that team members understand from the get-go what you expect from these meetings. Don't let them carry you down rabbit trails, but do allow time in your regularly scheduled team meetings to discuss status, problems, and what they expect to accomplish during the next time period before you meet again.

Now that everyone has been introduced, it's time for them to start working together. Once they do, they'll progress through several stages of team development, which we'll look at next.

Four Stages of Team Development

The process of team development and team building seems very simple — bring a diverse group of people from inside and outside the organization onto the same team and get them to work together in the most effective and efficient way possible. Although this is easier to say than it is to do, there are ways to make it happen.

One of the first things to recognize when working with your project team is that they'll progress through several stages of development. Dr. Bruce Tuckman and Mary Ann Jensen developed a model that describes how teams develop and mature throughout several stages. These stages occur with any group of people who work together, and it doesn't matter whether the people know each other. In fact, many times your project team members will not know each other prior to working on the project. You'll want to make certain that you hold project team meetings to allow the team members time to get to know one another and to progress through the stages working as a group. It's important for you as the project manager to understand these stages so that you can help them progress to the most effective stage of development. Let's take a look at the Tuckman/Jensen five stages of development:

Stage 1: Forming   The forming stage occurs when all the team members have been brought together and introduced. Here they'll be told about the project objectives, the tasks they've been assigned, and the expectations that the project manager has regarding the project and the team. At this point, team members are asking themselves several questions:

- Why have I been assigned to this project?
- What's expected of me?
- What roles do the other team members have on this project?
- Will I be able to successfully complete the assignments given to me?
- Will I get the resources I need to perform the job satisfactorily?
- Can I work well with the project manager?

During this stage of team development, people will be somewhat reserved. They'll usually be polite and have a formal business approach communication style. Teams progress through this stage rapidly.

Your role as the project manager in this stage of development is communication. If the team is small, I recommend meeting with each of the members one-on-one and as a group to discuss the questions (and answers) outlined earlier. In my experience, team members who clearly understand why they are assigned to the project, their expectations regarding individual and team deliverables, and how to inform the project manager of their needs and issues will generally out-perform their peers who do not have or understand this information.

Stage 2: Storming   The storming stage is where the team starts to realize what the work of the project entails. The team members become more comfortable around one another and start challenging one another for position and status within the team. Then the sparks start to fly. Conflicts arise about the task assignments, and team members start asking these types of questions:

- Who is going to do what?
- How will the work get completed?

- ◆ What process should we use to do the work?
- ◆ Who should do it?

You'll know you've entered the storming stage when conflicts start to occur. We'll discuss some conflict-resolution techniques in the next section that you can use to help the team work through these issues. Your role as the project manager during this stage is to remind the team of the project goals and keep everyone centered on those goals. Conflicts aren't bad in this case; they're actually necessary to get the team into the next stage. It's best during this stage if you can limit your intervention and let team members resolve their own issues as often as possible. Team members need to get a feel for where they stand, where the extent of their responsibility lies, and how they'll accomplish their tasks working with the other personalities of the team, and that usually involves some tussles. Questioning and conflict help clarify the goals of the project for everyone on the team, not just the person in conflict, so encourage your team members to ask questions and discuss conflicts openly. But you won't progress to the next stage until the team has resolved the conflicts.

Some teams never progress out of the storming stage. It's difficult to manage a team in this stage, and it could have a negative impact on the project if relations are particularly nasty among team members. Consider replacing team members who are not cooperating or are the cause of unnecessary conflicts if the team doesn't seem to be making any progress.

NOTE

Stage 3: Norming   The norming stage is where the team starts to calm down, settle in, and do the work of the project. They know what's expected of them, and they have accepted and understand the goals of the project. The team members are comfortable with one another and with their own positions within the team, and they'll exhibit affection and familiarity with one another. Conflicts subside, and the team members confront the project concerns and problems instead of one another. And they make decisions jointly, getting input from all the team members.

As the project manager, you should continue to hold team meetings, especially during this stage, because team members can fall back into the storming stage if left to their own devices. During this stage, you should intervene more often when conflicts arise to keep the team moving forward. Monitor each team member's participation, and encourage the team to continue to remain focused on the project's goals and alert you of any problems as soon as they arise.

Teams in the norming stage are efficient, functioning teams. If your team has progressed to this stage, they'll likely be productive and work effectively toward meeting the project goals. But they still aren't performing at their absolute best — that happens in the next stage.

Stage 4: Performing   The performing stage is the most mature stage of all the development stages. The team functions in the most productive and effective ways possible. They support one another, they monitor themselves, and they achieve great things in this stage. Teams that operate in the performing stage are almost unstoppable.

However, not all teams make it to this stage. If you're lucky enough to manage one or two teams during your career that are functioning in this stage, you'll never want to work any other way. There's a harmony and a synergy among the team members and in their relationship with you that cannot be duplicated.

This stage cannot be forced. It happens because team members have mutual respect for one another and for you and are fully dedicated to the goals of the project. They've accepted the project as their personal responsibility and hold themselves accountable for doing the job well.

Your role as project manager during this stage should be more focused on the project management processes than on the team itself. Teams in this stage are usually self-directed and will hum along smoothly provided you are continuing to update them on project progress and are keeping the lines of communication open.

Stage 5: Adjourning   As the name implies, this phase refers to the breakup of the team after the work is completed. As the project manager, it's important for you to realize that many team members may be experiencing a sense of loss at the end of the project, particularly long-term projects. Guide the team through a closure process. Team celebrations at the conclusion of the project are one way to accomplish this. Acknowledge their contributions, and let them know you are grateful for their efforts and for any sacrifices they've made during the course of the project.

The most effective teams perform at stage 4. As we stated, you can't force this stage on the team. There are some things you can do as the project manager to help the team progress to this stage, though, including communicating effectively, asking team members for input, and using effective conflict-resolution techniques. Each of these ideas is recapped as follows:

Communicating Effectively   Schedule regular team meetings and individual meetings with each team member. Encourage them to bring concerns and problems to the meetings. Be certain to inform the team of anything that impacts them directly as soon as possible.

Soliciting Input   Ask team members to participate and contribute. Teams that feel they have some control over the project and project decisions will be more productive than those that feel they have no control. The project manager can give them decision-making authority over day-to-day activities to help encourage support and buy-in.

Resolving Conflict Effectively   Encourage the team to try to resolve their own conflicts as they arise. Whatever they cannot resolve on their own should be escalated to you. Encourage the team members to voice their concerns and attempt to reach mutual agreements concerning alternatives whenever possible. Remember to start by getting all the facts, and then examine the facts for possible solutions.

Effective Team Characteristics

Effective teams are those that function in the norming or performing stage of team development. They're energetic and enthusiastic about the work of the project, and they become good problem solvers. Effective teams are a joy to work with and will amaze you with their creativity. Encouraging individual participation, maintaining an open-door policy, and engaging the team in team-building activities will go a long way toward making your next team a smoothly running team. We'll talk more about the project manager's role in team development in a later section.

Some of the characteristics of effective teams are listed here:

- Good conflict resolution
- Enthusiastic commitment to the project
- Dedication and commitment to the project team members and project managers
- Creative problem solving
- High job satisfaction
- Productive team members who have a sense of belonging and purpose
- Enhanced communication
- Decisions made jointly by all team members

Dysfunctional teams operate with the opposite characteristics of effective teams. This is not the kind of team you want on your next project. Be aware of the warning signs of dysfunctional teams:

- Status meetings that turn into gripe sessions
- Lack of motivation and apathetic attitudes
- Team members not finding the work of the project satisfying
- Poor communication
- Lack of respect for one another
- Lack of respect for the project manager

I've had the experience of working with both types of teams, and the effective team is much more fun to work with. Successful project results happen because of the energy and focus the team pays to the project goals.

Problems are resolved almost effortlessly, and everything just seems to click. Dysfunctional teams, on the other hand, take up all of your time and all of your energy, and there is little benefit in return. Sometimes you have no choice but to tough it out with the team you've been given, even if it is dysfunctional. If you're working with a dysfunctional team, my best advice to you is to get your team into team-building activities and open up the lines of communication.

Also consider whether your team members are misplaced. Do they need training? Have they been asked to perform tasks they aren't prepared to work on? Do they have the resources they need to perform the task? If team members don't feel as though they're prepared to handle the tasks they've been given or they don't feel like they're a valuable part of the team, they'll likely take on "don't care" attitudes, which leads to dysfunctional teams.

NOTE **A poor attitude is like the common cold. Once one member of your team catches it, they all catch it. You'll want to cure or help prevent a poor attitude before other team members catch it.**

You can help prevent and correct your team's dysfunctional behavior by following the guidelines outlined in the next few sections of this chapter.

Negotiation and Problem-Solving Techniques

One of the things I can promise that you'll encounter on your next project is problems or conflicts, unless you're working on the project all by yourself. But even then, you have the customer to consider, and where there's a customer, there's a person. Where there are people, there'll be differences of opinion, differences in communication skills, and differences in needs, goals, and desires.

Conflict happens when one person's needs, goals, or desires differ from another's. (This can happen at the corporate level also, not just at the individual level.) Sometimes, conflicts are easily resolved by simply meeting with the person or people who have an issue and discussing the situation and possible alternatives until a reasonable resolution is reached. Other times, it's not that easy.

The most likely areas that will require problem-solving skills or negotiation are the project schedule, resource assignments, issues regarding contract elements or price, issues regarding your or another's authority and responsibility, and problems surrounding the use of business or technical processes. An example of this last one might be the project management methodology you'll use for the project. Someone may challenge the process you're using or the way you're implementing the processes of the chosen methodology that will require negotiation to resolve.

Every good project manager will have to use problem-solving and negotiation techniques; it's guaranteed. Good communication skills and good problem-solving skills go hand in hand, so you'll want to fine-tune these skills and include them in your project management tool bag. There are several techniques you can use to negotiate and resolve project issues, and we'll touch on a few of those here. If you're interested in digging into this area further, there are books devoted to the topics of problem solving and negotiation.

Start at the Beginning

The time to start solving problems is when they first begin to arise. Tackling your problems early on will many times be enough to keep them from escalating into out-of-control octopuses. Problems, like octopuses, can have many arms, and just when you think you've taken care of one of those arms, another one will grab you from behind when you're not looking!

When it's evident that you have a problem or an issue on your hands that's going to require negotiation, you should first document the problem. Define the issue, in writing, detailing as much as you can. Break it down into smaller parts and try to focus on the problem, not the symptoms of the problem. Defining the problem, and asking the other party to do the same, may bring to light a miscommunication or misunderstanding that's easily cleared after everyone understands what the real issue is.

In addition to documenting the problem, document the assumptions about the problem. This is another potential problem area. If you assume that I need a certain employee from your department for six months starting June 1 and I assume that I need that employee starting next week, we might discover that there isn't a problem after all. We both understand, or assume in this case, something different, and the issue is easily resolved.

Next, document your proposed solutions. These can be ideas at this point and not full-fledged plans for detailing all the aspects of the solution. The point is to start thinking about how the problem can be resolved. Offering solutions to the other party shows that you're willing to work together toward a resolution and aren't going to camp on the "It's your problem" approach. Early in my career, I had a manager who would not allow me to approach him with a problem unless I had at least one suggestion for a resolution to the problem. I remember wondering at the time what the company paid him to do, but this technique of thinking through problems and coming up with possible alternatives before confronting someone has helped me come to a quick resolution many times.

Documenting the problem, your assumptions about the problem, and possible alternatives will help prepare you for the face-to-face meeting and will keep you focused on the issues at hand during the discussions.   *NOTE*

After documenting the problem, assumptions, and possible solutions, arrange to meet with the people you're having the conflict with to discuss the

mediator
Acts as a third party to negotiate settlements between two or more parties involved in a dispute. The mediator should be a disinterested party with nothing to gain from the outcome of the decision.

problem face to face. I recommend doing this on neutral territory; in other words, meet with them in a conference room or even an off-site location, not in your office.

If there is a potential for this meeting to get a little heated, consider using a mediator. A *mediator* should be someone who is not involved in the conflict and has nothing to gain from the outcome. The mediator will keep the meeting on track, make sure everyone understands the issues at hand, and ensure that everyone has the chance to state their side of the problem and any proposed solutions. Day-to-day project issues you'll encounter won't usually require the use of a mediator, but it is an option if you're having difficulty reaching a resolution that's agreeable to all the parties involved.

Allow each party to discuss the problem from their perspective and to offer alternative solutions. Make sure everyone gets an equal opportunity to state their case. After each person has had the chance to describe the problem from their own perspective, switch roles and let the first person describe, in their own words, what they believe the problem is from the second person's point of view. This is a lot like the listening technique I described in Chapter 2, "Developing Project Management Skills," where you paraphrase what you heard the speaker say so that you're sure you understand what was said. Restating the problem from the other person's perspective might also lead to a quick resolution.

Problem solving and negotiation takes practice. Don't worry that you'll lack opportunity, however. The project management arena will give you lots of chances to perfect your problem-solving skills. I believe the most important factor in problem solving is accurately and thoroughly defining the problem. Don't jump to conclusions too quickly though; allow alternative solutions to surface so that all the possibilities can be explored.

Before we leave this topic, we'll look at the six different methods of problem resolution.

The Six Approaches to Problem Resolution

The PMI recognizes six approaches to problem resolution, and I think you'll agree that these cover the range of possible behaviors from all the participants. If you can spot people using these techniques during your next confrontation, you can help steer them toward a successful resolution by keeping everyone in the problem-solving technique (the last one described in this section) as much as possible.

Forcing Forcing is when one person, the King or Queen, says, "This is the way it's going to be," and all the subjects agree. The subjects may go away mumbling under their breath that this was the dumbest idea they've heard in a long time, but they publicly agree for fear of losing their head. Forcing happens whenever one person forces their decision on others. Usually the person doing the forcing is someone in power but not always.

Lead technicians and highly skilled employees whom management is in fear of losing can sometimes wield this power. Decisions made using the forcing technique aren't necessarily the best decisions, but they are usually permanent ones because, after all, the boss is the boss and what she says goes.

Forcing typically creates an atmosphere of strife and an "us versus them" mentality. I recommend you use this technique only when it's absolutely necessary. That means resolution cannot be reached any other way, so you, or your executive manager, are forced to make the decision and impose it on the group.

Smoothing/Accommodating   This technique involves some sleight of hand. You've probably heard the opening line for this technique in meetings you've attended. It goes something like this: "I don't understand what everyone is so upset about. This isn't a big deal. You have all blown this way out of proportion." After the person who started this is finished with their very convincing speech, everyone in the room looks at one another and wonders why this was such a big deal. As a result, everyone quickly comes to a resolution, only to go back to their desks later in the day and begin thinking about what happened. They'll realize that the real issue was pushed under the carpet and the problem still exists. At the next meeting, the issue will surface again, and the problem-solving merry-go-round will start again unless someone recognizes what's happening and shifts the group to the problem-solving technique.

Compromise   Compromise is where both parties agree to give up something to reach a solution. On the surface, this may sound like a good technique, but if neither party is enthusiastic about the decision that was reached, they may drag their feet or even change their mind later in the project. Neither side wins or loses in this situation. However, if both parties are committed to the compromise and the solution, it can be a workable technique.

Collaborating   Collaborating occurs when multiple viewpoints are discussed and shared and team members have the opportunity to examine all the perspectives of the issue. Collaborating will lead to true consensus where team members commit to the decision.

Withdrawal/Avoidance   This technique never results in resolution because one of the parties picks up their toys and goes home. They may physically get up and leave the meeting, or they may check out emotionally, but either way they're not participating in finding a resolution. This is probably the worst of all techniques, because no lasting resolution can be reached when one party refuses to cooperate.

Keep in mind that this isn't the same thing as leaving a meeting when one party becomes hot-headed and out of control. I know a project manager who got into a tangle with a key stakeholder in a public meeting and walked out. The key stakeholder decided that he was going to take out all his problems on the unsuspecting project manager and proceeded to vent all kinds of nasty things, using some colorful language. The project manager looked the stakeholder squarely in the eye and said, "This meeting is over. When you're ready to act like a professional, call me," and then left the meeting. I wish I could tell you that this never happens, but it does. It isn't an everyday occurrence, but sometime during the course of your career you'll find yourself sitting across from someone like this. Never subject yourself or your team members to the irate ranting of stakeholders. This is a case where it is OK to ask them to knock it off or leave the meeting.

Confrontation/Problem Solving   This technique is the best technique for reaching a resolution. The idea behind this technique is that one correct solution exists for the problem, and it's the team's responsibility to dig out all the facts and find that solution. Many times, the act of finding all the facts will reveal the solution. This is the process I described in the opening of this section. Document the problem, let the facts reveal what's really going on, and then work together to come up with a resolution everyone can live with. This is the technique you should use most often.

NOTE   The problem-solving technique is the technique used most often by project managers for conflict resolution.

When you're in the midst of problem solving or decision making, you should keep the number of lines of communication in mind. (We talked about that in Chapter 2.) Ideal group sizes are between five and eleven people — anything more than that and you run the risk of not being able to make a decision or of making inaccurate decisions.

Remember that conflict resolution involves communication and listening skills as well. You'll find that your work as a project manager encompasses these areas more than anything else you'll do. Good communication skills and excellent project planning techniques are the keys to successful projects. Now let's examine what project managers need to know about effective team development.

Project Manager's Role in Team Development

Project managers have a tough job. Since projects exist to create a unique product, service, or result, every new project they undertake puts their reputation on the line. Even when the projects are similar in size and scope to projects they've worked on in the past, they're still a different animal with different risks, outcomes, and project teams. Every new project has the potential to succeed or fail, and every team has the potential to be an effective team functioning at the performing stage or to be a dysfunctional team.

One of your roles as project manager includes motivating your team members and encouraging the most effective performance from your team as possible. Everyone likes to be recognized for a job well done, and recognition is one of the motivators that drives people and teams to perform at their best. In the next section, we'll look at what motivates team members and how to appropriately reward the behaviors you'd like to see repeated.

Rewarding Experiences

Why do people do the things they do? How do you encourage positive behaviors, outstanding performance, and team collaboration from your team members? Get out your magic wand...what, you don't have one of those? Then the next best thing is to learn some of the basic theories of motivation, including how to reward and recognize team members to help drive your team to perfection. We'll start with a definition of motivation.

Motivation

Motivation is the result of some type of incentive that drives us to perform, and the incentive comes in two forms: intrinsic motivators and extrinsic motivators. *Intrinsic motivators* are personal things internal to the individual that drive them to perform. For example, some people are naturally driven to achieve. It's a personal matter for them to be the best they can be and perform at their best all the time. They receive personal satisfaction from doing the best job they can. There isn't anything external that drives them to perform like this; it comes from inside.

intrinsic motivators
Motivators that are specific to an individual or are derived from within the individual to spur them to perform.

Extrinsic motivators are typically external to the individual and are usually material in nature. Promises of bonuses, raises, stock options, vacations, and so on, are examples of extrinsic motivators. The person performs the task for the benefit of receiving something they perceive has value.

extrinsic motivators
Incentives that are external to the individual such as money, gifts, and rewards that spur them to perform.

Rewards and recognition are types of extrinsic motivators. Let's look at some examples.

Rewards and Recognition

Rewards and recognition at both the individual level and the team level are important team motivators. They are a way for the project manager to encourage desirable behavior and performance from team members.

Rewards and recognition should be in proportion to the accomplishment or achievement. I used to have a boss who had this saying written across the top of his office whiteboard: "Never confuse activity with accomplishment." I don't know the author of this saying, but the message is clear: Being busy isn't the same thing as being productive. You may have team members who put in long hours and seem to have a flurry of activity going on around them all the time. That doesn't mean they're productive. You should gauge the productivity of all team members according to their task assignments, the goals associated with those assignments, and their due dates and budget constraints if they apply.

Other softer skills apply as well, such as innovative problem solving, good communication skills, team participation, and so on.

Linking Rewards to Performance

You always want to link rewards to the desired performance. Perhaps your project is time-constrained. If so, you'll want to reward team members for meeting the key deliverable dates. If you reward employees for bad behavior (don't laugh, I've seen it happen), you'll get more of that bad behavior, and you'll soon find other team members repeating that bad behavior.

Let's say you've made it clear that the project is time-constrained and that you intend to reward employees for meeting key dates. Kit is a team member who consistently meets her dates on time or earlier than scheduled. Linda consistently misses her dates by a day or two, sometimes longer, because of poor work habits. However, you're a really nice project manager, so you let Linda's dates slide, granting her a grace period time and again. When the other team members catch on to what's happening, they don't take their due dates seriously. They've learned that the rewards are not linked to the performance you've specified (meeting key dates) because due dates are extended when their work is late. Be certain that the performance you're rewarding is the performance you want to see more of in the future, and make sure to reward consistently, and without showing favoritism, every team member who performs accordingly.

You'll also want to make certain that the reward is realistic. Let's say you promised your team members bonus checks of $10,000 at the end of the project, provided the project is delivered earlier than scheduled while still meeting all the project and quality requirements. If the team members know up front that there is no way the company could afford or ever would reward their employees with bonus checks like this, the promise of a bonus does nothing for them. In other words, the motivator is useless. It has no impact on their performance because they know they aren't going to receive it. However, let's say your company is known for generously rewarding employees on past projects for a job well done. Then the reward is realistic, and team members will work with the expectation that the reward will be granted if they meet the criteria.

NOTE **Recognize achievements, even small ones, with appropriate rewards. Recognizing employees with rewards that are linked to performance is a powerful motivator.**

You'll have to use your own judgment when determining what rewards are appropriate. Base your judgment on the cultural atmosphere at your organization, past rewards, and the complexity of the accomplishment. For example, at one organization, meeting a milestone earlier than planned may have the project manager handing out gift certificates for a latte at the local coffee shop, while another organization may approve of your giving out gift certificates for a dinner at a nice restaurant.

The important thing here is that you don't give someone a reward that far surpasses the achievement or effort they expended. Bonus checks of $10,000 may be perfectly appropriate for a two-year project that's expected to bring in millions in revenue to the company and was completed four months ahead of schedule. Bonus checks of this size probably wouldn't be appropriate for delivering a small project with minimal benefits to the company.

Be aware that your company policies may limit the types and amounts of rewards you can give. If policy dictates that you can give no more than $100 per employee per project, you'll have to work within that limit. It doesn't mean you should hold back rewards because you think they're too small or don't measure up to the level of effort that the employees expended. Recognition and reward are good motivators even if the reward is small. The fact that you took the time to thank the employees and recognize them means a lot.

If you work in an organization that prohibits monetary rewards, consider some of these ideas to use as rewards. These are good rewards to use for small achievements that you want to recognize as well:

◆ Paid-time-off certificates

◆ Leave-early or come-late-to-work passes

◆ Handwritten thank-you notes from the project manager

◆ Printed and framed certificates of achievement (created on your computer)

◆ Email congratulations addressed to the recipient and copied to the other team members, the project sponsor, and the management staff when appropriate

◆ Catered lunch at a project team meeting

◆ Decorating the employee's cube with a "You're a Star Performer" theme

When publicly recognizing individuals, consider preferences and cultural differences. Some people do not like to be recognized in front of others and would prefer that the project manager approach them one-on-one. Others love to have the attention of the group lavished on them. Be aware that some cultures do not encourage individual recognition, so these folks may find it difficult to accept a personal reward.

WARNING

Employee Recognition

Having employees recognize one another's accomplishments or acknowledge the help they've received from someone else is another good motivation technique. You can set this up in several ways. Employees can nominate each other via a form or email that explains what the recognition is for and how the team member helped them. The project manager can announce these once a month in team meetings and congratulate each person for their participation and help. Or you could use a designated object, like a trophy, a decorative shoe, a stuffed animal, and so on, to represent a job well done. The idea here is that employees recognize outstanding performance by presenting one another with the trophy and a note that describes the accomplishment. The recipient of the award holds on to it for a set period of time, perhaps a month, and then they must pass it on to another team member in the fashion they received it.

Rewards and recognition can be used to help influence employee behavior and to encourage team members to perform at their best. If you're not particularly good at rewarding and recognizing team members yourself, consider appointing someone else with this duty so that it doesn't get swept under the carpet altogether. Dozens of books are available on motivation and employee behaviors if you're really interested in learning more about this topic. As the project manager, you have to win the respect and trust of every new team you lead, and that takes time. If you're a great project leader, your reputation will precede you, but it isn't a guarantee that folks on the new team will instantly respect and trust you. They need time to form their own opinions.

Leadership is granted to project managers by default — they've been appointed by an executive sponsor to lead the project. But it doesn't mean they are a leader or that team members will respect their leadership. Project teams typically have informal leaders as well. You'll want to firmly establish yourself as the leader of the project, or else the informal leaders will have all the control behind the scenes. We'll talk about how to do that in the next section. But before we get into some specific things you can do to win the respect and trust of your team members, let's look at the different forms of leadership power.

Leadership Power

Project managers, leaders, senior managers, team members, and others use power to influence others to do things or perform tasks in specific ways. Each of us uses different forms of power at different times depending on our personality, our personal values, and the company culture. You don't have to be in a position of power to be a leader. Teams may have informal leaders who wield a lot of power. Conversely, a senior manager who waves a magic wand over some unsuspecting team member and says "Poof, you're a project manager!" does not make that person a leader.

There are several different types of leadership power. Let's explore each of them and their characteristics in more depth:

Reward Power   We talked about rewards and recognition earlier. Reward power is the ability to grant incentives or bonuses to team members who perform their job functions well. Team members respond to this type of power by performing the desired behaviors for the reward (provided the reward is realistic and is linked to the performance, as explained earlier).

Punishment Power   Punishment power involves the use of penalties or consequences as a threat for not performing up to expectations. This is the kind of power we talked about in Chapter 1, "Building the Foundation," when the ruler of the kingdom picked a "volunteer" to act as the project manager. The volunteer accepted the role out of fear of some dreadful form of punishment that, fortunately, project managers don't have to face today. Sometimes good project managers will be required to use punishment power when team members are out of line or not performing the duties of their job. Work with your manager and human resources department to determine how to appropriately use this type of power in your organization.

Expert Power   This type of power comes about as a result of a person's knowledge, or perceived knowledge, of a subject. The person being influenced believes the expert knows what they're talking about and will go along with the direction and decisions made by the expert because of their knowledge. Special skills and abilities are another way people receive expert power. Be careful with this one because some people come across as experts because of the confidence they show when they speak about the subject or what their body language conveys, but they aren't experts at all. They may have book knowledge but no hands-on knowledge. If you have doubts about what someone like this is telling you, especially if they're providing technical leadership or advice on your project, get a second opinion.

Legitimate Power   Legitimate, or formal, power comes about as a result of the influencer's position. Because that person is the project manager, executive vice president, or CEO, they have the power to call the shots and make decisions.

Referent Power   Referent power is the power team members give one another because of the respect they have for the individual. One member of the team may be highly respected and trusted by the others and as a result is given referent power by their teammates — when this person voices an opinion, the others listen. Project managers who are held in high regard by the project team receive referent power from the team members. Project managers who have referent power are powerful indeed, because they have the most loyal of all project teams and the members will do most anything the project manager asks of them.

I've had the opportunity to operate under each of these types of power, and referent power is by far my favorite form of leadership power. Referent power isn't something you can manufacture. It happens as a result of the rapport you have with the team and their respect for you and your abilities.

Gaining Trust and Respect from Team Members

Have you ever worked in an organization where almost all the people working within one department seemed to be unhappy, disgruntled, and particularly critical of others? I've witnessed this phenomenon a couple of times in my career, and I've come to attribute this to two factors: the leader at the head of the department and the lack of communication from and to the leader, which goes back to the leader at the top.

It looks like the common denominator here is the leader. Team members emulate the behavior they see coming from you, so it's important for you to set the example you'd like your team members to follow. If you're typically critical of others, have a poor customer service attitude, and never listen to team member input or suggestions, you can expect your team members to act the same way. If you treat your team members with respect and value their input and participation on the project, they will likely treat you and others the same way.

Examine your own organization to see whether this isn't true. Departments or teams with dynamic leaders who value their employees, communicate well, have strong customer service ethics, and are good decision makers are usually the ones with the teams that are the most productive and satisfied with their work. When new team members who have sour attitudes are introduced into teams like this, they don't usually last long and will leave on their own accord. It's no fun to have sour attitudes by themselves, so they move on.

You can do several things to gain the respect and trust of your team members. A nice benefit of gaining the respect and trust of your team members is motivation. Teams that respect their project managers will usually be motivated to perform their best because of their respect for you. Let's look at some of the tactics you can put into practice today to help build trust and respect with your teams.

Do What You Say You Will Do   You've probably heard this one a thousand times, but it's worth repeating. Nothing builds trust and respect faster than doing what you said you would do. If you're the forgetful type, write the promise down. Make an appointment on your calendar to give yourself the time or to remind yourself to complete the promised action. This goes hand-in-hand with follow-through. When someone brings an issue to you and you agree to handle it, do just that and get back to the person with a response.

Lead by Example   As stated earlier in this section, team members will mimic your behavior. Act the way you'd like to see your team members act.

Communicate and Then Communicate Some More   We covered communication skills in Chapter 2. Pay particular attention to the active listening skills. Don't do all the talking. Get input from your team members and consider their suggestions. If they aren't good suggestions — and some of them won't be — still thank them for their input and ask them to keep the ideas coming.

Maintain an Open-Door Policy   This one goes with communication. If team members find you unapproachable or hard to talk to, they won't be eager to alert you of problems or issues on the project. Let folks know that you encourage them to talk with you, and then make yourself available. (Remember the "Do what you say you'll do" action item!)

Be Honest   Being honest builds credibility with your team members, and they'll quickly develop respect for you as a leader when they find out you are a truth teller. Sometimes being honest means that you have to deliver bad news. That's OK. Don't sugarcoat the bad news. Lay out the facts for the team, let them know the alternatives being considered, and ask them for their input if appropriate. And by all means, keep confidences. If your team members feel that everything they tell you is going to make the rounds at wildfire speed, you'll end up being the last to know of problems and issues on the team.

Be on Time   When you set up meetings, start them on time. When you agree to attend meetings others have set up, show up on time. This shows a respect for others' time. Some managers think showing up late to meetings makes them look important because others have to wait on them. On the contrary, it makes others feel as though they aren't valued by the manager and causes frustration and resentment. If you consistently wait for all team members to show up at the meeting before starting, you're rewarding the wrong behavior. In other words, the folks who were there on time are punished for showing up on time by having to wait for the latecomers because you won't start the meeting until they get there. Reward the folks who showed up on time by starting on time. The latecomers will quickly learn to get to the meeting at the scheduled time or risk being embarrassed by coming in late.

Clearly Define the Goals of the Project   Project team members who have a firm understanding of the goals of the project are more likely to be committed to the project, and team members who are committed to the project are more productive than those who are not.

Clearly Define Team Member Roles   This ties back to communication; make sure every team member knows and understands their role and responsibilities on the project. Let them know what measures you'll use to gauge their performance, and give them feedback often.

Hold Team Members Accountable   This sometimes means you'll have to play the heavy and discipline team members or dismiss them. This doesn't negate all the other tactics listed in this section. Be honest, communicate expectations with your team members, and when they don't measure up, hold them accountable. It's beyond the scope of this book to go into all the possibilities for disciplining and releasing employees. Before things ever get to this point, I strongly urge you to work with your manager and your human resources department to find out how you go about disciplining employees. You should always document unwanted employee behavior, but if you wait until the last minute when you're at the breaking point with the person, you won't recall the kind of details you're going to need to justify your action. Start documenting as soon as you start having problems, and contact human resources.

Most of these things are second nature to those folks who have natural project management and leadership abilities, but it never hurts to refresh your options for team building. Put these ideas into practice with your next project team.

Professional Responsibility

Part of your responsibility as a project manager is to ensure the integrity of the project management process and your own personal integrity. To have personal integrity means that you abide by an ethical code. If you're thinking of becoming a certified project manager through PMI, for example, you'll be required to adhere to their code of conduct. Most of the things you'll find in the code of conduct are intuitive, but again, it never hurts to refresh your memory.

Regardless of whether you are certified or ever intend to be, you should always strive for some personal integrity goals, including keeping the organization's interests at the forefront as opposed to your own personal interests, eliminating all possibilities of conflict-of-interest situations, and acting professionally. Let's look at each of these areas in a little more depth.

Personal Gain

Your own personal gain should never be a factor in project decisions or when working with your customers or stakeholders on project issues. Truthfulness and integrity should be reflective not only of your own professional experiences but of the circumstances of the project as well.

You should never consider your own personal gain or bettering your own position by compromising project deliverables or milestones. For example, if you've been promised a bonus for finishing the project earlier than scheduled, it would be inappropriate to skip tasks or only partially complete the tasks in order to make it look as though the project was completed early. This would be putting your own personal gain over the best interest of the project. Not only does it show a lack of integrity on your part, but actions like this could also cost you your job.

Personal gain doesn't have to be monetary. For example, a stakeholder may promise you a promotion if you sway the selection committee or if you make sure that their interests in the project are dealt with in specific ways. Working toward your own promotion instead of keeping the integrity of the project process and the product of the project as your top priority would call your personal integrity into question.

Conflict of Interest

A *conflict of interest* occurs when personal interests are put above the interests of the project or when you use your influence to cause others to make decisions in your favor regardless of the impact on the project. Conflict-of-interest situations can occur with friends, family members, vendors, stakeholders, or anyone else who has an interest in the project. Keep in mind that any circumstance where the possibility for abusing the situation exists can also be considered a conflict of interest. For example, suppose one of your family members works for a consulting company that will be bidding on the project you're managing. This is a conflict of interest because you could potentially share information with that family member that other bidders don't have access to, thereby using your relationship for personal gain. Even if you don't share the information, the situation is still considered a conflict of interest because the possibility for sharing information exists. The best thing to do in this case is to let your project sponsor know about the situation, don't share information that isn't available to all the bidders, and decline to participate as a selection committee member.

Vendor gifts are another potential area for conflicts of interest. Check with your organizational policies before accepting any gifts from vendors. Most organizations have dollar limits on the gifts, meals, and other items vendors can give you. If you're starting or are in the midst of a bidding process and you're part of the selection committee or have influence over the selection committee, don't accept any gifts from any vendors, including lunches. This can be misconstrued as a conflict of interest by other vendors and can call your integrity into question.

If you're in doubt regarding whether to accept a gift, you're better off to decline it than put the project at risk. Not only do you put your own reputation on the line in these situations, but you could put the entire project in jeopardy. Vendors who think other vendors were given unfair advantages or who can pin you with a conflict of interest can protest the winning bid and delay the start of the project for weeks or months.

Stakeholder influence can also be a cause of conflict of interest. For example, stakeholders may have an interest in one particular vendor and may try to convince you or bribe you with offers of favoritism or promotion if you'll choose the vendor they recommend. Always opt to make decisions with the objectives of the project in mind and not your own, or someone else's, personal interests.

Not only should you not accept gifts, favors, or promises of personal gain from others in exchange for favorable decisions, you should not offer gifts or promises to others to sway their decisions.

conflict of interest
A potential for personal gain where personal interests are at odds with the best interests of the project outcomes.

TIP

Act Professionally

Everyone in the business world is required to act in a professional manner.
That involves all the things we've talked about so far and includes controlling
yourself and your reactions to situations you'll encounter on a day-to-day basis.
You've probably heard this before, but I'm going to remind you of it one more
time — the only thing you truly have control over is your own reactions to situations. You cannot control what others will do or say, but you can control your
own reactions to what they do and say. When that unruly customer or stakeholder decides to vent on you, take the upper road and remain calm. Practice
active listening, ask some clarifying questions, and let them know that you'll
research the issue and get back with them. If they're especially up in arms, ask
whether you can schedule a meeting with them at a later time to go over the
issues, and drop the topic until everyone has had a chance to cool down.

Here are some of the things you should keep in mind when working on
any project:

◆ Respect confidential information, and do not use it for your own gain.

◆ Respect company data and any information developed by the organization that has a commercial value.

◆ Coach your team members to conform to professional standards of conduct.

◆ We all lead by example, so don't forget that your actions speak louder
than words.

◆ Stay abreast of new project management practices and techniques.

◆ Stay abreast of the trends in your industry.

◆ Don't mislead others regarding your work experience, certification, or
educational status.

◆ Be honest about what you do know and about what you don't know.

◆ Report all project information truthfully.

◆ Respect cultural differences.

NOTE   **Team members represent you and the project. They should act professionally at
all times, and it's your job to ensure that they do. If team members are acting
out of turn, coach them regarding the standards of conduct you expect. Make
sure you're leading by example so that they witness the standards of conduct
you expect in action.**

Progress Reporting

We're going to shift gears a bit and talk about another important area in the
Executing process of the project — progress reporting. Project managers are
responsible for reporting on the progress of the project. In order to do that,

you'll need information from the team members, vendors, and other key personnel on the project. There are two ways to gather this information: formally and informally.

Make it a habit to walk around during the day and chat informally with team members to keep yourself up-to-date on where things are. Remember that body language can tell you a lot. Get to know your team members, and build that trust level so that they feel comfortable telling you what's up. Stay alert for signs that trouble may be brewing, and often ask the team how their work is going.

Who Gets What?

The communications plan we talked about in Chapter 4, "Defining the Project Goals," outlines who should receive information about the project, what type of project information they get, and how often they get it. During the Planning process, however, you may not have identified all the information the stakeholders want to see now that the project is underway.

Aside from the regular status reports, stakeholders may request information regarding schedule changes, scope changes, variance reports, resource usage, revised cost estimates, quality measurements, and so on. As the project manager, you'll have to produce the information they've requested. It's a good idea to ask the stakeholders requesting the new reports a few questions to keep yourself from spinning your wheels producing information they don't find useful. Ask them to describe the purpose of the report, what specific types of information they're looking for in the report, how often they'd like to have the information reported, and who should get the information. I suggest setting up a time to meet with the key stakeholders to fine-tune the details after you've come up with a draft of the report.

Don't forget to update the communications plan to include the new report and who gets copies of it.

Well, you knew it was coming. I've never worked on a project yet that did not require status reports, so let's get to it.

Status Reports and Action Logs

I recommend requiring your team members to send status reports to you on a weekly basis in written form. This is the best method of collecting project status and gives you a way to condense and consolidate the information for the stakeholder meetings we'll talk about shortly.

Many project management software programs have status-reporting features built in. If you're not using one of their tools, you could use a form like the one in the following graphic. Use this template to build your own status reports. Email the forms to your team members, set a date and time the status report is due, and then hold them accountable for getting the information to you on time.

Most of these sections are self-explanatory. Section III refers to reporting on scheduled dates for tasks or deliverables. For example, if you have task due dates coming up within this reporting period, list the tasks here, showing their due dates and their actual completion dates, or refer readers to the project schedule if there are too many tasks to list here.

You should take each of your team members' reports and create one overall project status from their combined information. Once you've consolidated all the status reports into one, you could use this form to report status to the project team during your team meetings. It's important for the team to know that the project is making progress, because it will keep them motivated and committed to the goals of the project. You should start off every project team meeting with an updated status and also note any progress on the project schedule. Report to the team when milestones are met or deliverables are completed. You might want to consider having celebrations when important milestones or deliverables are met to keep the team motivated and get them focused and enthused about the next set of deliverables.

Project Status Report

I. General Information

Project name:_____   Project number:_____

Project Manager name:_____   Report period ending:_____

II. Progress Made Since Last Reporting Period

III. Scheduled and Actual Completion Dates

IV. Progress Expected This Reporting Period Not Completed

V. Progress Expected Next Reporting Period

VI. Issues

You can also download the project status report at www.sybex.com/go/
projectmanagementjumpstart3.

NOTE

Consider keeping a copy of the project schedule in a place where the team
can see the progress that's being made. As tasks are completed, check them off
or highlight them. You could use the network diagram to note progress as well.
Tape up a copy on the wall in the project team meeting room. Everyone can see
the progress at a glance as you check the boxes on the network diagram that
have been completed.

I recommend adding one additional report to your status updates when reporting at project team meetings and stakeholder status meetings called Action Items.
These are issues, problems, or questions that need to be researched and resolved.
Track action items and report on them at every meeting. Let those who are
responsible for action items know that you're going to ask for the status of their
action items at the meeting (or before). This report should contain the elements
shown in the following graphic:

Action Item Log

I. General Information

Project name:_____   Project number:_____
Project Manager name:_____

II. Action Item Log

ID:	Date reported:	Action item:	Assigned to:	Date resolved:

───── *NOTE* ─────
You can also download the action item log at www.sybex.com/go/ projectmanagementjumpstart3.

As your action items are resolved, roll them off this report onto a separate list to keep for reference purposes. I like to keep resolved items on the current status report for two weeks (or two reporting periods) and then roll them off to an archived list. As always, keep a copy of the action item log with your project documents. This can be a great tool to use for future projects when you're identifying constraints, risks, and tasks.

Stakeholder Status Meetings

You'll want to hold status meetings with the key stakeholders, sponsor, and customers on a regular basis as well with your project team. Set up your stakeholder status meetings at regularly scheduled times, just like the project meetings. Send out an agenda before every meeting. What you report during these meetings depends on the complexity of the project and the makeup of your stakeholder group. At a minimum, you'll want to report on the following project items:

- Project status, as shown in the graphics you saw earlier in this section
- Schedule updates, including changes
- Milestone achievements
- Budget expenditures and budget status
- Change requests this period
- Major issues that could impede progress of the project

You could use the status report template in this section to report to the stakeholders if the project is small in size. Otherwise, you could use a milestone chart like the one we talked about in Chapter 5, "Breaking Down the Project Activities." This shows the progress of the milestone delivery dates and shows, at least in a high-level view, whether the project is progressing as expected.

Leave time at the end of the meeting for questions. If you don't know the answers, don't bluff. Let them know you'll research the answer and get back to them, and then follow through.

Taking Corrective Action

corrective action
Any action taken to ensure that the product of the project meets the requirements of the project as described in the scope document.

One of the functions of the Executing process of the project is taking corrective action. Things do go wrong on the project, and it's the job of the project manager to take the right actions to keep the project on track. *Corrective action* includes any actions taken to keep the project in line with the project plan. These might include reducing the scope, changing the schedule, adding or reassigning resources, and other similar actions.

Perhaps you're working on a project that requires parts for the hardware you're building to be manufactured to certain specifications. When the first shipment of parts arrives, you discover that they're a half an inch too small. You notify the vendor of the problem and ask them to correct the process and send new parts in the specified size. Another example of a corrective action might include rearranging equipment delivery dates so that the project tasks stay on schedule. Any action you take to keep the project on track with the project plan is a corrective action.

Corrective actions are outputs of the Monitoring and Controlling process (which comes after the Executing process), but remember that they're inputs into the Executing process because once you decide on the corrective action, you have to execute that action. We'll talk about the Monitoring and Controlling processes in the next chapter.

Terms to Know

conflict of interest	intrinsic motivators
corrective action	mediator
extrinsic motivators	

Review Questions

1. Name the five stages of team development.

2. At what stage of team development do team members struggle with conflicts and questions regarding their position or status on the team?

3. What are some of the things you can do to prepare for conflict-resolution meetings?

4. What are the six approaches to problem solving, and which one should project manager's use most often?

5. Describe the two types of motivators.

6. Why is it important to link the reward to performance and to make the reward realistic?

7. Which of the four types of leadership power is a result of a person's specialized knowledge or abilities?

8. Suppose you're in the midst of receiving bids for work on an upcoming project. Your favorite vendor contact, whom you've used many times in the past, offers you and your family tickets to box seats at the upcoming ball game. The box seats include a catered dinner. You decline, explaining to the vendor that this could be construed as what?

9. What types of project information will stakeholders normally want updates on during the course of the project?

10. Corrective actions are an output of what project process?

Chapter 11

Controlling the Project Outcome

We'll spend a good deal of this chapter discussing project changes, how to manage change, and how to assess the impacts of change. The change control process kicks in during the Monitoring and Controlling process of a project. Remember that change can also occur during the Planning and Executing processes, as mentioned in previous chapters. For clarity's sake, we'll cover all the change processes here.

Change can have positive or negative effects on your project, and it's important that you understand how to handle the change, what it means to the progress of the project, and how to communicate the change to the project team while maintaining their enthusiasm and focus on the project goals.

This chapter will also look at performance-monitoring techniques to determine whether the project is on track with the plan. We'll wrap up with a section on the warning signs of a project in trouble.

Change Happens

There's an old saying that says nothing is certain but change. This definitely applies to your projects. I've never had the experience of working on a project that went from Initiating to Closing according to the original project plan without making any changes. You need to be flexible when dealing with change, communicate the change properly, and know when to say no.

The Monitoring and Controlling process group is about managing change. As you progress through this process, the team members, stakeholders, and customers will request changes. You'll measure and inspect project performance, which may also turn up the need for change or require some action to get the project back on track. And change requests can occur regarding any aspect of the project including budget, scope, schedule, risk mitigation, corrective actions, and more. You'll want to manage all those changes in an integrated fashion so that all changes are reviewed, approved, implemented, and tracked in the same way. (We'll look at all the aspects of change management in the remainder of this section.) According to the *PMBOK Guide*, these are the key elements you'll want to focus on when performing change control:

- Influencing the factors that cause change control processes to be circumvented
- Promptly reviewing and analyzing change requests
- Managing approved changes
- Maintaining the integrity of the project baselines (including scope, quality, schedule, cost, and performance measurement baseline) and incorporating approved changes into the project management plan and other project documents
- Promptly reviewing and analyzing corrective and preventive actions
- Coordinating and managing changes across the project
- Documenting requested changes and their impacts

We'll discuss each of these activities later in this section and the next. But first let's take a closer look at how changes come about on projects. If you understand how or why changes come about, it will help you come up with good change control procedures to manage the process, which we'll cover in the next section.

How Changes Come About

Changes occur for many reasons. Some changes are requested by stakeholders and team members, and others come about as a result of measurements and inspections performed during the course of the project. Here are some of the ways that changes may occur on the project. This isn't an exhaustive list, but it should get you thinking about the ways changes occur so that you can then figure out how to deal with them when they do:

Stakeholder and Customer Requests   Stakeholders and customers may request changes to the requirements of the project, they may ask for the project schedule to be shortened, they may add new deliverables, or they may have other requests that impact the project. Stakeholders and customers never seem to be short of ideas for project change.

Project Team Member Requests   As the project progresses, team members may recommend changes as they discover more efficient ways of doing the tasks. They may recommend ways to change the process to shorten the schedule or ways to combine tasks for better efficiency.

Key Members Leaving the Project   Team members who leave the project can cause changes to the project. Their expertise may be such that their departure will hold up the progress of the project until another expert can be hired or found. This requires a change to the project schedule.

Budget Cuts   Budget cuts mean the scope, schedule, resource allocation, or quality aspects of the project have to change.

Organizational Changes   Reorganizations and realignments of business units can bring about changes to the project as can mergers and acquisitions. These types of change usually delay the project schedule. New senior management personnel can also change the direction of the project. This one is even a potential project killer.

Measurement and Inspection   Errors discovered during inspection processes in the Monitoring and Controlling process will necessitate changes to correct the process and will impact the project. Variances in measurements, processes, or controls will likely force changes as well.

Indirect Changes   Changes may occur to the project indirectly as a result of implementing contingency plans or risk response plans. Also, be on the lookout for changes that team members make without telling you. They may be doing a favor for a stakeholder or end user and decide to make a change without telling anyone else. While you don't want to discourage good working relationships between the team and stakeholders, you do want to make sure that everyone knows and follows the established change control process. Undocumented changes can add up and eventually will impact the schedule or the budget.

Responding to Change

Many people do not like change. We all have different tolerances for change, and some adapt better than others. As a general rule, folks like the status quo. Keep this in mind when working with your project team regarding changes.

Change, whether its impacts are positive or negative, can have a demoralizing effect on the team. The last thing you want to have happen at this stage of the project is to kill the team's motivation.

Let your team members know that there is a process in place to document and approve changes and that only valid changes will be approved, because they want to be assured that you're not going to jump every time someone suggests a change and derail their hard work. Be certain to document the justification for the change and share that with the team. Team members should clearly understand the need for the change and how it's going to be implemented and incorporated into the project. But if changes keep coming their way without any communication from you, they may throw up their hands and say, "What are we doing this for?" If they begin to feel that their efforts are in vain, they'll lose their motivation and will no longer maintain their commitment to the goals of the project. Remember those bad attitudes that we talked about? Here's where they'll really catch on and spread if you're not careful to communicate well with the team and support them.

NOTE
Honesty is the best policy when explaining changes to the team. Don't make the changes out to be worse than they really are, but don't keep bad news from the team either. They'll find out some other way, and then you'll have to deal with a loss of credibility as well as with the impact of the changes.

Explain the changes to the team in full detail and don't cover up unpleasant news. Help them understand the impact on the project and let them know you're in this with them to make it work. Include the team in the brainstorming sessions to work through alternatives to deal with the changes. Let them know that you support the changes and that you support their ideas as well. Then rally their support for the changes.

As the project manager, you'll want to keep change to a minimum whenever possible. We'll talk about how to assess the impacts of change later in this chapter. First, let's look at the mechanics of the change control process and how change requests are generated.

Establishing Change Management Control Procedures

Change control is an important process in the project life cycle. And change requests should come about in a formal manner. If you haven't done a good job establishing a change control process and communicating that process to the stakeholders and team members, you'll likely end up with email going directly to project team members asking for changes or stakeholders grabbing you in the hallway and asking for something "they must have" to consider the project successful.

Here's your first rule regarding change: Always require change requests in writing.

TIP

No one has a perfect memory. Undocumented changes can cause big conflicts. If you don't remember the change the way it was described or the stakeholders thought they said what they meant but that's not what the project team implements, you'll have even more setbacks and changes to deal with than the original requested change. Undocumented changes could end up affecting the project schedule or the product quality or costing the organization money or loss of business, so always get change requests in writing.

Change control procedures are normally documented during the Planning process and implemented during the Executing and Monitoring and Controlling processes. For the sake of clarity, I've included the change management process and change management plan in this chapter. I think it will be easier for you to see the logical progression of the change process if it's described all in one place.

Forming a Change Management Plan

A *change management plan* helps you accomplish three things:

change management plan
The plan that describes how change requests are submitted, reviewed, and approved or denied.

◆ It helps you understand what causes change to come about; we talked about that in the opening section.

◆ It helps you understand when or why a change is needed.

◆ It helps you manage the change by establishing procedures for change.

Good change management plans should describe such processes as submitting change requests, managing change requests, deciding who will review the change requests, and determining how they're approved. It's a good idea to provide users with forms for submitting change requests, because this will ensure that you capture all the information you need to make a decision regarding the change. (I'll give you an example change request template later in this chapter.)

Your organization may already have a change management process in place. If so, use the existing policies and modify them — with permission, of course — if you need a process that is specific to your project.

The following list shows most of the elements you should include in your change management plan. You could modify these for use as headings in the change management plan and then fill in the information according to your project needs or organizational policies:

◆ Where to obtain change request forms

◆ How change requests are submitted

◆ The person or team responsible for accepting change request forms for review

Also include a section that describes how the change control processes work. This should outline the following processes:

- How changes are approved
- How the preliminary review works
- How recommendations for approval, rejection, or delay are made
- How the change control board process works, their authority level, and their meeting dates
- Sign-off by the project manager and/or change control board

change control board
A group of individuals including the project manager and key stakeholders responsible for reviewing, approving, and denying change requests.

The change management plan should describe the level of authority needed to approve a change, as noted in the preceding list. Some change requests may be approved by the project manager, depending on the nature and size of the change and the organization's policies. Others need to go before a review committee, often called a *change control board* (discussed in the following section), that reviews and approves all changes outside the project manager's authority.

NOTE   Here is your second rule regarding change: All change requests must follow the change management process. They should be submitted according to the change management plan, approved or denied by the appropriate level of authority, and signed off. Changes that are not submitted according to the rules of the process are automatically denied.

It's important that stakeholders and team members follow the established change management process. Undocumented changes are also known as scope creep. As we've previously discussed, scope creep can get out of hand quickly, escalate the costs of the project, lengthen the project schedule, or distort the quality of the product. All of these things add up to an unsuccessful project. Projects that are unsuccessful because the project manager failed to implement processes and project plans foretell an unsuccessful project management career, so do everything you can to make sure these processes are followed.

The change management plan should be distributed to all key stakeholders, project team members, customers, vendors, and anyone else outlined in your communications plan who gets project information. File a copy of this plan in your project notebook as well.

Establishing a Change Control Board

The change control board consists of key stakeholders, the project manager, key project team members, and functional managers and customer representatives when appropriate. The purpose of the change control board is to review change requests and approve, reject, or delay them. The board's authority should be outlined in the project management plan, as mentioned earlier.

The change control board should meet at regularly established times. Their meeting schedule will depend on the project; once a week may be necessary for some projects, while once a month is enough for others. Establish the meeting schedule at the end of the Planning process, and start holding your meetings shortly after Executing begins.

Make certain there are procedures in place for emergency changes. If the change control board meets only once a month, for example, and the project manager has an issue that must be dealt with on the spot, procedures should be outlined in the change management plan that give the project manager the authority to make the change. After making the emergency change, the project manager should still submit the change request to the board as a formality to show that the change has occurred, to log the change, and to include documentation of the change with the project information.

There are several ways to administer the change process and deliver change requests to the change control board. Your procedures may require that all changes go through a preliminary review by the project manager so that a high-level impact analysis can be recorded right on the change request form. After the high-level impact analysis is completed, the change control board reviews the change request and makes their decision. Alternatively, large projects may have a full-time change manager who reviews all change requests and is responsible for the first level of approval before the change request goes to the change control board. Requests denied by the change manager go no further. Or the change control board may review all change requests first. Those they think have potential to improve the product or project processes are given to the project manager to perform an impact analysis. The project manager turns in the impact analysis at the next change control board meeting, where a final decision is made. Yet another method is for the project team to review all change requests and only those recommended for approval will go to the change control board. Again, the change management plan should outline your procedure, including when and how impact analysis should be performed. (We'll get to impact analysis later in this chapter.)

Tracking Changes

Change control procedures should include a tracking system to track the date the change was requested, the status of the change, and the approval status. This could be a simple change log or spreadsheet like the one shown in Table 11.1. This example shows a sample portion of a change control log for a software development project.

Table 11.1 Change control log

Project name:						
Project number:						
Project Manager's name:						
ID	Change request description	Submit date	Status	Approve/ reject/delay date	Implement date	
1	Add new edit module to accounting program.	1/20	Researching schedule and resource impacts	Pending		
2	Change the content of the audit report in the accounting program.	1/30	Approved	2/03	2/10	

Use this log at your change control board meetings to keep track of change requests and their status. The meetings shouldn't take long because your only purpose is to discuss changes. If you're working on large projects, the meetings may get more involved. But if they're getting too lengthy, consider having them more often. The control board meeting agenda looks something like this:

1. Review outstanding change requests.

2. Discuss impacts and benefits of the changes.

3. Approve or deny the changes.

4. Review progress of changes previously approved.

All approved change requests should be signed by a member of the change control board. This gives you the authority to implement the change or to file the denied change request in the project notebook.

After the change meeting, you'll communicate the disposition of the changes to the project team and modify the project plans to include the approved change. Changes to the scope, the project schedule, the quality, or the budget will require updates to these project plans. Don't forget to submit the modified project plans to the key stakeholders and project sponsor for signatures when the changes are significant in nature.

Assessing the Impacts of Change

Once a change has been requested, at some point in the process someone is going to ask you what the impact of the change is on the project. You'll be required to assess the impact of the change and report on the impacts it will have on the various project plans. Changes will almost always affect at least one of the following, if not several of the following:

◆ Scope

◆ Project schedule

◆ Budget

◆ Resource requirements

◆ Quality

◆ Risk response plans

Here's the third rule of change: Budget changes almost always require changes to the project schedule, scope, or quality, or a combination of the three. Schedule changes almost always require changes to the budget, scope, or quality, or a combination of the three. Scope changes almost always require changes to the project schedule and may require changes to the budget, or quality, or any combination of the three.

NOTE

Keep in mind that just because a change is requested doesn't mean it has to be implemented. That's one of the reasons you go through the effort to create a scope statement. Perhaps your stakeholders are asking for a change that is out of scope for the project and is recorded as an out-of-scope requirement in the scope statement document. You can remind them, by showing them a signed copy of the scope statement if needed, that their request is documented as out of scope for this project.

Remember that time equals money, so even if the change doesn't impact the budget directly but it impacts the time required to complete the tasks, it still indirectly impacts the cost of the project. If all your project team members are on staff and the tasks take longer than originally planned, their salaries are charged to the work of the project longer than originally planned, so indirectly the cost of the project has risen. And the end product doesn't reach the customer, or the marketplace, until the delayed completion date, which means that the ability of the company to collect revenue on the product of the project is delayed.

Calling in Reinforcements

Your first step in examining how changes will impact the project is to get the project planning documents together. You begin by reviewing the change requested against the associated planning documents. The impact of some changes will be obvious. Start by noting those changes, and ask yourself how they may impact other parts of the project that are not so obvious.

Use some of the techniques we discussed in previous chapters such as brainstorming to come up with ideas, impacts, and all the project areas that may be affected. Involve stakeholders and project team members to help you uncover all the possible impacts of change and any risks associated with the change.

Usually you'll find that change requests fall into one of three areas: scope change, schedule change, or budget change. We'll look at these categories of change to see how changes in these areas may impact the project, how to assess their impact, and how to make adjustments to accommodate the changes.

Three questions should be examined for each of the changes we'll discuss:

◆ Why is the change needed?

◆ What will be the impact on the project or product of the project if the change is not implemented?

◆ Are there alternatives to the change?

Start examining how the change affects the project by asking these three questions. The third question should be examined by the project team to determine whether there are ways to accommodate the results of the change while reducing the impact or coming up with other ways to get the same results.

Adjusting for Scope and Schedule Changes

Scope changes are probably the most frequent type of change requested on a project. In this section, we'll look at how scope changes are requested, what questions to ask to help you assess their impact, and how they affect the schedule. Remember that scope changes always require schedule changes, so we'll cover both of those types of changes here.

Scope changes include any changes to the deliverables or requirements of the project. Chapter 4, "Defining the Project Goals," discussed how any modification to the agreed-upon WBS is considered a scope change. You'll recall that the WBS details the project deliverables, summary tasks, and tasks. Therefore, changes to any of these items constitute a change in scope.

First, let's look at how scope changes are requested and what types of information you need to assess their impact. The following shows a sample change request form. Your project team or stakeholders can use this template to request any type of change, including scope changes. We've already discussed most of the elements on this form. Each heading has a brief explanation beneath it describing the kinds of information the requestor and project manager should provide.

```
                              Change Request Form

  I. General Information

  Project name:_____     Project number:_____
  Requestor name:_____   Requestor's contact information: _____   Date of request:_____
  Change request tracking number:_____   Date request approved/denied:_____

  Section One—To Be Completed by the Requestor

  II. Description of Change Request    Include a detailed description of the requested scope change.


  III. Business Justification for Change   Describe how the business, project, or product will benefit from the
                                           requested change.

  IV. Impacts of Not Making the Change   Describe how the business, project, or product will be impacted if the
                                         change is not made.

  V. Alternatives to Change            Describe any known alternatives to the change.


  Section Two—To Be Completed by the Project Manager

  VI. Impacts of the Change       Describe the impacts of this change to the project schedule, budget, and quality.


  VII. Alternatives to Change    Describe alternative solutions to the change.


  VIII. Recommendation to the    Describe the project manager's recommendation to approve or
        Change Control Board     deny the change. Include justification for the recommendation.

  Section Three—To Be Completed by the Change Control Board

  Recommendation:     Include a discussion concerning the goals of the project. Does this change significantly
  Date of Review:     impact the goals of the project such that the project goals can no longer be met?
                      Should this change be considered a new project or phase two of the existing project, etc.?

  Signature:
```

NOTE   **You can also download the change request form template at** www.sybex.com/
go/projectmanagementjumpstart3.

Modify this template for use on your projects. And don't forget to post these
to your project site on the network. I recommend creating a directory just for
change requests and the change request-tracking log. Be sure to note the tracking number from the change request log on the top of this form.

Modifying the Scope and Schedule

When the scope change is approved, you'll need to adjust the project schedule
and budget to accommodate the change. Remember that changes to scope
always require changes to the project schedule. To do this, you'll need to assess
how the changes affect the project and what adjustments you need to make to
accommodate the changes. Things you can do to help make adjustments for
scope and schedule changes include the following. Keep in mind that many of
these items were probably already documented in the change request.

◆ Ask functional managers for suggestions and assistance with changes.

◆ Examine resource allocation and ask for more resources — human and
equipment — to meet the new requirements and dates.

◆ Determine whether working overtime is an option for existing team
members to meet new requirements and dates.

◆ Examine vendor options. Are there services you can purchase or parts
you can buy that the team was originally going to produce, or can you
outsource some of the deliverables to the vendor to complete?

◆ Reduce the project scope to accommodate schedule changes, including
modifying goals and deliverables.

◆ Move some deliverables to the second phase of the project to accommodate schedule changes.

Once the changes have been approved, the project manager should adjust
the project schedule to account for the changes. Communicate those changes
— including new tasks, new due dates, modified tasks or dates, and so on — to
the project team members. Discuss scope and schedule changes as part of your
regular team meetings.

Adjusting the Project Schedule

Sometimes you'll be asked to shorten the project schedule even after it's been
approved and the Executing process has begun. Reasons for this new urgency
may include a new marketing opportunity, the sponsor's fear of a budget cut
before the project can be completed, or a scope change that may require shortening the schedule.

There are two techniques for shortening, or compressing, the schedule. The first is called *fast tracking*. As an example, let's say that the team writing the technical users guide for a software programming project starts writing the manual at the same time the testing team is testing the modules. Originally, the writers were not going to start until the testing phase was complete, but by starting the two activities at the same time, the schedule is shortened. This technique can also be applied to project phases. For example, the construction industry sometimes uses a "design-build" approach to shorten the overall length of a project. In this example, the design phase of the project overlaps the building phase. That means as soon as a portion of the design is finished, the building phase begins, even though design isn't completely finished.

The second technique for shortening the schedule is called *crashing*. Crashing is a technique that weighs cost and schedule trade-offs. For example, you may consider adding resources to the critical-path tasks to crash the schedule. Adding resources will shorten the amount of time needed to complete these tasks. (Remember that adding resources to the non-critical-path tasks won't help because non-critical-path tasks don't impact the schedule.) Another technique of crashing is limiting or reducing the project requirements. This will also sometimes shorten the project schedule if the tasks related to these requirements are on the critical path.

The primary goal behind schedule crashing is to gain the greatest schedule compression with the least cost.

Crashing isn't always an option, because the results may negatively impact the project. Always check the critical path after using this technique because the critical path may change. You may have some tasks drop off the critical path while others that were not critical are now considered critical. Fast tracking doesn't always work either. There is often a reason for tasks starting one after another, especially for quality control or completeness of the product.

fast tracking
A schedule compression technique that overlaps project processes or starts two tasks at the same time that were originally scheduled to start sequentially.

crashing
A schedule compression technique that examines ways to reduce the duration of critical-path tasks.

TIP

Managing and Revising Costs

Changes to the budget come about for several reasons, including incorrect estimating techniques, schedule overruns, and inadequate WBS development. These items are within your control as the project manager, and they underscore the importance of proper project Planning techniques.

Budget changes that come about because of circumstances you can't control include the schedule and scope changes we discussed in the previous section, fixed budgets that are set from the beginning of the project, and corrective actions taken to get the project back in line with the project plan. All of these conditions may lead to budget revisions.

The first step in adjusting the budget is to determine the revised cost estimates. Review the original estimates, and confirm your assumptions regarding those estimates. Realize that the product or service you planned to purchase may have changed, been upgraded, or been modified somehow, which affects the original estimate and the cost of the product today. If you're bringing in new resources or materials that weren't previously included in the budget plan, you need to acquire estimates for those items and include them in the updated budget.

Next, you must update the budget with the new costs. Include narrative information that describes why the updates or additions are necessary, and note the change request tracking number associated with the budget update. Get approval of the updated budget from the project sponsor, and distribute copies of the new budget to the appropriate folks.

Monitoring and Controlling Project Processes

The Monitoring and Controlling process group involves monitoring the project outcomes to make certain that they're in keeping with the project plans and that the project continues according to the plan throughout the life of the project. This includes managing and controlling change (as we've already discussed), measuring and inspecting the project performance for adherence to the project plans, taking action to get the project back on track when variances occur, and evaluating the effectiveness of corrective actions.

Successful projects are those that fulfill the requirements of the project to the stakeholders' satisfaction while keeping the project on time and on budget. To maintain the schedule and the budget, you'll have to monitor the performance of the project. We've already discussed managing change; now we'll look at how you'll measure outcomes and control performance.

As you might imagine, there are several ways to monitor the performance of the project. Communication between you and the project team is certainly one of your best defenses against unforeseen problems or problems running out of control. There are other tools and techniques you can use as well to monitor project outcomes, and we'll look at those in this section.

Obviously, the project plan will serve as your measurement baseline for all project performance. We've spent a great deal of time discussing the project plan and its importance, and it comes into play again in this process as our baseline for project performance. During the Monitoring and Controlling process, you'll regularly monitor the project's outcomes against the plan to make certain that everything progresses according to plan. The four things you'll monitor closely for performance during this process are the project schedule, budget, scope, and quality.

Performance-Reporting Tools

Several techniques are available that you can use to monitor project outcomes. We'll take a brief look at each of these techniques in this section. It's beyond the scope of this book to go into the details of these techniques, because many of them involve complex math calculations, graphs, and methods that are at an advanced level of project management. If you're interested in further study, several books on the market deal with these techniques.

Monitoring project outcomes and taking measurements occurs during the Monitoring and Controlling process. However, you should establish what to measure, how to measure, and what project outcomes to monitor during the Planning process of the project. If you have waited until the Monitoring and Controlling process to determine what to measure, you may be too late; you could end up measuring on the fly and producing results with little value or meaning. Or you may have already missed opportunities to correct poor project performance because some of the work is already completed.

NOTE

Status Review Meetings Project status meetings allow you to collect information from the project team members regarding progress. We discussed status review meetings in Chapter 10, "Executing the Project." Don't forget to visit informally with your team members as well to maintain up-to-date information on project performance.

Variance Analysis This technique compares the expected project plan results with the actual results to determine whether variances exist. You'll use this technique primarily to determine schedule variances, budget variances, and quality variances. Variance analysis can be used for risks, scope, and performance specification measurements as well.

Trend Analysis Trend analysis involves analyzing project results periodically to determine whether the project performance is improving or getting worse. Mathematical formulas are used in this technique to forecast project outcomes based on historical information.

Earned Value Analysis Earned value analysis is the technique used most often to determine project performance. Earned value is unique because it calculates cost, schedule, and scope measurements together to determine various indexes, performance measures, and variances. Several formulas and measurements are used in this technique to determine the forecasted costs of the project at completion, the actual costs of the project to date versus what was budgeted, schedule variances, performance indexes, and so on. There are entire books available on this technique alone.

Inspection Inspection is most often used in quality control. This involves physically looking at the results and measuring them or testing them to determine whether the results meet the requirements or quality standards outlined in the plan.

Control Charts Control charts are used to measure and plot the results of processes over time. You can measure and display variances, track measurements, compare variables, and so on. There are several forms of control charts, including variance control charts, flowcharts, Pareto diagrams, scatter diagrams, and numerous industry-specific controls.

The goal of gathering data and measuring the results is to control the project outcomes so that they conform to the requirements and so that the project process conforms to the project plan. When you've taken some of these measurements and determined that variances do exist, you'll need to take corrective action to put the project back on track.

corrective actions
Actions taken to align project performance with the project plan.

Corrective actions involve a variety of options and depend on the project and the problem you've encountered. For example, say you've performed some variance analysis on your project schedule. Prior to conducting the analysis, you determined that the control limit for schedule variances for this project is 10 days. If schedule variances are less than 10 days, no action is needed. If you discover that the variances are greater than 10 days, you'll have to take action to get the project performance back in line with the plan so that the variances are minimized or eliminated. You could add resources to the project, move some deliverables to the second phase, eliminate some of the requirements and the tasks associated with them, and so on, to get the schedule back on track. Remember that updates to the project's Planning documents will be required when corrective actions are taken.

NOTE

After you've taken corrective action, it's important to measure the results to make certain that the action was effective and that you're getting the outcome you planned.

The project's Planning, Executing, and Monitoring and Controlling processes are revisited several times throughout the project. Updates to the plan require the execution of the new plans. Controls and corrective actions require changes to the plan that require new tasks to be carried out and measured against the plan. Corrective actions may not always require new project plan updates, but they will require a trip back through the Executing process as the corrective actions are put into place.

Not all projects require formal measurement techniques. However, the most important Monitoring and Controlling technique you can use is to regularly gather information regarding the project status, meet with team members formally and informally, and remain aware of all the activity on your project. This all goes back to communication. Taking an active role in knowing where the project is compared to the project schedule and other project plans is your best defense against project problems taking you by surprise.

Risk Monitoring

Another important part of the Monitoring and Controlling process is monitoring the project for the occurrence of potential risk events. (We identified risks and developed risk response plans in Chapter 7, "Assessing Risk.") Schedule periodic reviews to check the risks identified in the risk plan and reexamine their impacts. Monitor the risks and their status to determine whether the impacts you identified in the risk response plan are still realistic. It could be that some of the risk events now have reduced impacts while others have increased impacts.

Be on the alert throughout the Monitoring and Controlling process for risk events. Actively review all the identified risks, and remind your project team members to keep you informed of any risk triggers.

TIP

New risks might come to light as a result of measuring and monitoring project performance. When this occurs, document the risks in the risk plan and create response plans for them. Remember to update the existing risk response plan with the newly created responses.

Is the Project in Trouble?

Not only is change a guarantee on your next project, so are problems. Problems aren't always bad, and they don't always mean an end to life as you know it. But if you aren't careful, problems can quickly get out of control and wreak havoc on your project. The monitoring process we discussed, in which you put on your eagle eyes and watch for every sign that something may be amiss, is one way to determine whether problems are about to get out of control. Monitoring and controlling project changes will also keep problems at a manageable level.

Unfortunately, there are times when schedules or budgets or key personnel do run amuck and the damage to the project is not repairable. This section should alert you to some of the warning signs that the project is headed the wrong way down a one-way street. If you recognize these signs early enough and deal with them correctly, you may avert a head-on collision with an unsuccessful project.

Just Say No

Before we look at some of those early warning signs, let's talk about flatlined projects. Sometimes it's time to pack up the project management tool bag and go home. You and the team have put a lot of time and effort into the project, but it is so far out of control that there's no coming back. When that's the case, sometimes the best call to make is to end the project.

Most of the factors that will cause the project to get to this point are the same as the warning signs we'll cover next. If you've done a good job creating the project plan, communicating with stakeholders and the project team, and monitoring and controlling the performance of the project, you have nothing to be ashamed of. Sometimes projects end on their own accord; they outlive their usefulness, and the organization drops interest in the project. Other times projects are killed by overzealous stakeholders attempting to make a career-boosting move that will propel them into the Big Boss seat.

Let's take a look at some of the other warning signs of project problems that could become project killers.

Early Warning Signs

Lest I sound redundant, you've seen many of these signs before. I just want one last chance to tell you how important it is to keep your eyes peeled for these signs. It's not unusual for seasoned project managers to have a failed project or two under their belt, but projects that fail as a result of the project manager's error, lack of preparation, or oversight are not going to win you that promotion to the project management director's position anytime soon. Here we go:

Poor Planning Techniques Are Starting to Influence the Scope, Schedule, Quality, or Budget of the Project   How many more ways can this one be said? The better your project planning skills and the better your documentation, the easier it will be to manage your project and the higher the chances of completing a successful project. Poor project planning techniques are a sure indicator of an unsuccessful project.

You and Your Team Start Telling Key Stakeholders What They Want to Hear Instead of the True Project Status and Issues   Never tell the sponsor and the key stakeholders only what they want to hear. This is a sure sign the project is headed for disaster. They might not want to know about the problems and want only the good stuff reported to them, but it's your job to tell them anyway. If you don't inform them of problems and issues, they'll make you the scapegoat when it all crashes in, and I think you know what happens after that.

People Don't Know What's Going On, They Don't Understand Their Jobs or Deliverables, and Rumors Are Spreading   Communicate well and communicate the right information to the right people. Be an active listener, watch for nonverbal cues, and let the sponsor and key stakeholders know about important project information almost as soon as you learn it yourself. Many times they can help you resolve problems in ways you wouldn't have thought about. And don't forget the honesty factor: Tell them the truth, even if it hurts. They can't help you resolve problems they aren't fully informed about.

The Project Started Late But Is Still Expected to Finish on Time   This can cause problems later in the project. Delayed starts aren't uncommon because key personnel may not be ready for the new assignments, the budget may not receive approval prior to the planned start date, and so on. If no schedule changes are permitted, use some of the techniques we discussed earlier such as crashing and reducing scope to help meet the project schedule.

Budget Cuts Are Impacting the Project Dramatically   This can be a sure project killer. This might be one of those situations where it's time to pack up and call it quits. But don't come to that conclusion too quickly. Assess the impact on the scope and schedule and see whether there are ways to work within the new limits. If not, just say no. Let the sponsor and stakeholders know that it's not possible to complete the project with the existing requirements with the budget cuts they've proposed.

The Team Is Starting to Lag Behind Due to Poor Duration Estimates or Lack of Skill, or They're Motivated and Committed But Don't Possess the Skills Needed to Do the Work of the Project   Consider hiring subject-matter experts to help with the lack of skills problem, and encourage these experts to mentor your team members. If poor duration estimates are the problem, consider having the estimates examined by a third party or a knowledgeable expert from another department before using the estimates to complete the project schedule. If you're already in the midst of a project with this problem, consider changing the project priorities, asking for more resources, or requiring overtime to catch up with the schedule. This is another problem area where you may reach a point of no return. If it becomes evident that the team has taken on more than they're capable of, you'll need to be honest and inform the sponsor that the existing team isn't going to be able to complete the project.

Your Team Members Start Regularly Stating, "I'm Almost Finished"   This is an award-winning line in the information technology industry. There is no good way to measure how far along a programming task has progressed, so you have to rely on the lead programmers to judge (by their experience) how close they think they or their team members are to completing the task. The problem comes when you've heard this statement for the past six weeks from the same team member. The only way out of this one is to communicate and stress the importance of honest reporting.

You Have Too Many Changes   Too many changes can cause the project to end up very differently from what it started out as. Manage changes and stick to the agreed-upon scope of the project, as discussed in the previous section.

You and Your Team Realize That the Project Should Never Have Been Started in the First Place   The objectives are beyond the ability of the project team to perform, the time expectations are unrealistic, or the budget is unrealistic. When you know this up front, inform the sponsor and decline to manage the project if they aren't willing to work with you to correct the problems. If you don't realize this until later, you'll have to document your findings and recommend to the sponsor shutting down the project.

Stay informed of problems and meet them head on when they occur. Remember to keep the sponsor and key stakeholders informed, because they will often be able to help you resolve problems or obtain resources that are outside your authority.

Terms to Know

change control board   crashing

change management plan   fast tracking

corrective actions

Review Questions

1. Name three ways that change comes about on projects.

2. Why should change requests be submitted in writing?

3. What is the purpose of a change management plan, and when in the project life cycle should it be created?

4. What types of information should be included in the change management plan?

5. What is the purpose of a change control board?

6. Scope changes always require changes to what other Planning document?

7. Name two options you can examine when faced with scope or schedule changes.

8. Name the two schedule compression techniques.

9. What is fast tracking?

10. What is the most important Monitoring and Controlling technique you can use when monitoring the performance of the project?

Chapter 12

Closing the Books

Congratulations! You've made it to the end of the project, the stake-holders are ecstatic, and you've received great praise for a job well done. Now it's time to kick back, put your feet up, and relax — right?

Not quite yet. Even though the work of the project is finished, your job isn't over yet. The Closing process of the project life cycle involves closing out the books, paying the vendors, documenting the final project outcomes, and evaluating the project. During this process, you will examine all the things that went right and all the things that didn't go quite so right on the project, learn from those things, and document them. All the documents you created on this project will serve as a reference for your next project.

Happy Endings

I don't know about you, but I like happy endings. When I'm closing in on the last chapter or two of the novel I'm reading, I want things to work out. I want the guy to get the girl, I want the bad guy to get caught, and I want the revenge to be sweet. I feel the same way about my project endings. Especially the revenge part...all those stakeholders who thought the project would never be successful. Ha! We fooled them. Oh...um...back to project closeout.

We started off our study of project management by stating that a project is considered successful when it meets or exceeds the stakeholders' expectations. This means the deliverables have been completed, the requirements have been met, and the budget and schedule have been followed closely throughout the project. It also means you've applied good project management techniques and communicated with the stakeholders throughout the process.

Everything we've talked about up until this point will help you meet or exceed customer expectations at the end of your project. As we've stated many times, project planning and communication are the two biggest allies you have in your camp. When you fight the daily project management battles with a good plan as your foundation and you have the ability to communicate honestly and can resolve conflict, you can conquer the world. (OK, maybe not the world, but certainly your next project!)

Details, Details

project approval
Verification and formal acceptance of the product or service of the project.

The Closing process is often hurried through at best or skipped altogether. Closing has several purposes that will help you on your next project. Here you'll get formal *project approval* of the product or service of the project, close out the contracts, pay the vendors, and close out the financial records for this project. You'll file away the project documentation for future reference and take some lessons learned from this project with you to the next project. You'll also take one last look back and examine the work of the project and make sure everything is complete.

Remember the checklist we started with in Chapter 1, "Building the Foundation"? Table 12.1 shows an updated version of that checklist, with some new items added that you've learned about throughout the course of this book. Use this checklist to help you manage your next project through the project life-cycle phases.

NOTE   **You can also download the project process checklist at** www.sybex.com/go/
projectmanagementjumpstart3.

Table 12.1   Project process checklist

Project name:						
Project number:						
Project Manager's name:						
Complete	**Process or document name**	**Responsibility**	**Notes**	**Project life cycle**		
☐	Project charter	Project sponsor	Describes project purpose, business justification, and outcomes.	Initiation		
☐	Cost-benefit analysis	Project manager with input from stakeholders	Determines whether project is financially (or otherwise) beneficial to the organization. Included in the project charter and project scope statement.	Planning		
☐	Assumptions and constraints	Project manager with input from stakeholders	Describes project assumptions and any constraints limiting the project team. Included in the project scope statement.	Planning		
☐	Project scope statement	Project manager with input from stakeholders	Describes project goals, contains a comprehensive list of deliverables, and describes the specific requirements of the product, service, or result of the project. Signed by project sponsor, project manager, and stakeholders.	Planning		

Table 12.1 Project process checklist *(continued)*

Complete	Process or document name	Responsibility	Notes	Project life cycle
☐	Critical success factors	Project manager with input from stakeholders	Describes those things that must be completed accurately in order to consider the project a success. These may include project deliverables or requirements. Can be included with the project scope statement.	Planning
☐	Communications plan	Project manager	Describes the information needs of stakeholders and the project team and how the information is distributed.	Planning
☐	Work breakdown structure (WBS)	Project manager	Formatted as a deliverables-oriented hierarchy that defines the work of the project.	Planning
☐	Responsibility assignment matrix	Project manager	Ties roles and responsibilities of project team members with WBS elements.	Planning
☐	Resource plan	Project manager	Describes physical resources and human resources needed to complete the project.	Planning
☐	Procurement plan	Project manager and/or procurement department	Describes resources or services to be purchased from an outside provider.	Planning

Complete	Process or document name	Responsibility	Notes	Project life cycle
☐	Risk management plan	Project manager with input from stakeholders, risk analysis team, and project team members	Identifies, describes, ranks, and plans for project risks. Includes risk response plans for high-ranking risks.	Planning
☐	Quality plan	Project manager and/or quality team	Describes how quality will be assured and measured.	Planning
☐	Project schedule	Project manager	Displays task dependencies, task durations, and milestones. Used to determine the critical path.	Planning
☐	Project budget	Project manager and/or finance manager	Determines targeted costs of the project.	Planning
☐	Project team kick-off meeting	Project manager	Assigns all team members to their responsibilities.	Executing
☐	Status meetings and status reports	Project manager	Provides updates regarding project progress, issues, change requests, and more to stakeholders and team members.	Executing, and Monitoring and Controlling
☐	Change management plan	Project manager and change control board	Describes how changes to the project plan will be identified and managed.	Planning, and used in Monitoring and Controlling

Table 12.1   Project process checklist (*continued*)

Complete	Process or document name	Responsibility	Notes	Project life cycle
☐	Monitoring project performance and taking corrective action	Project manager	Oversees project performance. May require updates to project Planning documents.	Monitoring and Controlling
☐	Closing the accounting records and finalizing the contracts	Project manager and finance manager	Project manager notifies finance manager to close all project accounts so that no more charges are incurred against the project budget.	Closing
☐	Implementation checklist	Project manager	Describes issues to be discussed or information to be turned over regarding the product, service, or result of the project to internal departments or the customer.	Closing
☐	Lessons learned document	Project manager with input from stakeholders and team members	Documents processes, plans, communications, and so on, that worked well. Also documents things that did not work well so that they will not be repeated in future projects and, if practical, integrates them into the standard company project management processes or templates.	Monitoring and Controlling, and Closing
☐	Obtaining project sign-off and sending formal notice of closure	Project manager	Assures acceptance of the product, service, or result of the project and notifies all parties that the project is officially closed.	Closing

Complete	Process or document name	Responsibility	Notes	Project life cycle
☐	Project feedback	Project manager, stakeholders, and team members	Provides information to improve performance on future projects. Can be included in the lessons learned document.	Closing
☐	Archiving project documents	Project manager	Archives project records for future reference.	Closing
☐	Celebrating your success	Project manager and project team	Provides a means to publicly thank team members for their hard work and recognize success. Brings closure to the project and helps team members make the transition to new assignments.	Closing

This checklist shows the primary documents you're responsible for creating and the processes you'll follow throughout the project life cycle. All the Executing, Monitoring and Controlling, and Closing processes have now been added to the list. You can use this checklist template when starting your next project as a reminder of the important documents and activities you'll need to complete as you manage the project. You should periodically review this list throughout the project to make certain you've covered all the bases.

It also serves as a good reminder or reference for what's to come, so you should review the checklist as you approach the end of each life-cycle phase to remind yourself of what needs to happen during the next process. File this checklist in the front of the project notebook, and use it as an informal measure of your progress throughout the project by checking off each process as you complete it.

You can see from this checklist that we have several things left to complete in the Closing process. The first item we'll talk about is closing the accounts and finalizing the contracts. We'll deal with the remaining items throughout this chapter.

Closing the Accounts

When the project is completed, you'll want to make sure the accounts for the project are closed so that no more spending is charged against the project budget. Your accounting staff or finance manager usually does this. We talked about the unique account identifiers or codes associated with the WBS elements back in Chapter 5, "Breaking Down the Project Activities." These codes associate the accounts with the project budget and were used by the accounting office to track expenditures. When the finance manager closes the accounts, the codes are closed out also, and no additional charges will be approved against the project's code of accounts.

TIP — **Stop runaway charging and over-budget conditions by closing the project accounts when the work of the project is completed.**

If you're working on a small project, you're probably the only one approving orders and invoices, so you'll know when to stop charging items against the project budget. But large projects may have several approvers, or your finance manager may be the one who has managed the budget throughout the project. Make certain that you formally communicate to them that the project is over and the books should be closed out, so no more spending goes against your project.

Finalizing the Contracts

During the Closing process, contracts are finalized and closed out. When projects are completed under contract or you've used contract help to do the work of the project, you'll want to verify that the work of the contract was completed accurately and satisfactorily according to the terms of the contract prior to closing them out. Review the contract and the statement of work, and compare them against the project outcome to make certain that all the requirements have been fulfilled. This should be a fairly easy step because you would have monitored the work of the project and requested that the vendor make corrections when needed during the Monitoring and Controlling phase. Now you'll make one more pass through the SOW and make certain that none of the requirements has been missed.

One of the most important activities you'll fulfill during this process is the formal notification to the seller that the contract is complete and the product or service is satisfactory and accepted. This notification should be put in writing. If the product or service doesn't meet your expectations, inform the vendor that there are outstanding issues they need to resolve before you can issue a final acceptance notice. This usually happens in the Monitoring and Controlling process as you monitor and measure the project outcomes and at that time notify the vendor of problems. Sometimes, though, you don't have the final product until the Closing phase. If that's the case and the product isn't acceptable, let the vendor know as soon as possible.

Be aware that some contracts have specific conditions or terms that you must meet in order to close out the contract. Review the contract, or ask your procurement department to make you aware of these conditions, so that you can fulfill the requirements of closeout and don't hold up the project.

Breaking Up Is Hard to Do

As the project comes to a close, you'll release team members back to their functional duties or to assignments on other projects. This will likely happen slowly and may even begin in the Monitoring and Controlling phase as tasks are completed and approved.

This process involves good communication on your part. You'll want to keep the functional managers informed prior to the release of team members so that they have a chance to prepare for their return. If the team members are being released to another project, let the project manager know the dates the team members will be released. This gives the other managers time to plan activities and schedule due dates for activities for the new work. Start informing the managers about four to six weeks prior to the team members' release, and keep them posted as you approach the date for their return.

Watch for signs of project slowdown toward the end of the project. Team members may not want to move on to new assignments and will try to extend the fun on the current project by making up problems or delaying final due dates.

WARNING

Team members may begin to drag their feet as the end of the project approaches. Keep an eye out for this situation, especially with teams in the performing stage. They've formed friendships, are committed to the goals of the project, and are generally having a great deal of fun doing the work of the project. As the end approaches, they know that the camaraderie and the synergy they've created as a team are coming to an end. This may cause them to slow down their work in order to prolong the project and postpone their reassignment. Communicate openly with the team during this time, and let them know how valuable their work has been on this project. Assure them that their new assignments are important to the organization and that they'll have many opportunities to form relationships with their new team members. Remind them that they'll have a chance now to educate others in the organization on how good teams function and that they'll have the ability to help form great teams in other parts of the organization because of their experience on this team.

Prior to sending team members on their way, you should write up performance reviews and hold one-on-one meetings with each team member to discuss their performance on the project. These reviews will be given to their functional managers or to their new project managers and will become part of their overall performance rating for the year.

Training and Warranty Period

Have you ever brought home a new gadget or appliance you couldn't wait to try? It hums along fine the first day or two and then quits, right when you need it most. "Thank goodness for the warranty," you think. Project warranties work the same way.

warranty period
A period of time when the stakeholders can notify the team of problems and have them corrected immediately.

Some projects, particularly those in the information technology arena, require that some of the primary team members remain assigned to the team, or at a minimum are available for assistance, for a specified length of time after the project is completed and turned over to the customer. This time period is called the *warranty period*. (Some vendors offer warranty periods on their work as well.) It's inevitable that problems will creep up on newly written programs or newly installed hardware. The idea is, as the user works with the new programs or hardware, they can report problems to the team and have them addressed immediately during the warranty period. This is not a time for the team to work on additional features or enhancements. The warranty period is for bug fixes only, and once the warranty period expires, problems are prioritized and handled according to the organizational policies designed to handle day-to-day problems.

NOTE — If you don't establish a warranty period and the customer finds problems, it can be frustrating for them to have to wait for these problems to make it to the top of the priority list before being addressed. The warranty period gives them a buffer period when problems can be addressed as soon as they occur.

Some projects require training upon completion. If this is the case, the training activity is included as part of the overall project plan. Once training is completed, the product is turned over to the customer. Again, you might choose to institute a warranty period to answer training questions and issues as they come up.

Implementing the Project

At the end of the warranty period, it's time to turn the product of the project over to the customer. You'll want to make sure that all the processes are complete and the proper information is turned over to the customer. Table 12.2 shows a sample checklist that you can use at the end of the project to make certain that the product is ready to be delivered and the customer receives all the information they need regarding the product. As the project manager, you should verify that these items are complete and correct prior to delivering the product to the customer.

You can also download the implementation checklist at www.sybex.com/go/ projectmanagementjumpstart3.

NOTE

Table 12.2   Implementation checklist

Project name:		
Project number:		
Project Manager's name:		
Completed	**Description**	**Comments**
❏	Deliverables completed	
❏	Deliverables accepted and approved	
❏	Contracts closed out	
❏	Vendors paid	
❏	Customer training completed	
❏	Product documentation provided to customer	
❏	Warranty information given to customer	
❏	Contact information provided to customer	
❏	Final product delivered	

Documenting Lessons Learned

You're a lot smarter now that you've made it to the end of the project than you were before you started. You've learned some things simply by performing the project management practices throughout the project and watching the life-cycle processes play out. Now what you need to do, and should do throughout the project, is document those things you learned that will help you perform the next project more efficiently.

My dad, while giving me lecture number 343, would often tell me I was lucky to be able to benefit from his experience. He was happy to help me out by passing on valuable information so that I wouldn't have to "learn the hard way." It's taken me a while, but I've come to see the wisdom in this, especially in the project management field. Why should you repeat the same mistakes a former project manager made, or even ones you made in the past, when you can avoid them and have your next project run more smoothly than the last one?

lessons learned
The documented successes and failures of the project.

The *lessons learned* document contains information about all the project life-cycle processes but most important, the Executing and Monitoring and Controlling processes. These two processes are when the work of the project is performed and when you'll likely find mistakes that were made in the Planning documents or processes. Anything you discover that could have been clearer or any additional information that would have helped to avoid confusion should be noted here. Process improvements, communication glitches, or any other information that will help you perform the next project better should be noted here.

Ask your team members, stakeholders, and the project sponsor to help you compile the lessons learned document. Ask them what went well on the project and what could have gone better. Don't wait until the end of the project to start making notes, however. Start this document during the Executing phase and begin making notes to yourself as soon as problems occur. Document how the situation could have been handled differently to avoid these same types of problem on future projects. The following is the information you should include in your lessons learned document:

- How the project management processes were used throughout the project and how successful they were in planning and tracking progress

- How well the project plan and project schedule reflected the actual work of the project

- How well the change management process worked and what might have worked better

- Why corrective actions were taken and whether they were effective

- Causes of performance variances and how they could have been avoided

◆ Outcomes of corrective actions

◆ Risk response plans that were implemented and whether they adequately addressed the risk events

◆ Unplanned risk events that occurred

◆ Mistakes that occurred and how they could have been avoided

◆ Team dynamics, including what could have helped the team perform more efficiently

Don't limit your lessons learned document to only the items on this list. Anything that worked well, or didn't work well, that will help you perform your next project better or smooth out problems before they get out of hand should be documented here. That means positive and negative feedback. This process is particularly useful for failed projects, because there are many things you can learn from projects that fail that will help prevent your next project from suffering the same fate.

Many project managers skip this step because, let's face it, most of us don't like to admit our mistakes and we don't want others knowing that we made them. Encourage your team to be honest and forthcoming about their lessons learned. If you've spent the time throughout the project building their trust and creating an open atmosphere of communication, documenting lessons learned won't be that difficult. Assure your employees that this is for the benefit of future projects and is not a means to punish or judge their work. Establish some ground rules that say no one may blame someone else for anything that went wrong and that no names will be taken. Documenting lessons learned allows you to bring a wealth of knowledge to future projects, and you'll benefit by learning from past mistakes without having to repeat them.

The lessons learned document should get filed in the project notebook with all the other project information. This is one of the first documents you'll want to review when starting your next project.

Obtaining Project Sign-off

Now it's time to formalize project closure and obtain sign-off on the final product or service of the project. This process ensures that the customer and stakeholders have formally accepted the product by verifying that the outcomes meet all the requirements outlined in the project scope statement.

One way to obtain sign-off is to produce and distribute a final status report for the project that includes a section for acceptance signatures. The final status report looks different from the periodic status reports you've been producing all along. The final report should recap the goals of the project and detail the major milestones and deliverables accepted and completed.

A final status report template is shown in the following graphic. Use this template for your projects and modify it to meet the needs of your projects.

Final Status Report

I. General Information

Project name:_____   Project number:_____
Project Manager name:_____   Date of report:_____

II. Project Overview	Describe the final product or service of the project, the reason the project was undertaken, and the purpose of the project. Include a description of the business problem that was solved by implementing this project.

III. Project Goals and Objectives	Identify the goals that were met during this project and compare them to the goals on the scope statement.

IV. Project Deliverables and Milestones	Identify the major deliverables or milestones met, their due dates according to the final plan, their actual delivery dates, and stakeholder acceptance dates.

V. Project Budget	Give a final overview of the project budget and variances from the budget.

VI. Quality Assurance	Document acceptance of the quality criteria and inspections.

VII. Comments	Include any information that reminds stakeholders of agreements made concerning deliverables that were moved to phase two of the project, major problems that were encountered and how they were resolved, risk events that need further explanation, and so on.

VIII. Final Acceptance and Signatures	Provide a way for each stakeholder to indicate their acceptance of the project and sign their name.
Accept/Decline	Stakeholder name_____

The idea here is to provide a high-level overview of the project, including its successes and problems, and to note the dates when stakeholders accepted the key deliverables for the project. This report is for public consumption, so keep it honest but not brutally honest. If major problems occurred on the project because of certain stakeholders or team members who were particularly difficult to deal with, consider creating a confidential report or briefing to give to the project sponsor or appropriate executive managers. If other political hot potatoes arose during the project that you don't feel should be noted publicly in this status report, put them in the confidential report.

Once the stakeholders sign the acceptance document, the process concludes with a formal notice of the acceptance to the stakeholders, customers, and project sponsor. The project manager is responsible for distributing this last piece of communication. This notice should be written, dated, and sent according to the communications plan. If the project is internal to the organization, an email notification might work. If the project was completed on contract, I recommend sending formal notice through the post office the old-fashioned way. This is the last time you'll hear me say this: File the acceptance document in the project notebook.

You can also download the final status report template at www.sybex.com/go/ projectmanagementjumpstart3.

Is the Customer Happy?

By the time you reach this point in the project, you know whether the stakeholders' expectations have been met. Part of the Monitoring and Controlling process involves reviewing the project plan, deliverables, and requirements and making certain the actions of the project team are satisfying the requirements and thus satisfying the stakeholders. But another part of stakeholder satisfaction includes the softer skills of communication, customer service, and problem resolution. The only way to get the answers to these questions is to ask them.

If the project is small with only a handful of stakeholders involved, hold one-on-one interviews to ask them their opinions on the progress of the project and project management processes. Or consider creating a questionnaire to hand out to your stakeholders and customers to determine their level of satisfaction with the project. You can also use this technique to help you with the lessons learned document we discussed earlier.

Here are some sample questions you can use in your interviews, or questionnaire, to determine stakeholder satisfaction. If you're creating a questionnaire, provide them with a scale of 1 to 5, where 1 is not at all satisfied and 5 is very satisfied, or a similar scale.

- Are you satisfied that the deliverable dates were met according to the final project plan?
- Are you satisfied with the level of involvement you had on the project?
- How satisfied are you that the status reports were clear and concise and contained enough information to determine project progress?
- Are you satisfied with the change management process?
- Do you think that problems were addressed and resolved in a timely manner?
- What is your overall level of satisfaction with the product or service of the project?
- Are you satisfied with the quality process used during the project?
- What is your overall level of satisfaction with the project management process?
- Overall, are you satisfied with the amount of information you received during the project regarding status, problems, and progress?

Tailor this questionnaire to your specific project, and always give the respondents room for free-form comments and feedback.

You should also interview your project sponsor. Ask them the same questions you asked the stakeholders, and also ask them about your working relationship. Were there things either of you could have done differently to help the project progress more efficiently? Were the communication channels open? Did they have enough information to report the status to executive managers and answer questions regarding the project when confronted?

And don't forget the team members. While some of the questions in the preceding list won't apply to them, you should ask them how they think the project progressed. Were communication channels open between you and the team? Did they feel adequately informed of progress, changes, and new information? What do they think of the change control process? What do they think of the team effectiveness, and what are their suggestions for future team enhancements? All of this information will help you improve your next project if you take the time to analyze what they've told you and initiate changes where needed.

NOTE   **Each project is a learning experience. Even though each project exists to create a unique product or service and no two projects will ever be the same, the processes you use to manage the projects will be similar, and there is always room for improvement.**

Back in Chapter 1, we talked about how our ancient project management counterparts probably followed processes that are similar to the processes we use today. We've cleaned them up and made them more efficient, and we've certainly made our job easier through the use of computer software programs, but the management processes we use to ensure that the outcomes of the project meet the requirements are basically the same. So, take the time to learn from the good and bad on every project, get feedback from your stakeholders and team members, and then apply these ideas to your next project.

Archiving Project Documents

You've created a lot of project information, documents, and processes throughout the project. Since you, or other project managers, can benefit from this information when creating the same documents for future projects, you'll want to archive all the project documents so that they will be accessible when needed. This includes everything you've created during the life of this project: the project charter, project scope statement, project planning documents, quality plan, risk response plans, status reports, lessons learned, final acceptance document, and so on.

If you've used the intranet or some other electronic means to maintain your project document library, archiving should be an easy process. But you may find that you have some paper documents, especially those with signatures, that didn't get scanned or uploaded to the project directory. Search through your project papers to make sure you've captured everything.

I recommend keeping project files accessible for as long as possible provided you have the space. Archiving in this case is a simple matter of moving the project documents to a folder called "Closed Projects." If that's not possible, archive your documents in a manner that makes them easy to retrieve. Use the same process for all your archives and similar naming conventions for all the project files. It's a good idea to add a date at the beginning or end of the project folder name for search purposes. There's only one official project function remaining. Let's get to it.

It's Party Time!

Celebrate your success! Throw a party, take the team to lunch, or buy noise-makers and set them off at the last project team meeting. Recognize the success of the team, no matter how small the project.

This is also the time for you to officially thank the team members for their participation on the project. If significant accomplishments were made during the course of the project, consider giving awards to those who made the contributions. If the project was successful, this recognition should be done publicly. Keep in mind this isn't the first time you will have recognized team members who've done an exemplary job, but it does give you one last opportunity to recognize individual excellence as well as team effort. And reflecting on a job well done builds confidence and encourages you and the team members to stretch your skills and take on even more complex projects.

Celebration brings closure to the project and helps the team formally recognize the project's end. It helps smooth the transition and lets team members know that their contributions were appreciated. Remember the adjourning stage in the Tuckman/Jensen team formation model? That's what this celebration accomplishes. It also helps them cut the ties and begin thinking about their new assignments, so don't skip this process. Now, go celebrate your own success! You've finished this book and learned some new things about project management that will help you manage your coming projects more efficiently and should grant you much success in your project management endeavors. Even if you never work under the title of "project manager," you'll no doubt be involved in several projects during the course of your career. What you've learned here will help you successfully see these projects through to completion.

Terms to Know

lessons learned   warranty period

project approval

Review Questions

1. What is the definition of a successful project?

2. Describe the purpose of the Closing process.

3. Why should you close the project accounts at the end of the project?

4. What should the project manager do after contract closeout?

5. What sometimes happens with team members in the performing stage of development as they approach the end of the project?

6. Describe the purpose of a warranty period.

7. What are lessons learned?

8. Why should the project manager get formal project sign-off?

9. What information should be archived at the close of the project?

10. Why is celebration important for team members?

Appendix A

Answers to Review Questions

Chapter 1

1. What is project management?

   Answer: Project management involves applying skills, knowledge, and established project management tools and techniques to your project to fulfill the requirements of the project to the customer's satisfaction.

2. What are some of the benefits of a projectized organization?

   Answer: The benefits of a projectized organization are the project manager has ultimate authority over the project and that the focus of the organization is on project work.

3. What are the five project management process groups?

   Answer: Initiating, Planning, Executing, Monitoring and Controlling, and Closing are the five process groups.

4. Name three of the things that you'll accomplish during the Planning process.

   Answer: During project planning, you'll define project deliverables, define project activities and estimates, and publish the scope statement.

5. Name three of the things that you'll accomplish during the Executing process.

   Answer: The Executing process involves developing, leading, and directing the project team, communicating project progress, and implementing quality assurance procedures.

6. Which project management process is the one most often skipped?

   Answer: The Closing process is the one most often skipped.

7. Name at least three criteria for determining whether your work assignment is a project.

   Answer: A work assignment is a project if the project has definite beginning and ending dates, it's temporary in nature, it produces a unique product or service, and resources are dedicated to the work of the project.

8. What is the definition of a constraint?

   Answer: Constraints are anything that restricts or dictates the actions of the project team.

9. Name the triple constraints and other common competing demands.

Answer: The triple constraints are scope, schedule, and budget. Risk, quality, resources, and customer satisfaction are other examples of competing demands or constraints.

10. What does it mean when a person has a PMP?

Answer: PMP stands for Project Management Professional. PMPs are people who have received certification in project management processes from the Project Management Institute.

Chapter 2

1. What is the most important skill that a project manager can possess?

Answer: The most important skill that a project manager can possess is communication skills.

2. Why is time management important?

Answer: Good time management practices allow you to control the priorities over your time instead of letting the day's happenings control you.

3. What are some examples of firefighting priorities?

Answer: Some examples of firefighting priorities include emergencies, unplanned risks, and service interruptions.

4. What are some examples of looking-for-a-new-job zone activities, and why should you avoid them?

Answer: Some examples of low-importance/low-urgency activities include extraneous documentation, cube hopping, and web surfing. You should avoid these activities because they are time wasters and will prevent you from completing the things you should be working on in the planning zone. (Note: The name of the zone should provide a clue.)

5. What is an excellent rule to remember for information management?

Answer: The rule for information management is to handle every piece of information one time and then do something with it.

6. Name the elements involved in information exchange.

Answer: The elements involved in information exchange are sender, message, and receiver.

7. What are some of the things senders are responsible for when communicating with team members or stakeholders?

Answer: Senders are responsible for making messages clear and concise and targeting the information for the right audience.

8. What are some of the things receivers are responsible for in receiving information?

Answer: Receivers are responsible for understanding the information, making certain they have received all the information, and asking clarifying questions.

9. Name three effective listening techniques.

Answer: Three effective listening techniques are to make eye contact, paraphrase what you heard, and not interrupt.

10. Name three effective communication techniques.

    Answer: Effective communication techniques include making the messages clear and to the point, combining communication methods (such as using visual aids during a project meeting), and eliminating noise.

Chapter 3

1. Name the primary output of the Initiating process.

    Answer: The outputs of the Initiating process are the project charter (which appoints the project manager), the stakeholder register, and the stakeholder management strategy.

2. Name at least three needs or demands (also known as strategic considerations) that bring about projects.

    Answer: The needs or demands that bring about projects include business need, market demand, customer request, legal requirement, technological advance, and social need.

3. What is the purpose of the project concept document?

    Answer: The project concept document is used to formally request a project. It outlines the purpose and objectives of the project at a high level for review by the selection committee. The selection committee uses the project concept document to make a go/no-go decision.

4. What are the most common financial methods used to weigh project selection criteria?

    Answer: The most common financial methods used to select projects include payback period, discounted cash flow, cost-benefit analysis, internal rate of return, and return on investment.

5. Describe the role of the project sponsor.

    Answer: The project sponsor is usually an executive in the corporation who rallies support for the project. This executive has the authority to commit resources to the project, make decisions, and settle disputes. The project sponsor is a partner with the project manager and shares responsibility for a successful outcome.

6. Where should the stakeholder roles and responsibilities chart be documented and filed?

    Answer: The roles and responsibilities of the stakeholders should be documented in the project charter and filed in the project notebook folder or posted on the intranet site.

7. State the purpose of the project charter.

    Answer: The purpose of the project charter is to acknowledge the existence of the project and appoint the project manager. The project charter should be a written document that's filed in the project notebook folder or posted on the intranet site.

8. Who should publish the project charter?

    Answer: The project charter is published by the project sponsor or another executive manager in the organization.

9. Who should sign the project charter, and why?

    Answer: The project charter should be signed by the project sponsor, the project manager, the key stakeholders, the customer, and vendors, if appropriate. Signing the document shows support and endorsement of the project. It should also signify that the stakeholders understand the purpose and intent of the project and are ready to participate as needed on the project.

10. What happens at a project kickoff meeting?

    Answer: The project kickoff meeting establishes verbally what the project charter establishes in writing. The project kickoff meeting allows participants to ask questions, and it assures the project sponsor and project manager that all the project participants have the same understanding regarding the project objectives and that they understand their roles in the project.

Chapter 4

1. What criteria should you use to define project goals?

   Answer: The acronym SMART describes the criteria for defining project goals. Goals should be specific, measurable, attainable, and agreed to, realistic, and time bound.

2. Describe project deliverables.

   Answer: Deliverables are the specific items or services that must be produced in order to fulfill the goals of the project. Deliverables must have measurable results and measurable outcomes, or they must detail specific products or services to be produced. Deliverables, like goals, should be specific and measurable.

3. How are requirements different from deliverables or goals?

   Answer: Requirements are the specifications of the goal or deliverable. They describe the characteristics of the deliverable. Requirements cannot be broken down further, whereas goals and deliverables can.

4. What are critical success factors?

   Answer: Critical success factors are the things that absolutely must be completed correctly in order to consider the project a success.

5. Why are assumptions often overlooked in the project planning process?

   Answer: Assumptions are often overlooked because we presume that things will continue to operate in the future as they have in the past. We assume that key team members will be available or vendors will deliver on time because they have in the past. These items should be documented so that you can develop a plan to deal with the assumptions that turn out to be false and can have severe impacts later in the project's Planning process.

6. Name three potential constraints for projects other than the triple constraints.

   Answer: Lack of commitment from the executive team or project sponsor, poor communications, and unrealistic expectations of project outcomes can also hamper a project.

7. What is the purpose of a project scope statement?

   Answer: The purpose of the project scope statement is to document the goals, deliverables, and requirements of the project. The scope statement will be used as a baseline for future project decisions and as the criteria for determining project success when the project ends.

8. What is the purpose of the project scope management plan?

   Answer: The project scope management plan describes the process that you'll use to define the project scope; how the work breakdown structure will be defined, maintained, and approved; the process that describes how deliverable verification and acceptance will occur; and the process requestors must go through to request changes and how those changes will be incorporated into the project.

9. Why is it important to obtain sign-off of the project scope statement?

   Answer: Sign-off of the scope statement ensures that all the stakeholders are in agreement of and support the goals, deliverables, and requirements of the project. It also serves as a handy reminder when memories get foggy later in the project. The project manager can refer to the project scope statement to determine whether the request is a change or is part of the original requirements.

10. What does the communications plan document?

   Answer: The communications plan documents who will receive project communications, how they will receive them, when they will receive them, and how to access project information. It also describes how project information will be collected, stored, filed, and archived.

Chapter 5

1. What is the purpose of activity definition?

   Answer: The purpose of activity definition is to break down the work of the project into manageable components in order to establish time, resource, and cost estimates.

2. Name some of the purposes of activity sequencing.

   Answer: Activity sequencing puts the activities in a logical order. This will help you build the project schedule. It's also a means of grouping similar types of work together.

3. What are milestones, and what significance do they have to the project?

   Answer: Milestones signify important accomplishments that have been achieved on the project. They are not work in themselves but consist of a grouping of activities that, when completed, are a significant portion of the project.

4. Describe a work breakdown structure.

   Answer: A WBS is a tool used to graphically display the deliverables of the project in a hierarchical fashion. They can be displayed in tree form, much like an organizational chart, or in outline form.

5. What is a work package?

   Answer: A work package is the lowest level of a WBS. This is the level where resource assignments, time estimates, and costs are assigned.

6. Why are codes used to identify elements in the WBS?

   Answer: Codes are to track the cost of each element in the WBS, generally at the work package level. They also serve as a reference number to identify the WBS element and tie it to explanatory information.

7. Define a RAM and explain how it's used.

   Answer: A RAM is a responsibility assignment matrix. It's used to show what types of resources are needed for each element of the WBS. These are constructed in chart form, and the intersection of a row and a column indicates the level of activity needed by the resource for that WBS activity.

8. Name two methods of determining activity duration estimates.

   Answer: Two methods used to determine activity duration estimates are expert judgment and parametric estimating.

9. Describe the four types of dependency relationships, and indicate which one is used most often.

   Answer: The four types of dependency relationships are Finish to Start, Finish to Finish, Start to Start, and Start to Finish. The most often used dependency is Finish to Start, which says that the independent activity must finish before the dependent activity can start.

10. Name two ways to display network diagrams and briefly describe each.

    Answer: Precedence diagramming is a method of placing activities in the correct sequential order, taking their dependencies into account. There are two ways to display precedence diagrams. One technique displays activities in boxes or nodes (AON), with arrows showing the dependencies between the nodes. Activity on arrow (AOA) displays the activities on the arrows, with milestones or events represented on the nodes.

Chapter 6

1. What policies should you consult before putting together your project team?

   Answer: You should review your organizational policies and recruitment policies before organizing your project team. There may be specific requirements regarding job descriptions or transferring employees that should be followed.

2. Name at least four things you should consider when choosing project team members.

   Answer: When choosing project team members, you should consider skills, personality, experience, ability to work with others, and knowledge.

3. What tools can you use to help determine human resource needs for the project?

   Answer: Skills assessments and skills definition charts are useful tools for outlining the type and level of skills needed for the tasks of the project.

4. What document should you look at first to help you determine the supplies, materials, and equipment needed for the work of the project?

   Answer: The WBS is one of the first documents you should review when determining what supplies, materials, and equipment are needed for the work of the project.

5. What is the purpose of the project team directory?

   Answer: The project team directory is a quick reference for locating the names and contact information for everyone involved on the project, including the project sponsor, stakeholders, project manager, project team members, and vendors.

6. What is the purpose of a make-or-buy decision?

Answer: The purpose of a make-or-buy decision is to determine whether it's more cost-effective and efficient for the organization to make or buy the products or services needed.

7. Describe the resource plan and its purpose.

Answer: The resource plan describes all the resources needed for the project, including people, supplies, materials, and equipment. The resource plan documents in one place the skills needed for the tasks of the project, the resources assigned to the tasks, and a materials list. This, as well as all the other project planning documentation, can be used in the future to help plan projects of similar size and scope.

8. Why is it important for project managers to understand contracts?

Answer: The project manager is the person who communicates with the vendor regarding their performance and fulfillment of the terms of the contract. The project manager also reports the status of the vendor's work to the procurement department so that payment can be made to the vendor.

9. What is the purpose of the requisition process in the contract lifecycle?

Answer: The purpose of the requisition process in the contract lifecycle is to prepare the RFP, RFI, or RFQ, which contains information regarding the project objectives and deliverables for the vendors who will be bidding on the project work.

10. Name two processes used in the selection or award process of the contract lifecycle

Answer: Weighted scoring models and screening systems are tools used to evaluate RFP responses, select a vendor, and award a contract during the award phase of the contract lifecycle.

Chapter 7

1. What is a risk?

Answer: A risk is the possibility of a problem occurring on the project that threatens the project's successful outcome in some way or poses an opportunity the project team should investigate.

2. Name some of the planning documents or elements of the planning documents that you can use to start identifying risk.

Answer: Some documents you can use to help start identifying risks are the WBS, the task list, the list of project constraints, and critical success factors.

3. Name three of the most common project risks.

Answer: The three most common project risks are associated with the triple constraints: time, budget, and scope.

4. Name five types of participants who should assist in the risk-identification process.

Answer: Participants in the risk-identification process should consist of the project manager, key project team members, key stakeholders, subject-matter experts, and people with previous experience on similar projects.

5. Which risk-identification technique places all the participants together in the same room with a facilitator, has each participant record risks on sticky notes, one per round, and then posts the notes to a white board?

   Answer: The Nominal Group technique is like brainstorming in that all the participants are together in the same room, but they write risks, one at a time, on sticky notes and give them to the facilitator to post. When all the risks are identified, the group then ranks the risks.

6. What are three other techniques, in addition to the Nominal Group technique, that you can use to identify risks?

   Answer: Some techniques you can use to help with the risk-identification process are brainstorming, the Delphi technique, interviewing, using checklists, and researching historical information.

7. Briefly describe a probability impact matrix and the purpose it serves.

   Answer: A probability impact matrix is a way to assign probability values and impact values to each risk event to determine an overall risk score. The overall risk score is used to determine which risks need risk response plans.

8. What is risk tolerance?

   Answer: Risk tolerance is the amount of risk that an individual or an organization is willing to tolerate in exchange for the benefits of partaking in the activity.

9. Name the seven risk response strategies.

   Answer: The seven risk response strategies are accepting, avoiding, transferring, mitigating, exploit, share, and enhance.

10. What are contingency reserves used for?

    Answer: Contingency reserves are used to handle risks that have minimal impacts, such as secondary risks or residual risks, or for risks that are not addressed through any of the other strategies such as avoiding, transferring, mitigating, sharing, enhancing, or exploiting.

Chapter 8

1. Name three items completed previously in the project's Planning process that will assist you in building the project schedule.

   Answer: The Planning documents you can use to help produce the schedule include, but aren't limited to, the project scope statement, the WBS, the activity list, activity estimates, network diagrams, and resource needs.

2. What three estimates does the PERT calculation use to determine duration?

   Answer: PERT uses the optimistic, most likely, and pessimistic estimates to determine a weighted average duration.

3. What is expected value?

   Answer: Expected value is the weighted average of the three time estimates used in PERT.

4. What is the formula for determining the expected value of PERT estimates?

   Answer: The formula for determining the expected value of PERT estimates is Expected Value = (Optimistic + (4 × Most Likely) + Pessimistic) / 6.

5. What is a confidence factor?

   Answer: A confidence factor is the level of confidence that the estimate given is accurate.

6. Describe the critical path.

   Answer: The critical path is the longest full path on the project.

7. Describe the two types of float time.

   Answer: Total float is the amount of time you can delay the earliest start of a task without delaying the end of the project. Free float is the amount of time you can delay the start of a task without delaying the earliest start of a successor task.

8. Name two things you can do to shorten a project's duration.

   Answer: Things you can do to shorten project duration include adding more resources, changing the project scope, rescheduling the tasks in a different order, bringing in more skilled resources, asking for more time, and starting two tasks in parallel that were originally scheduled to start successively.

9. What is resource leveling, and why do you use it?

   Answer: Resource leveling evens out the task assignments so that overloading and underutilization problems are lessened or eliminated.

10. What is the cost of quality?

   Answer: The cost of quality is the cost to produce the product or service of the project according to the quality standards and or the cost to fix or make a product or service that is nonconforming meet the quality requirements.

Chapter 9

1. What is a project budget?

   Answer: A project budget is an itemized list of estimated expenses needed to complete the work of the project.

2. Name the three categories of project costs.

   Answer: The three categories of project costs are human resource costs, administrative costs, and non-human resource costs.

3. Describe the two types of project costs and give an example of each.

   Answer: The two types of project costs are direct costs and indirect costs. Direct costs are costs that are specifically related to the project such as team salaries, equipment rentals, and training. Indirect costs are not specifically related to the project but are necessary to complete the work of the project. Indirect costs include building leases, administrative support expenses, and management salaries.

4. Describe the analogous estimating technique.

   Answer: Analogous estimating establishes an estimate for the project based on the actual costs of previous projects similar in size and scope to the project being estimated.

5. Describe the bottom-up estimating technique.

   Answer: Bottom-up estimating establishes individual estimates for each task and then adds together all the estimates to come up with a total estimate for the project.

6. What is a contingency reserve used for?

   Answer: A contingency reserve is an extra percentage of the total budget added into the budget to account for unknown and unplanned events or risks that may occur on the project. Most project managers build contingency reserves into the project budget.

7. Your project budget has been approved, but it's been approved at a lower amount than the original request. What are some of the things you can do to deal with this situation?

   Answer: Some of the ways you can adjust the project for a reduced budget are reducing the project scope, reducing the features or functionality of the deliverables, and reducing the number of team members.

8. What is a cost baseline and what is it used for?

   Answer: A cost baseline is the expected cost of the project. It's used to track and measure future project performance to make sure that actual expenses are in line with the project budget.

9. Changes in project scope typically require changes to what other two project's Planning processes?

   Answer: Changes in project scope usually require changes to the project schedule and project budget.

10. Does approval of each of the Planning documents guarantee overall project plan approval? Why or why not?

   Answer: Approval of all Planning documents does not guarantee overall project plan approval. Organizational changes, budget changes, personnel changes, and risk tolerance changes are just some of the factors that could kill a project even if all the plans up to this point have been approved.

Chapter 10

1. Name the five stages of team development.

   Answer: The five stages of team development are forming, storming, norming, performing, and adjourning.

2. At what stage of team development do team members struggle with conflicts and questions regarding their position or status on the team?

   Answer: The storming stage is where conflicts arise and team members struggle with one another to determine position or status within the team.

3. What are some of the things you can do to prepare for conflict-resolution meetings?

   Answer: Documenting the problem, your assumptions about the problem, and alternative solutions will help you prepare for face-to-face meetings where negotiations or problem resolution must take place.

4. What are the six approaches to problem solving, and which one should project managers use most often?

   Answer: The six approaches to problem solving are forcing, smoothing/accommodating, compromise, collaborating, withdrawal/avoidance, and confrontation/problem solving. Confrontation/problem solving is the technique project managers should use most often.

5. Describe the two types of motivators.

   Answer: Intrinsic motivators are things that are internal or specific to the individual that drive them to perform. Extrinsic motivators originate from outside the individual and include things such as bonuses, stock options, and so on.

6. Why is it important to link the reward to performance and to make the reward realistic?

   Answer: Rewards linked to desired performance will produce more of that behavior in the future. The reverse is true also. If you reward bad performance or behavior, you'll get more of it in the future. Rewards should be realistic or they lose their power to motivate.

7. Which of the four types of leadership power is a result of a person's specialized knowledge or abilities?

   Answer: Expert power comes about as a result of a person's knowledge of a subject or as a result of specialized skills they have. The other types of leadership power are punishment power, reward power, and referent power.

8. Suppose you're in the midst of receiving bids for work on an upcoming project. Your favorite vendor contact, whom you've used many times in the past, offers you and your family tickets to box seats at the upcoming ball game. The box seats include a catered dinner. You decline, explaining to the vendor that this could be construed as what?

   Answer: In this situation, a conflict of interest would have occurred if you had accepted the tickets from the vendor. You'd have experienced a personal gain while allowing the vendor to influence you to make a decision in their favor regarding the project work.

9. What types of project information will stakeholders normally want updates on during the course of the project?

   Answer: Stakeholders require status updates on the progress of the project, and status usually includes updates on work completed this period, project schedule updates (changes, dates that were met, and dates that were missed), project issues, budget updates, and change requests.

10. Corrective actions are an output of what project process?

    Answer: Corrective actions are an output of the Monitoring and Controlling process but an input to the Executing process.

Chapter 11

1. Name three ways that change comes about on projects.

   Answer: Change comes about on projects for many reasons: stakeholder requests, customer requests, team member recommendations, business changes, the result of risks, and so on.

2. Why should change requests be submitted in writing?

   Answer: Change requests should be written down to avoid miscommunication and confusion and so that they can be tracked, reviewed, and analyzed for their impact on the project.

3. What is the purpose of a change management plan, and when in the project lifecycle should it be created?

   Answer: A change management plan helps you understand what causes change to come about and when and why the change is needed, and it establishes the procedures for change. It should be created in the Planning process of the project lifecycle.

4. What types of information should be included in the change management plan?

   Answer: The change management plan should describe where to obtain forms for change requests, how to submit change requests, how the changes are approved, and the authority level of the project manager and change control board.

5. What is the purpose of a change control board?

   Answer: The change control board is responsible for reviewing, approving, rejecting, or delaying change requests.

6. Scope changes always require changes to what other Planning document?

   Answer: Scope changes always require changes to the project schedule and include any changes to the agreed-upon WBS.

7. Name two options you can examine when faced with scope or schedule changes.

   Answer: When faced with scope or schedule changes, you can consider bringing in more resources, modifying the scope of the tasks, or reducing the scope of the project by moving deliverables to another phase of the project.

8. Name the two schedule compression techniques.

   Answer: Schedule compression can be accomplished with fast tracking or crashing the schedule.

9. What is fast tracking?

   Answer: Fast tracking means overlapping project phases or starting two tasks at the same time that were originally scheduled to start sequentially.

10. What is the most important Monitoring and Controlling technique you can use when monitoring the performance of the project?

    Answer: The most important technique you can use to monitor the progress of the project in the Monitoring and Controlling process is to stay up-to-date on project status by holding regular team meetings and maintaining open communication with project team members by meeting with them informally.

Chapter 12

1. What is the definition of a successful project?

   Answer: A successful project meets or exceeds the expectations of the stakeholders.

2. Describe the purpose of the Closing process.

   Answer: The Closing process involves getting final approval of the product of the project, closing out the accounts, documenting lessons learned, and archiving project information.

3. Why should you close the project accounts at the end of the project?

   Answer: The project accounts should be closed at the end of the project so that no more spending is charged against the project budget. If more charges are applied to the budget than what are called for in the plan, you'll have budget variances.

4. What should the project manager do after contract closeout?

   Answer: After performing contract closeout, the project manager should formally notify the seller in writing that the contract is complete and the product or service of the project is satisfactory and acceptable.

5. What sometimes happens with team members in the performing stage of development as they approach the end of the project?

   Answer: Teams in the performing stage of development sometimes delay the close of the project by creating problems or dragging out due dates. They're reluctant to move on because they are enjoying their work on the project and don't want it to come to an end.

6. Describe the purpose of a warranty period.

   Answer: A warranty period provides a period of time after the implementation of the project when stakeholders or customers can report problems and have them addressed immediately.

7. What are lessons learned?

   Answer: Lessons learned are the successes and failures of the project, and they should be noted and archived with the project documentation for future reference.

8. Why should the project manager get formal project sign-off?

   Answer: Final, formal sign-off on the project ensures that the customer and stakeholders have verified that the outcomes of the project meet all the requirements outlined in the scope statement.

9. What information should be archived at the close of the project?

   Answer: All project documentation should be archived at the close of the project. This includes the project charter, all project planning documents, lessons learned, and more.

10. Why is celebration important for team members?

    Answer: Celebration brings closure to the project and helps the team members formally recognize the end of the project. It's also a chance for the project manager to recognize the contributions of the team members and thank them for their participation.

Appendix B

Sample Project Management Forms

Here are the forms covered throughout *Project Management JumpStart.* You can use them as is or adapt them to your particular project needs.

Project concept document (from Chapter 3):

Project Concept Document

I. General Information

Project name:_____   Project number:_____

Requestor name: _____   Date of request:_____

Requestor's contact information:_____

Section One — To be completed by the requestor

II. Business Justification	*State the reason this project is needed and what problem or issue the project will resolve. Describe the impacts to the organization if the project is not approved.*

III. Project Description	*Provide a high-level overview of the project objectives. Include a brief list of desired project outcomes.*

IV. Project Costs	*Provide high-level estimates if known.*

V. Timeframe	*Is there a critical completion date?* Y/N *Date required:_____*
	Desired completion date if not critical:_____

Project Concept Document—page 2

Section Two — To be completed by the business unit manager or project manager

VI. Planning Estimates   *Provide a high-level estimate of project completion.*

VII. Business Areas Impacted   *List all business units impacted by this project.*

Section Three — To be completed by the review committee

VIII. Selection Committee Review

Date of review:
Comments:
Project reviewed/denied:
Project priority:

IX. Signatures of Review Committee

Project charter (from Chapter 3):

Project Charter

I. General Information

Project name:_____   Project number:_____
Sponsor name:_____   Date:_____

II. Project Overview	*Describe the product or service of the project, the reason the project was undertaken, and the purpose of the project.*

III. Project Objectives	*Describe the overall objectives of the project and what factors will determine the success of the project.*

IV. Requirements	*Describe the expectations and requirements of the customer, sponsor, and stakeholders.*

V. Business Justification	*State the reason this project is needed and what problem or issue the project will resolve. Describe the impacts to the organization if the project is not approved.*

VI. Resource Costs and Estimates	*Provide cost estimates if known, including monies already expended such as a feasibility study or consulting time.*

VII. Roles and Responsibilities	*List the stakeholders and their responsibilities.*

VIII. Signatures	*Include signature lines for the project sponsor, project manager, key stakeholders, customers, and vendors.*

IX. Attachments	*List the attachments to the charter here.*

Project kickoff meeting agenda (from Chapter 3):

Project Kickoff Meeting Agenda

I. General Information

Project name:_____   Project number:_____

Project Manager name:_____   Date:_____

II. Agenda Items

1. *Introductions*
2. *Project charter*
3. *Project purpose*
4. *Project objectives*
5. *Roles and responsibilities*
6. *Questions*

Project scope statement (from Chapter 4):

Project Scope Statement

I. General Information

Project name:_____   Project number:_____

Project Manager name: _____   Date:_____

II. Project Overview	*Describe the product or service of the project, the reason the project was undertaken, and the purpose of the project.*
III. Project Goals and Objectives	*Describe the project goals using the SMART (Specific, Measurable, Accurate and Agreed to, Realistic, Time Bound) formula. These goals will be used to measure and determine the project's success at its conclusion.*
IV. Comprehensive List of Project Deliverables	*These are the products or services that must be produced in order to fulfill the goals of the project. Deliverables should have measurable, verifiable results and outcomes. Identify critical success factors.*
V. Comprehensive List of Project Requirements	*Requirements are the specifications of the deliverables.*
VI. Exclusions from Scope	*List all deliverables or requirements that are not part of this project.*
VII. Time and Cost Estimates	*Include initial estimates of time and resources. These are estimates only and will be updated after additional project planning activities are completed.*
VIII. Roles and Responsibilities	*Include a roles-and-responsibilities chart, detailing project responsibilities.*
IX. Assumptions	*List all project assumptions.*
X. Product Acceptance Criteria	*List all project acceptance criteria.*
XI. Constraints	*List all project constraints.*
XII. Signatures	*Include signature lines for the project sponsor, project manager, key stakeholders, customers, and vendors.*

Communications plan (from Chapter 4):

Communications Plan

I. General Information

Project name:_____

Project number:_____

Project Manager name: _____

Date:_____

Communication	Recipients	Method	Timing	Prepared By

Materials, supplies, and equipment list (from Chapter 6):

Materials, Supplies, and Equipment List

I. General Information

Project name:_____   Project number:_____
Project Manager name:_____   Date:_____

II. Materials, Supplies, and Equipment Needed

Task	Materials Needed	Quantity	Available/Procure	Approximate Cost
Design program modules	New PCs	4	Procure	$2,100 each
	Software licenses	6	Procure	$42,000 total
Write programs	Programming software	6	Procure	$62,000 total
	Sample handhelds	2	Procure	$1,900 total
	Training	10	Procure	$2,500 each

Quality management plan (from Chapter 8):

Quality Management Plan

I. General Information

Project name:_____   Project number:_____

Project Manager name:_____   Date:_____

II. Project Overview   *Provide an overview of the project, including its primary goals.*

III. Quality Standards and Regulations   *Note any quality policies, standards, or regulations the project team will be required to follow.*

IV. Quality Criteria   *Provide a detailed list of the quality criteria needed to consider the deliverables complete and correct. Include each deliverable and its quality criteria.*

V. Quality Assurance Procedures   *List the activities and processes that will be used to monitor adherence to the quality criteria.*

VI. Quality Management Roles and Responsibilities   *Include a roles and responsibility chart detailing who's responsible for which quality activities.*

VII. Signatures   *Include signature lines for the project sponsor, project manager, and those responsible for quality assurance and review.*

Project status report (from Chapter 10):

Project Status Report

I. General Information

Project name:_____   Project number:_____

Project Manager name:_____   Report period ending:_____

II. Progress Made Since Last Reporting Period

III. Scheduled and Actual Completion Dates

IV. Progress Expected This Reporting Period Not Completed

V. Progress Expected Next Reporting Period

VI. Issues

Action item log (from Chapter 10):

Action Item Log

I. General Information

Project name:_____   Project number:_____

Project Manager name:_____

II. Action Item Log

ID:	Date reported:	Action item:	Assigned to:	Date resolved:

Change request form (from Chapter 11):

Change Request Form

I. General Information

Project name:_____   Project number:_____

Requestor name:_____   Requestor's contact information:_____   Date of request:_____

Change request tracking number:_____   Date request approved/denied:_____

Section One—To Be Completed by the Requestor

II. Description of Change Request	*Include a detailed description of the requested scope change.*

III. Business Justification for Change	*Describe how the business, project, or product will benefit from the requested change.*

IV. Impacts of Not Making the Change	*Describe how the business, project, or product will be impacted if the change is not made.*

V. Alternatives to Change	*Describe any known alternatives to the change.*

Section Two—To Be Completed by the Project Manager

VI. Impacts of the Change	*Describe the impacts of this change to the project schedule, budget, and quality.*

VII. Alternatives to Change	*Describe alternative solutions to the change.*

VIII. Recommendation to the Change Control Board	*Describe the project manager's recommendation to approve or deny the change. Include justification for the recommendation.*

Section Three—To Be Completed by the Change Control Board

Recommendation: Date of Review:	*Include a discussion concerning the goals of the project. Does this change significantly impact the goals of the project such that the project goals can no longer be met? Should this change be considered a new project or phase two of the existing project, etc.?*

Signature:	

Final status report (from Chapter 12):

Final Status Report

I. General Information

Project name:_____   Project number:_____

Project Manager name:_____   Date of report:_____

II. Project Overview	Describe the final product or service of the project, the reason the project was undertaken, and the purpose of the project. Include a description of the business problem that was solved by implementing this project.

III. Project Goals and Objectives	Identify the goals that were met during this project and compare them to the goals on the scope statement.

IV. Project Deliverables and Milestones	Identify the major deliverables or milestones met, their due dates according to the final plan, their actual delivery dates, and stakeholder acceptance dates.

V. Project Budget	Give a final overview of the project budget and variances from the budget.

VI. Quality Assurance	Document acceptance of the quality criteria and inspections.

VII. Comments	Include any information that reminds stakeholders of agreements made concerning deliverables that were moved to phase two of the project, major problems that were encountered and how they were resolved, risk events that need further explanation, and so on.

VIII. Final Acceptance and Signatures	Provide a way for each stakeholder to indicate their acceptance of the project and sign their name.
Accept/Decline	Stakeholder name_____

Appendix C

Sample Project Management Checklists

Here are the checklists that we mentioned throughout *Project Management JumpStart*. You can use them as is or adapt them to your particular project needs.

See Chapter 7, "Assessing Risk," for a detailed discussion of the checklist shown in Table C.1.

Table C.1   Checklist of common project risks

Project name:		
Project number:		
Project Manager's name:		
Type of risk	**Describe the impact or characteristics**	**Examined**
Project schedule	Increased project time	❏
Budgets/funding	Increased cost	❏
Personnel issues	Loss of key team member, not enough team members assigned to project	❏
Quality	Doesn't meet standards	❏
Key stakeholder consensus	Conflicts and project delays	❏
Scope changes	Increased project time and costs	❏
Project plans	Increased project time and costs, impact on quality, poor direction and communication	❏
Project management methodology	Increased project time and costs	❏
Business risk	Poor public image	❏
Management risk	Reorganization resulting in loss of team members	❏
Vendor issues	Delivery delays	❏
Contract risks	Project delays, increased costs	❏

Table C.1 Checklist of common project risks *(continued)*

Type of risk	Describe the impact or characteristics	Examined
Legal issues	Increased costs, poor public image	❑
Political issues	Poor public image	❑
Environmental risk	Increased costs, delays to schedule, poor public image	❑
Weather or natural disasters	Schedule delays, delivery delays, increased costs	❑
Technology risks	Not available when needed	❑
Project complexity	Inexperience of project team	❑
Project manager skills	Inexperience of project manager	❑
Team skills and abilities	Inexperience of team members, lack of training	❑

See Chapter 9, "Budgeting 101," for a detailed discussion of the checklist shown in Table C.2.

Table C.2 Project planning processes

Project name:		
Project number:		
Project Manager's name:		
Project planning activity	**Inputs**	**Outputs**
Project scope management plan	Project scope statement	Scope management plan that outlines how scope will be defined and how changes to scope will be handled
Project scope statement	Project charter	Project goals and objectives, assumptions and constraints, critical success factors
Work breakdown structure (WBS)	Project scope statement, project scope management plan	Deliverables-oriented breakdown of the work of the project
Activity identification	Project scope statement, WBS	WBS, task list
Communication planning	Project charter, project scope statement	Communication plan
Resource identification	Project scope statement, WBS, task list	Resource plan that identifies physical and human resources needed for the project

Table C.2   Project planning processes *(continued)*

Project planning activity	Inputs	Outputs
Task dependencies	WBS, task list	Logical dependencies of tasks
Network diagram	WBS, task list, dependencies	Graphical picture of tasks in dependency order
Task duration estimates	WBS, task list, resource plan, network diagram	Time needed to complete each task
Procurement planning	WBS, task list, network diagram, resource plan	Procurement plan
Risk planning	Project scope statement, WBS, task list, network diagram, resource plan	Risk plan
Quality planning	Project scope statement, project scope management plan, WBS, task list, network diagram	Quality plan
Project scheduling	Project scope statement, WBS, task list, network diagram, resource plan	Project schedule
Budgeting	Project scope statement, WBS, task list, network diagram, resource plan, procurement plan, risk plan, project schedule	Project budget

See Chapter 9, "Budgeting 101," for a detailed discussion of the checklist shown in Table C.3.

Table C.3   Budget items

Project name:	
Project number:	
Project Manager's name:	
Item	
Project team salaries	❏
Equipment and materials expense	❏
Rent or lease costs for facilities	❏
Marketing costs, including focus group and market research costs	❏
Legal costs	❏

Table C.3   Budget items *(continued)*

Item	
Travel expenses	❑
Advertising costs	❑
Research costs	❑
Feasibility study costs	❑
Consulting services for subject-matter expertise or as project participants	❑
Phone, fax, and long-distance charges	❑
Office supplies	❑
Internet access charges and/or website hosting fees	❑
Software	❑
Hardware	❑
Training	❑

See Chapter 12, "Closing the Books," for a detailed discussion about the checklist shown in Table C.4.

Table C.4   Project process checklist

Project name:				
Project number:				
Project Manager's name:				
Complete	**Process or document name**	**Responsibility**	**Notes**	**Project life cycle**
❑	Project charter	Project sponsor	Describes project purpose, business justification, and outcomes.	Initiation
❑	Cost-benefit analysis	Project manager with input from stakeholders	Determines whether project is financially (or otherwise) beneficial to the organization. Included in the project charter and project scope statement.	Planning

Table C.4   Project process checklist *(continued)*

Complete	Process or document name	Responsibility	Notes	Project life cycle
❑	Assumptions and constraints	Project manager with input from stakeholders	Describes project assumptions and any constraints limiting the project team. Included in the project scope statement.	Planning
❑	Project scope statement	Project manager with input from stakeholders	Describes project goals, contains a comprehensive list of deliverables, and describes the specific requirements of the product, service, or result of the project. Signed by project sponsor, project manager, and stakeholders.	Planning
❑	Critical success factors	Project manager with input from stakeholders	Describes those things that must be completed accurately in order to consider the project a success. These may include project deliverables or requirements. Can be included with the project scope statement.	Planning
❑	Communications plan	Project manager	Describes the information needs of stakeholders and the project team and how the information is distributed.	Planning
❑	Work breakdown structure (WBS)	Project manager	Formatted as a deliverables-oriented hierarchy that defines the work of the project.	Planning
❑	Roles and responsibility matrix	Project manager	Ties roles and responsibilities of project team members with WBS elements.	Planning
❑	Resource plan	Project manager	Describes physical resources and human resources needed to complete the project.	Planning
❑	Procurement plan	Project manager and/or procurement department	Describes resources or services to be purchased from an outside provider.	Planning

Table C.4   Project process checklist *(continued)*

Complete	Process or document name	Responsibility	Notes	Project life cycle
❑	Risk management plan	Project manager with input from stakeholders, risk analysis team, and project team members	Identifies, describes, ranks, and plans for project risks. Includes risk response plans for high-ranking risks.	Planning
❑	Quality plan	Project manager and/or quality team	Describes how quality will be assured and measured.	Planning
❑	Project schedule	Project manager	Displays task dependencies, task durations, and milestones. Used to determine the critical path.	Planning
❑	Project budget	Project manager and/or finance manager	Determines targeted costs of the project.	Planning
❑	Project team kickoff meeting	Project manager	Assigns all team members to their responsibilities.	Executing
❑	Status meetings and status reports	Project manager	Provides updates regarding project progress, issues, change requests, and more to stakeholders and team members.	Executing, and Monitoring and Controlling
❑	Change management plan	Project manager and change control board	Describes how changes to the project plan will be identified and managed.	Planning, and used in Monitoring and Controlling
❑	Monitoring project performance and taking corrective action	Project manager	Oversees project performance. May require updates to the project's Planning documents.	Monitoring and Controlling
❑	Closing the accounting records and finalizing the contracts	Project manager and finance manager	Project manager notifies finance manager to close all project accounts so that no more charges are incurred against the project budget.	Closing

Table C.4 Project process checklist *(continued)*

Complete	Process or document name	Responsibility	Notes	Project life cycle
❏	Implementation checklist	Project manager	Describes issues to be discussed or information to be turned over regarding the product, service, or result of the project to internal departments or the customer.	Closing
❏	Lessons learned document	Project manager with input from stakeholders and team members	Documents processes, plans, communications, etc. that worked well. Also documents things that did not work well so that they will not be repeated in future projects and, if practical, integrates them into the standard company project management processes or templates.	Monitoring and Controlling, and Closing
❏	Obtaining project sign-off and sending formal notice of closure	Project manager	Assures acceptance of the product, service, or result of the project and notifies all parties that the project is officially closed.	Closing
❏	Project feedback	Project manager, stakeholders, and team members	Provides information to improve performance on future projects. Can be included in the lessons learned document.	Closing
❏	Archiving project documents	Project manager	Archives project records for future reference.	Closing
❏	Celebrating your success	Project manager and project team	Provides a means to publicly thank team members for their hard work and recognize success. Brings closure to the project and helps team members make the transition to new assignments.	Closing

See Chapter 12, "Closing the Books," for a detailed discussion of the checklist shown in Table C.5.

Table C.5 Implementation checklist

Project name:		
Project number:		
Project Manager's name:		
Completed	**Description**	**Comments**
❑	Deliverables completed	
❑	Deliverables accepted and approved	
❑	Contracts closed out	
❑	Vendors paid	
❑	Customer training completed	
❑	Product documentation provided to customer	
❑	Warranty information given to customer	
❑	Contact information provided to customer	
❑	Final product delivered	

Glossary

analogous estimating   This technique uses the actual duration of a similar, completed activity to determine the duration of the current activity. This is also called top-down estimating and uses both expert judgment and historical information.

assumptions   Events or actions believed to be true. Project assumptions should always be documented.

benchmarking   Compares previous similar activities to the current project activities to provide a standard against which to measure performance.

bottom-up estimating   Establishes individual estimates for each task and adds them all together to determine a total estimate for the project.

brainstorming   A method of discovering risk events, alternatives, requirements, or other project information with a group of people who have knowledge of the project, product, or processes used during the project. This process is intended to produce freeform ideas, and no restrictions are placed on the participants.

budget   An itemized list of estimated expenses needed to complete the work of the project.

business rule   Constraints to the project that are determined by company policy or institutional regulation.

change control board   A group of individuals, including the project manager and key stakeholders, who are responsible for reviewing, approving, and denying change requests.

change management plan   The plan that describes how change requests are submitted, reviewed, and approved or denied.

Closing process   The last process of the project life cycle, where all project activities are ended, canceled projects are closed, and the final product or service of the project is turned over to others.

collocated   Project team members are physically located together at the same site.

communications plan   Documents the types of information needs the stakeholders have, when the information should be distributed, and how the information will be delivered.

confidence factor   The level of confidence you have in the estimate that's been calculated.

conflict of interest   Conflict of interest occurs when personal interests are put above the interests of the project. It also occurs when personal influence is used to cause others to make decisions in favor of the influencer without regard for the project outcome.

constraint   Anything that limits or dictates the actions of the project team.

contingency planning   A process of planning for known risks to help ensure project success if a risk event occurs.

contingency reserves   Money added to the project budget to pay for unexpected events.

contract life cycle   Contract's progress through specific phases, similar to a project life cycle. The phases of a contract life cycle include requirement, requisition, solicitation, and award.

corrective action   Any action taken to ensure that the product of the project meets the requirements of the project as described in the scope document.

cost baseline   The expected cost of the project. The cost baseline is used to measure actual project expenses against the budgeted expenses.

cost of quality   The cost to produce the product or service of the project according to the quality standards set out in the plan or the cost to fix or make a product or service that is nonconforming meet the quality requirements.

crashing   A schedule compression technique that examines ways to reduce the duration of critical-path tasks.

critical path   The longest path through the project made up of activities with zero float.

critical-path method (CPM)   Determines a single early and late start date and an early and late finish date for each activity on the project.

critical success factors   The project deliverables or requirements that absolutely must be completed and must be completed correctly to consider the project a success.

customer   The end user or recipient of the product, service, or result of the project. Customers may be internal or external to the organization.

deliverables   A measurable outcome, measurable result, or specific item that must be produced to consider the project or project phase completed. Deliverables are tangible and can be measured and easily proved.

Delphi technique   A method of discovering risk events, alternatives, requirements, or other project information using a questionnaire format. This process uses a facilitator to solicit ideas, and participants' contributions or opinions remain anonymous.

direct costs   Costs specifically related to the work of the project.

discounted cash flow   A financial calculation used to determine the project's worth or profitability in today's value. Used as a selection criteria technique when choosing among competing projects.

Executing process   During this process, team members perform the work of the project. Teams are assembled, the task is assigned, and the work is carried out.

expected value   The weighted average of PERT's three estimates: most likely, pessimistic, and optimistic.

expert judgment   Using individuals or groups of people who have training, specialized knowledge, or skills to help assess information and determine estimates.

extrinsic motivators   Incentives that are external to the individual such as money, gifts, and rewards that spur them to perform.

fast tracking   A schedule compression technique that overlaps project phases or starts two tasks at the same time that were originally scheduled to start sequentially.

feasibility study   A preliminary study that examines the profitability of the project, the soundness or feasibility of the product of the project, the marketability of the product or service, alternative solutions, and the business demands that generated the request.

float time   Total float is the amount of time you can delay the early start of a task without delaying the end date of the project. This is also known as path float or slack. Free float is the amount of time you can delay the start of a task without delaying the earliest start of a successor task.

functional organizations   A traditional organizational structure that is hierarchical in nature. Employees report to one manager who reports to a higher-level manager.

handoff   The transition between each phase of the project life cycle.

indirect costs   Costs associated with the project but not directly related to the work of the project.

Initiating process   This is often the first phase in the project life cycle, and it's also the first project management process group, where project requests are generated and approved or denied. Once the project is approved, the project charter is produced in this phase, the project manager is appointed, and the organization recognizes that the project should begin.

internal rate of return (IRR) The discount rate when the present value of the cash inflows, or the value of the investment in today's dollar, equals the original investment. Used as a selection criteria technique when choosing among competing projects.

intrinsic motivators Motivators that are specific to an individual or are derived from within the individual to spur them to perform.

leaders Create and inspire vision while encouraging and motivating others to fulfill the vision.

lessons learned The documented successes and failures of the project.

lines of communication The number of channels between the people involved in the communication exchange.

managers Those who carry out the details of the leader's vision by completing the tasks and activities associated with the vision and by managing the day-to-day operations to the satisfaction of the stakeholders.

matrix organizations An organizational structure where employees report to multiple managers, including one functional manager and at least one project manager.

mediator Acts as a third party to negotiate settlements between two or more parties involved in a dispute. The mediator should be a disinterested party with nothing to gain from the outcome of the decision.

Monitoring and Controlling process This process group concerns monitoring project performance to make certain the outcomes meet the requirements of the project. Change requests are monitored and reviewed in this phase.

Nominal Group technique A method of discovering risk events, alternatives, requirements, or other project information. This process uses a facilitator to solicit ideas from the participants, similar to brainstorming.

payback period The amount of time it takes to recoup the original investment.

Planning process The process group where the project plans are documented, the project deliverables and requirements are defined, and the project schedule is created.

precedence diagramming A diagramming method that links project activities according to their dependency, using nodes or boxes to depict project activities and arrows to show dependencies.

probability The likelihood that an event will occur.

procurement plan Describes the resources or services to be purchased from an outside vendor.

product scope description Lists the characteristics of the product, including specifications, measurements, or other details that identify the product.

Program Evaluation and Review Technique (PERT) Uses the expected value, or weighted average, of critical-path tasks to determine project duration by establishing three estimates: most likely, pessimistic, and optimistic.

project approval Verification and formal acceptance of the product or service of the project.

project charter The official, written acknowledgment and recognition that a project exists. It gives the project manager the authority to proceed with the project and commits resources to the project.

project concept document Outlines the objectives and high-level goals of the project. Used in the selection process to determine whether the project should be approved or denied.

project life cycle All the phases of a project when taken together from the beginning of the project through the end.

project management The process of applying knowledge, skills, tools, and techniques to describe, organize, and monitor the work of the project in order to accomplish the goals of the project.

Project Management Institute (PMI)   Project Management Institute is U.S.-based worldwide organization dedicated to promoting the use of standardized project management techniques across industries.

project scope management plan   Describes how the project scope and work breakdown structure will be defined and describes and documents how project scope is managed throughout the project, including how changes to project scope will be managed.

project scope statement   Documents the project goals and deliverables and serves as a baseline for future project decisions.

project sponsor   An executive within the organization who has the authority to make decisions, assign resources, and assign a budget to the project.

project team directory   A directory of contact information for everyone involved in the project, their roles, and their communication needs.

projectized organizations   Projectized organizations focus on the project itself, not on the work of the functional department. Project managers have the most authority in this type of structure, and other functions, such as accounting or human resources, may report to the project manager.

receiver   The person or group the message is intended for.

request for proposal (RFP)   Procurement document used to solicit input from vendors when purchasing goods or services or outsourcing project work.

requirements   The specifications or characteristics of the deliverables that must be met in order to satisfy the needs of the project, broken down to their most basic components.

resource leveling   Attempts to smooth out the resource assignments so that tasks are completed without overloading individuals and without negatively impacting the project schedule.

resource plan   Describes all the resources needed for the project, including human resources and goods and materials.

responsibility assignment matrix (RAM)   A chart that ties roles and responsibilities with the WBS elements.

return on investment (ROI)   Measures the amount of savings or profit that the project will generate.

risk   An event that poses a potential threat or potential opportunity.

risk tolerance   The amount of risk that a person or organization is willing to tolerate in exchange for the perceived or actual benefits of partaking in the activity.

risk triggers   Symptoms that signal that a risk event is about to occur.

scope creep   A phenomenon where the scope of the project changes over time because of lack of agreement on the original scope statement, not sticking to the original scope statement, or not having a scope statement.

scope management plan   See *project scope management plan.*

scope statement   See *project scope statement.*

screening systems   Used in the procurement process to outline criteria that must be met in order for a proposal to make it to the next level in the selection process.

sender   The person or group formulating the content of the message.

skills assessment   A document that details the skills each team member possesses and their experience level in those skills.

stakeholder   Anyone who has a vested interest in the project.

statement of work (SOW)   Contains a description of the products or services produced as a result of the project, a description of the work of the project, and concise specifications of the product or services required. Often used with contracts to describe the work of the project. Used by the vendor to assess whether they should bid for the contract.

strategic plan   Describes the organization's long-term goals and plans.

three-point estimate   Three-point estimates are used to determine activity duration estimates. An average of three estimates, optimistic, most likely, and pessimistic, are used to derive the result.

triple constraints   Three constraints common to all projects: scope, schedule, and cost. Each of these constraints, or any combination of them, may also impact quality.

warranty period   A period of time when the stakeholders can notify the team of problems and have them corrected immediately.

WBS dictionary   A document that contains information about the activities or tasks listed on the WBS. It may include elements such as WBS number, WBS codes, descriptions, and resource names.

weighted scoring models   Used in the procurement process and the project-selection process to weight and rank various criteria and make a final selection.

work breakdown structure (WBS)   A deliverables-oriented hierarchy that defines all the work of the project. Each succeeding level has more detail than the level above it.

work package   The lowest level in a WBS. Resource assignments and time and cost estimates are established at this level.

Index

Note to the reader: Throughout this index **boldfaced** page numbers indicate primary discussions of a topic. *Italicized* page numbers indicate illustrations.

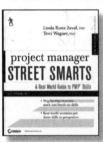